Paolina's Innocence

Paolina's Innocence

CHILD ABUSE
IN CASANOVA'S VENICE

Larry Wolff

STANFORD UNIVERSITY PRESS
STANFORD, CALIFORNIA

Stanford University Press
Stanford, California

Printed in the United States of America on acid-free, archival-quality paper

Library of Congress Cataloging-in-Publication Data

Wolff, Larry, author.
  Paolina's innocence : child abuse in Casanova's Venice / Larry Wolff.
    pages cm
  Includes bibliographical references and index.
    ISBN 978-0-8047-6261-8 (cloth : alk. paper) — ISBN 978-0-8047-6262-5 (pbk. : alk. paper)
    1. Franceschini, Gaetano, 1725?– —Trials, litigation, etc. 2. Lozaro, Paolina, 1777– —
Trials, litigation, etc. 3. Trials (Child sexual abuse)—Italy—Venice—History—18th century.
4. Child sexual abuse—Investigation—Italy—Venice—History—18th century. 5. Libertinism—Italy—Venice—History—18th century. 6. Sociological jurisprudence—Italy—Venice—History—18th century. I. Title.
    KKH41.F73W65 2012
    2011045204—dc23

                                  2011045204

Typeset by Bruce Lundquist in 10.5/14 Adobe Garamond

For Sheila Klass and in memory of Mort Klass—

"Always scribble, scribble, scribble! Eh, Mr. Gibbon?"

Contents

Acknowledgments

Although my research for many years has focused on Eastern Europe and the Habsburg monarchy, I have also maintained a strong interest in the history of childhood. I've taught a course on parents and children in European history and have published, over the years, articles on cultural conceptions of childhood, ranging in subject from Mme de Sévigné in the seventeenth century, to Jean-Jacques Rousseau in the eighteenth century, to Charles Dickens in the nineteenth century. In 1988 I published a book about child abuse in Freud's Vienna, and this new book on child abuse in Casanova's Venice is a closely related work. Each book attempts to understand abuse in a complex cultural context, which for all its complexity—in Casanova's Venice as in Freud's Vienna—did not include a clearly articulated sense of child abuse as a sociological phenomenon. The documentary basis for *Paolina's Innocence* is an unexpectedly fat archival file of some three hundred pages, which I came upon in the Archivio di Stato in Venice when I was working on an entirely different subject, Venetian rule over the Slavs of Dalmatia in the eighteenth century (eventually published in 2001 under the title *Venice and the Slavs*). I found this file at the very end of one of my archival visits to Venice. I remember beginning to read it, becoming instantly fascinated with the story of Paolina Lozaro and Gaetano Franceschini, and then having to make the tough decision as to whether I should keep on reading or send the entire file to be microfilmed and, eventually, mailed to me in Boston where I then lived. I requested the microfilm and therefore had to wait quite some time to learn the details of the case.

Over the last decade, first in Boston and then in New York, I have been looking for both the necessary time and the appropriate form in which to make this material into a book. I have enjoyed the support and encouragement of colleagues at both Boston College and NYU. I am likewise exceptionally grateful for the assistance and companionship of the archivists and scholars I encountered at the Archivio di Stato in Venice, as well as the kind assistance I have received at the Biblioteca Marciana and Biblioteca del Museo Correr in Venice, and the Archivio di Stato in Vicenza. I received financial support for my research from the Gladys Krieble Delmas Foundation.

I have greatly benefited from discussions of this project in particular, and the history of childhood more generally, with Maria Tatar, Paula Fass, and Tara Zahra. I have been glad to have the opportunity to discuss the early modern implications of this project with Mario Biagioli, Pierre Saint-Amand, and Andrei Zorin. I was fortunate to be able to present portions of this research at exceptionally stimulating conferences and seminars at the Princeton Cotsen Children's Library, at the École des Hautes Études en Sciences Sociales in Paris, at the Voltaire Foundation at Oxford, and at the University of Primorska in Koper, Slovenia. My work, as presented at these conferences, then benefited further from publications under the editorship of Andrew Kahn, Claudio Povolo, and Irina Prokhorova of the *New Literary Review* in Moscow.

In the early stages of this project I was given enthusiastic encouragement and advice by two scholars whose thoughts I hugely valued and who died before the book was complete: Morton Klass and Stephen Jay Gould. As always, I am grateful to my parents, Bob and Renee Wolff, for their spirited interest in my research. At NYU I have to thank Stefanos Geroulanos for helping me prepare the images to accompany the text. At Stanford I am very grateful to Norris Pope, not just for publishing this book but for publishing so handsomely five books over almost twenty years, and thus personally overseeing almost my entire academic career. Finally, at home, I could not have written this book without Perri Klass, who has lived with this project for a long time and who read and edited the entire manuscript. All my thoughts about children and the history of childhood owe just about everything to her.

Paolina's Innocence

Introduction

In the summer of 1785 a Venetian tribunal initiated the criminal investigation of a sixty-year-old man who had been accused of having sexual contact with an eight-year-old girl. In the eighteenth century there was no clear clinical or sociological concept of "child sexual abuse," as we understand it today, and the judicial investigation of this particular case kept growing in scope as the court attempted to determine what exactly had happened to the child, Paolina Lozaro, during a single night in the apartment, and the bed, of Gaetano Franceschini. She was the daughter of a poor laundress from the immigrant Friulian community in Venice; he came from a wealthy family of silk manufacturers in Vicenza. The details of the case were difficult to discover, and even more difficult to prove, for the child herself barely understood what had happened to her, but even the contested facts of the case were complicated by controversial cultural questions. The tribunal had to decide whether, and in what sense, the girl had actually been harmed; whether, and in what sense, the man's actions were criminal; and, if so, how he should be punished. There were no simple and straightforward answers to these questions in the eighteenth century. The case began with a single-page secret denunciation to the law, composed by a neighborhood priest who had heard that Franceschini slept with the girl "scandalously in his own bed."[1] The judicial dossier then accumulated testimonies of witnesses and documents of indictment and defense to the eventual length of some three hundred handwritten pages.

While it seems plausible to suppose that the mistreatment of children—what we call child abuse—was at least as common in earlier centuries as it is today, the absence of the modern concept of abuse meant that such mistreatment left relatively little documentary trace in the archival records. The three hundred–page dossier concerning the case of Gaetano Franceschini and Paolina Lozaro in 1785 may be, very possibly, the most detailed investigation of child abuse ever carried out and recorded in the world of the ancien régime. The dossier may be found in the records of the tribunal of the Esecutori contro la Bestemmia (Executors against Blasphemy), and that peculiar jurisdiction already suggests some of the difficulty in specifying and classifying the crime under consideration. Consistent with the denunciation that Franceschini kept the girl "scandalously in his own bed," the principal charge against him was the very generally conceived crime of causing scandal. Paradoxically, the case did not cause scandal because it was clearly criminal but rather was deemed judicially criminal because it was the cause of neighborhood scandal. Cultural and social perspectives on childhood thus partly conditioned the legal course of the prosecution.

The first part of the book focuses on the judicial aspects of the case and examines the mandate and procedure of the Bestemmia, dealing here with a case that was entirely unrelated to issues of blasphemy. Created in the sixteenth century to appease the wrath of God, the Bestemmia by the eighteenth century, from the perspective of the European Enlightenment, already appeared as an archaic relic. Yet in this case its conventions proved unexpectedly suited to confronting incipiently modern issues of law and society.

The early modern Venetian relation to sex and the law has been explored in the pioneering research of Guido Ruggiero, especially in *The Boundaries of Eros: Sex Crime and Sexuality in Renaissance Venice* (1985). More recently Ruggiero, together with Edward Muir, edited a collection of articles from *Quaderni storici* entitled *History from Crime* (1994), illustrating the methodological problem of studying society through criminal cases. Essential for understanding the implications of Venetian law is the work of Gaetano Cozzi; Claudio Povolo has further elaborated the historical implications of criminal and legal issues for understanding Venetian society, and Renzo Derosas has written specifically about the Bestemmia tribunal. The purposes of the tribunal can also be comprehended in the cultural context described by Alain Cabantous in his book on the history of blasphemy in Europe (1998). Most recently, in books on early modern Venice, Joanne Ferraro has broken new ground with her work on illicit sex and infanticide (2008), and Elizabeth Horodowich has published a very relevant study on the politics of language, including blasphemy (2008).[2] All these works offer important insights toward understanding the prosecution of Franceschini in 1785.

The second part of the book focuses on the institution of the Venetian coffeehouse, *bottega da caffè*, which turned out to be central to the judicial investigation. The apartment of Franceschini, where Paolina Lozaro spent that one night in his bed, was just upstairs from a coffeehouse, which helped to make the entire building into a center of community life and neighborhood discussion. What was most characteristic of an eighteenth-century European coffeehouse, and just as stimulating as the coffee for the customers, was the level of conversational buzz and exchange of news in a public forum. Ever since the appearance in 1962 of Jürgen Habermas's *The Structural Transformation of the Public Sphere*, the coffeehouse has been considered one of the fundamental institutions for the creation of a public sphere in eighteenth-century Europe. Coffee itself was a relatively new stimulant in Europe in the eighteenth century, and public discussion over cups of coffee seemed similarly new and equally addictive. One of the most celebrated Venetian dramas of the eighteenth century was Carlo Goldoni's *La bottega del caffè* (The Coffeehouse) of 1750, in which the proprietor, or *caffettiere*, Ridolfo, served coffee to the neighborhood gossip Don Marzio:

> DON MARZIO. Coffee.
> RIDOLFO. Immediately, at your service.
> DON MARZIO. What's new, Ridolfo?[3]

The coffeehouse itself was something new in Venice, but the conventional query "What's new?" became the prompt to public discussion of neighborhood news over cups of coffee. The Venetian tribunal of 1785, by soliciting the coffeehouse perspective on what was "new" in the neighborhood—including the testimony of the real-life *caffettiere*—was able to learn a great deal about what happened upstairs in the apartment of Gaetano Franceschini.

Danilo Reato has written a history of coffeehouses in Venice (1991), and Brian Cowan, writing about England, has explored the implications of the coffeehouse for society and community in *The Social Life of Coffee* (2005).

James Johnson, in *Venice Incognito* (2011), has analyzed the meanings of Venetian masking, including the wearing of masks in coffeehouses. Because of Habermas, the historical discussion of public life in the eighteenth century has invariably made reference to coffee. The public sphere of critical discussion, theorized by Habermas, however, was certainly not identical to the culture of coffeehouse gossip dramatized by Goldoni in the eighteenth century. The case of Franceschini suggests some of the ways that coffee and gossip were related to scandal and public life, and in this regard the work of Sarah Maza on the dynamics of scandal in the causes célèbres of eighteenth-century France is also illuminating.[4]

The third part of the book confronts the figure of the man accused, the man who resided upstairs from the coffeehouse. Gaetano Franceschini lived the life of an eighteenth-century libertine, pursuing a sex life without regard to conventional moral prejudices. Libertinism was both a celebrated and excoriated way of life in the eighteenth century, and Franceschini may be considered in relation to the most famous libertine of the century, the Venetian Casanova. The litany of seductions narrated in Casanova's memoirs suggests a question that has, perhaps, not yet been posed in the scholarly literature: How young was too young for Casanova? The answer to that question provides some clues to the meaning of Franceschini's conduct, for Casanova and Franceschini were exact contemporaries; Casanova was born in 1725 and turned sixty in 1785, the year of Franceschini's trial. The character of eighteenth-century libertinism may also be considered in relation to the iconic figure of Don Juan, or Don Giovanni, whose operatic incarnation was created by Mozart together with his Venetian librettist Lorenzo Da Ponte in the 1780s. The premiere of the opera in Prague took place in 1787, two years after Franceschini's trial. With reference to Franceschini, one may pose the question of how the eighteenth-century model of libertinism encompassed what the modern world would regard as sexual psychopathology. In 1886, a century after Franceschini's trial, the German psychiatrist Richard von Krafft-Ebing introduced the clinical category of "paedophilia erotica" in his *Psychopathia Sexualis*. The eighteenth-century world had some sense that Franceschini, with an eight-year-old girl in his bed, had done something exceptionally scandalous, but his contemporaries could not clearly articulate the exceptional deviation from the sexual norm.

The critical literature on libertinism includes major edited collections, such as *Eros philosophe: Discours libertins des lumières* (1984) and *Libertine*

Enlightenment: Sex, Liberty, and License in the Eighteenth Century (2004), exploring the diverse social, philosophical, and literary aspects of the subject. Pierre Saint-Amand's literary study of seduction in the Enlightenment appeared in Paris in 1987, translated into English as *The Libertine's Progress* in 1994. More recent monographs include *Le libertinage et l'histoire* by Stéphanie Genand (2005) and *Histoire du libertinage* by Didier Foucault (2007). The extensive scholarly literature on Casanova and Sade, and also on the opera *Don Giovanni*, further informs the discussion of libertinism in the 1780s. On the history of sexual predation important historical work has been done by Ruggiero, writing about sex crime in Venice, but also by Georges Vigarello in his history of rape, published in French in 1998 and in English translation in 2001.[5]

The final section of the book considers the girl herself, Paolina Lozaro, eight years old in 1785, the victim of Franceschini's sexual attentions. The testimony of witnesses offers evidence of how she fit into the context of contemporary perspectives on children and childhood's innocence. By considering Jean-Jacques Rousseau, his ideas about children, and even his own biographical experience in Venice in the 1740s, it is possible to see how the articulation of innocence in the case of Paolina Lozaro intersected with the Enlightenment's new conception of childhood. The entire field of the history of childhood received an enormous impetus with the publication in 1960 of the work of Philippe Ariès on family and childhood in the ancien régime; the research of the subsequent generation has been comprehensively consolidated within the *Encyclopedia of Children and Childhood in History and Society*, edited by Paula Fass (2004). Historical studies of individual children have pointed toward increasingly subtle understandings of childhood in historical context, such as Margaret King's book about Renaissance Venice, *The Death of the Child Valerio Marcello* (1994), and David Kertzer's book about Risorgimento Italy, *The Kidnapping of Edgardo Mortara* (1997).[6] The case of Paolina Lozaro may serve as a point of entry for analyzing the historical complexities of childhood in the context of the European Enlightenment.

The early modern structures of Venetian law and justice and the rise of the Venetian coffeehouse as a forum for gossip and public discussion conditioned a notable cultural combustibility in the prosecution of Gaetano Franceschini in 1785. Particularly explosive was the ideological encounter between the values of enlightened libertinism and the new Rousseauist perspective on childhood's innocence. In the case of Paolina Lozaro, this intersection of institutions and values—modern and early modern, enlightened and traditional—produced a historically unprecedented, intellectually confused, but retrospectively recognizable confrontation with the issues of child sexual abuse on the threshold of modern European history.

PART ONE

The Secret Denunciation

What are the reasons that justify secret accusations and punishments? Public safety, security, and maintaining the form of government? But what a strange constitution. . . . Can there be crimes, that is, public offenses, of which it is not in the interest of everyone that they be made a public example, that is, with a public judgment?

—Beccaria, *On Crimes and Punishments*

ONE

The Parish Priest

On September 2, 1785, Bortolo Fiorese, a priest at the church of Sant'Angelo in Venice, penned a secret denunciation to the Venetian government: "Yesterday I went to the apartment of Signore Gaetano Franceschini, a resident of this parish, and removed from that apartment, in the absence of the master, a girl of about eight years, Paolina Lozaro by name, and I delivered her into the hands of her mother Maria. I was driven by the reports I had obtained about the bad reputation and depraved inclinations of Signore Gaetano, and about his keeping the girl, the night before, scandalously in his own bed."[1] That same day, in immediate response to his denunciation, Father Fiorese was summoned to the Doge's Palace for questioning before a tribunal of the law. So began the legal investigation of Gaetano Franceschini in a case that would claim the attention of the Venetian judicial system for the rest of the year. A tribunal of four duly elected Venetian patricians fulfilled their civic responsibilities by overseeing the interrogation of an entire neighborhood in an attempt to determine exactly what happened to Paolina Lozaro during a single night in the home of Gaetano Franceschini before Father Fiorese removed her from the premises.

It all began on the last day of August, in the middle of the morning, according to Father Fiorese. "I happened to be in the sacristy of my church, and a woman wearing a silk shawl approached me and called me aside, and told me the following story. She said to me that she had just that moment come from confession." The woman in the silk shawl introduced herself to the priest as the housekeeper of Signore Gaetano Franceschini and confided that her master had recently made her an alarming proposition. The housekeeper, a recent widow, had two young daughters who were being raised outside the city, since their mother had to live as a servant in her master's house. Franceschini had suggested that he might employ one of the daughters in his household as well, especially since he had recently received some very particular medical advice: "He had been advised to find a young girl [*una tenera ragazza*] to sleep with him so that her warmth might reinvigorate his own." Not in the least deceived by this medical "pretext," the housekeeper declined the proposition and kept her daughters in the country, but she herself continued to work in Franceschini's service.[2]

This morning, however, as she told Father Fiorese, her master had ordered her to go to the church of Sant'Angelo where she was to meet a certain Friulian woman, a Furlana, with a young daughter. The housekeeper had no trouble recognizing the Furlana, who was lingering there in the church with her daughter and was obviously waiting to meet someone. Father Fiorese, testifying before the tribunal, explained the housekeeper's dilemma and his own reaction to her story.

> She was to meet a Furlana with a girl, and to bring the girl home, as a substitute for her own daughter to have with him in bed. She found the Furlana and the girl right there in the church, but, feeling herself constrained by the obligations of virtue and religion, she invoked my advice and assistance. Having heard about this interesting matter, I did not however believe that I should immediately give complete credence to the story, especially since the suspicion occurred to me that this woman actually wanted to put forward her own daughter and was seeking by this means to deprive the other girl of her good fortune [*provvidenza*]. Nevertheless, I took the expedient of advising that woman to go home and tell her master, of whom she seemed frightened [*dimostrava soggezione*], that she had not found the Furlana.[3]

The silk shawl was known variously in Venetian as the *zendale*, the *zendà*, or the *zendado*. It would probably have been black in eighteenth-century Venice, worn over the head, wrapped around the body, perhaps even partly covering the face, if a woman, for one reason or another, wished to conceal her identity. This woman, Franceschini's housekeeper, must certainly have hoped for some discretion as she revealed her master's intentions to Father Fiorese.

The priest immediately perceived the sinister aspect of the situation—that is, the recruitment of a warm young body—but nevertheless his first suspicion was directed against the housekeeper herself rather than her master. Even though Father Fiorese seemed to understand perfectly well that little girls should not be employed to reinvigorate old men in bed, he also had no doubt that for a girl from the lower levels of Venetian society it would be a piece of good fortune to be taken into the service and under the protection of a prosperous older gentleman. The housekeeper presented herself to the priest as reluctant to play the part of a procuress, professing to be too troubled to follow through on her master's order, but the priest thought she might be merely trying to procure the position for her own daughter by obstructing the other girl's opportunity with a smokescreen of sexual insinuations.

"Donne veneziane in zendà." Venetian women wearing black silk shawls, like that of Maria Bardini the housekeeper. From Pompeo Molmenti, *La storia di Venezia nella vita privata.*

Father Fiorese did not seem amazed at the brazenness of proposing to use a young body to warm an old one, and it may have seemed even unremarkable to a man who knew something about sinners in eighteenth-century Venice. If he was familiar with the Bible, which was not particularly likely for a Catholic priest at that time, he might have recalled the precedent of King David: "Now king David was old and stricken in years; and they covered him with clothes, but he gat no heat. Wherefore his servants said unto him, Let there be brought for my lord the king a young virgin: and let her stand before the king, and let her cherish him, and let her lie in thy bosom, that my lord the king may get heat." In the end, they delivered a virgin, who "cherished the king, and ministered to him: but the king knew her not."[4] Eighteenth-century medical notions still involved a significant measure of popular superstition, including an accumulated traditional wisdom about age and youth, heat and cold, health and debility, sex and virginity.

Church of Sant'Angelo with Campanile, in Campo Sant'Angelo. The engraving shows the campo before the demolition of the church and its bell tower in 1837. The leaning tower of San Stefano is visible in the background. From *Souvenirs de Venise* (1836), by Giovanni Pividor. By permission of the Biblioteca del Museo Correr, Venice.

At the same time, Venice in the eighteenth century was enlightened enough for a parish priest and a conscientious housekeeper to agree that the medical pursuit of a young girl's bodily warmth was surely the "pretext" for unspoken predatory intentions.

The urban landscape of Venice today is not altogether different from that which Father Fiorese inhabited in 1785. Many of the churches of his day still survive with their treasures of sacred art, but the church of Sant'Angelo does not. Dedicated to the Archangel Michael, the medieval church of Sant'Angelo was demolished in 1837, so today the Campo Sant'Angelo preserves only the memory of the church in the name of the square. The Campo Sant'Angelo lies between the Accademia bridge and the Rialto, a busy space in the heart of Venice; two beautiful Gothic palaces with delicately pointed arches at the windows, Palazzo Gritti and Palazzo Duodo, face each other across one end of the square.

Campo Sant'Angelo today, without the church and its bell tower. The leaning tower of San Stefano still stands in the background

In the eighteenth century the church of Sant'Angelo was known to contain Titian's last painting, the *Pietà* (1575), at one of the altars—but the painting is to be found today in the Accademia museum.[5] The *Pietà* shows the Virgin Mary with the body of Christ in a painted architectural niche, while Nicodemus kneels before them, and Mary Magdalene, one hand raised, seems to be stepping out of the painting toward the viewer—into the church of Sant'Angelo. The Titian *Pietà* would have been very familiar to Father Fiorese. It would certainly have been present in his church on that last day of August in 1785, the day that he received the unusual confidence of the woman in the silk shawl.

Having sent her away, Father Fiorese turned his attention to the Furlana and her daughter. The Furlana was Maria Lozaro, an immigrant from Friuli in the city of Venice. Friuli was a province of the Venetian Republic northeast of Venice, at the head of the Adriatic gulf, adjoining the Austrian and Slovenian provinces of the Habsburg monarchy. Within the Venetian state Friuli was also a border region between Venice's mainland Italian territories and the subject lands of the eastern Adriatic shore, Istria and Dalmatia, with their extensively Slavic populations. In the metropolis of Venice there was a significant immigrant population from Friuli, usually poor and often looking for employment in domestic service or menial labor. Friuli and the Friulians had a distinctive history and regional character. A Furlana would have spoken the regional Friulian language as her native tongue and would even perhaps have been characteristically dressed in provincial costume.

To someone like Father Fiorese, a native Venetian, Maria Lozaro was a humble provincial subject of Venice, ethnically distinct in her Friulian extraction, and he designated her simply as the Furlana.

> I called aside the Furlana, who was already in the church, and asked her the reason for which she was there. She replied to me that an older gentleman— though she didn't know who he was—had sought out her daughter, to keep her with him as an adoptive daughter [*come figlia d'anima*], and had promised to pay her a daily wage corresponding to eight lire monthly, for which reason he was coming to meet the girl, and the mother was waiting for him to come and take the girl away as agreed. I then tried opportunely [*destramente*] to get her to reflect, by telling her that entrusting a girl to someone she did not know could be too risky [*troppo azzardo*], that the excessively advantageous offer should have given her some well-founded suspicion, and that I too had some inkling of that sort. And so therefore I advised her for the moment to remove herself to the nearby church of San Stefano, and I would come half an hour later to tell her something more definite, since just

then I could not go, since I had to deal with another interesting matter—which was in fact true. My intention then was to increase her suspicions in such a way as to make her distance herself for that day, so as to preserve the secrecy of the other woman who had confided in me, and so I would have time to understand the matter properly. The Furlana was persuaded to leave, from which I recognized the innocence of her readiness to abandon her young daughter, and she headed toward San Stefano.[6]

If Father Fiorese's first suspicion was that the woman in the silk shawl was trying to obtain the position for her own daughter, his second suspicion was that the Furlana was no less eager to seize upon this good fortune. By leaving the church, and thus forgoing the rendezvous, she proved her "innocence" to him. Father Fiorese had clearly contemplated the guilty possibility that, in order to attain such good fortune as a wage of eight lire monthly, the Furlana might have been perfectly willing to install her young daughter in the old gentleman's bed. Suspicious of the housekeeper, suspicious of the mother, the priest was also, but not yet extremely or exclusively—suspicious of the gentleman himself, Gaetano Franceschini.

All through the priest's account of this episode in the church of Sant'Angelo, one person present in the church remained strangely invisible. Maria Lozaro must have been accompanied in the church by her daughter, the eight-year-old girl who was the object of all concerns and the reason for all suspicions. Yet Father Fiorese made no remark whatsoever about her age or appearance or demeanor, gave no clue as to whether the child seemed frightened or cheerful or bored or preoccupied. By the time Father Fiorese saw her again, she would have spent a night in Franceschini's bed, and the priest would have much more reason to be concerned about her. For the moment, however, he had some other "interesting matter" to attend to, and his mere half an hour of other business was going to prove to be all the time that was needed to precipitate the disaster of which he claimed to have an inkling.

The walk from the Campo Sant'Angelo to the Campo San Stefano takes only a matter of minutes, as they are almost adjacent squares. San Stefano is not a small church, and Father Fiorese might have had to spend a few minutes looking for the Furlana inside, in the magnificent Gothic structure with its Venetian celebrity tombs of the sixteenth-century composer Giovanni Gabrieli and the seventeenth-century military hero Francesco Morosini. The priest might even have noted the modern, that is, eighteenth-century, painting of *The Massacre of the Innocents* by Gaspare Diziani. The innocent child of Maria Lozaro, however, was not there in San Stefano. Father Fiorese had had half an hour to reflect upon the situation and may have now felt prepared to say "something more definite," but mother and daughter were nowhere to be found.

The church of Sant'Angelo defined a parish and marked the center of a Venetian neighborhood in which Father Fiorese, as the parish priest, would have been an important figure, occupied with many strands of church and community business.[7] His failure to find the Furlana in San Stefano seems not to have alarmed him immediately, and he probably put her problem out of his mind as he continued with his parochial responsibilities. Later that same day, however, Father Fiorese was taking a coffee break from his business when he encountered Maria Lozaro again, this time without her

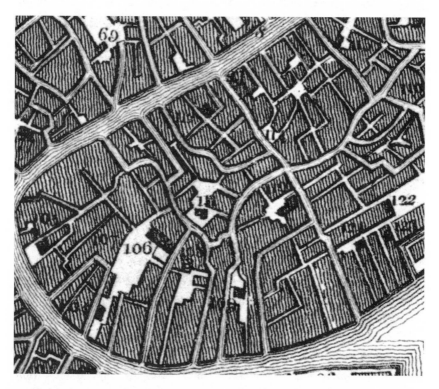

Neighborhood of Sant'Angelo: number 111 shows the Campo Sant'Angelo with the church in the middle of the Campo; number 106 shows the adjoining location of San Stefano; number 122 shows Piazza San Marco with the Doge's Palace. The drawing of the streets and squares does not appear to be absolutely accurate; the map also shows some canals that have been filled in since the eighteenth century and no longer exist. "A Plan of the City of Venice," London, John Stockdale (1776?; reprinted 1800).

daughter. "Having retired nearby to the coffeehouse, to chat with someone, I saw the Furlana approaching, agitated." She told him what had happened earlier in the day, how she had left the church of Sant'Angelo intending to go to San Stefano, as he had suggested, but Gaetano Franceschini had been waiting for her in the Campo Sant'Angelo as she came out of the church. Maria Lozaro was surprised to see him: "and being frightened [*per soggezione*], did not have the courage to avoid being led home by him." She was already anxious after Father Fiorese's warning, and she still did not know Franceschini's name. Franceschini, however, having brought her to his apartment, tried to be reassuring and made various promises in order to get her to leave the child with him, "suggesting however that the Furlana should instruct her daughter to obey him in everything, and advising her that she not come back to see the girl until the following Sunday."[8] In fact, Franceschini lived just upstairs from the coffeehouse, in the same building, and the girl was in his apartment at the very same time that Father Fiorese was chatting and drinking coffee below.

The priest was concerned but hesitant to intervene. "I did not have sufficient grounds to decide," he informed the tribunal, so he advised Maria Lozaro to make inquiries about Franceschini. He also made inquiries himself in the neighborhood but learned nothing definitive: "I could discover nothing more than abstract rumors that Franceschini was a sensual man [*uomo sensuale*]."[9] By the defensive quality of his testimony, his pleading of insufficient grounds, his insisting upon his many duties, Father Fiorese made it clear enough that he felt some qualms about his dilatory commitment to this matter in its earliest stages. While he was soliciting rumors from around the neighborhood, that last day of August waned into the Venetian summer evening. The child Paolina Lozaro was already installed in the home of Gaetano Franceschini, where her mother had nervously instructed her to obey him in everything. Night fell upon the lagoon, the canals, the churches, and the coffeehouses, the whole gorgeous city of islands with its crowded population of 140,000 men, women, and children.

The next morning was the first of September, and Father Fiorese, still gathering information about Gaetano Franceschini, learned that two women who had heard the story from Maria Lozaro had decided to take it upon themselves to intervene. They had gone to Franceschini's house while he was out, to try to rescue the girl, but had been thwarted by the resistance of his housekeeper. Though she, wrapped in her silk shawl, had discreetly tried to betray the scheme in church the day before, she could not now practice open insubordination from within her master's house. She could not simply let the young guest get away. The housekeeper, however, was not too intimidated to tell the other women exactly what had been going on in the apartment. They learned that the girl had spent the previous night in bed with Franceschini, and this alarming news was promptly communicated to Father Fiorese, offering new substance to the abstract rumors. Now he promised "all my commitment in this matter, which I recognized as necessarily concerning my sacred ministry."[10]

The principal job of a parish priest in eighteenth-century Venice was administering the sacraments, and religious historian Bruno Bertoli has noted that priests did not even usually preach during Mass.[11] Father Fiorese was sufficiently involved in the life of his community to feel some concern about what was taking place in Franceschini's apartment, but the priest was also clearly uncertain about the parameters of his own responsibility. His hesitations and equivocations during the preceding twenty-four hours may have revealed something about his own professional character, but they also testified to the threshold of reserve recognized by an eighteenth-century parish priest contemplating any serious intervention into the domestic arrangements and private lives of individual Venetians. The law itself, as embodied in the tribunal, would have to give similar consideration in this same case to the threshold of involvement for the state in Venetian private affairs.

Having learned that Franceschini was out of the house, Father Fiorese thought he would take advantage of that absence to knock on the door, and there he found himself again receiving the confidences of the housekeeper. Not only had the girl spent the night in bed with the master but the preceding afternoon as well, after lunch. The priest and the servant seem to have speculated quite explicitly about what happened in bed, and Father Fiorese was partly reassured.

> I could also infer that although decisive consequences had not yet occurred, nevertheless matters had moved far along. It was almost noon, and the certain danger of a greater evil was approaching. To carry her off with me I recognized as an act of violence, and to leave her there was contrary to charity, but there was no time for other recourses. Therefore, in this dilemma the duties of religion prevailed, and I took her away with me, preserving her thus from the plausible imminent danger, and him from the guilt. However, I first had her remove the silver buckles that she was wearing, given to her by Franceschini.[12]

It was the priest's Christian obligation to rescue the child from imminent sexual danger, but it was also a presumptuous intervention to take her
from the house where she had been installed by her own mother in the care
of the master. It would have been still worse to remove any valuables from
the premises, namely, the silver buckles, which might have been the child's
reward for compliant conduct. She was soon spirited away to the care of rela-
tives on the island of Murano. Having thus rescued the child, Father Fiorese
proceeded to make his secret denunciation and was immediately summoned
to testify before the tribunal.

In fact, he had been summoned by the same tribunal once before, six
years earlier in the summer of 1779, as part of the judicial investigation into
the life of a Roman barber named Giuseppe Terrizzo, then living in the
Campo Sant'Angelo and suspected of supporting himself as a pimp. His was
apparently a prominent and even prestigious operation, for he was seen in
the company of foreign ambassadors and supposedly befriended the secretary of the papal nuncio. In addition to pimping, Terrizzo was occupied with
other aspects of the sex trade, pretending to have special medical remedies
for venereal disease and even treatments to restore a girl's virginity. Father
Fiorese was summoned simply as a character witness to testify that though
Terrizzo lived in the parish, actually on the piazza right behind the church
of Sant'Angelo, he never attended Mass or received the sacraments. Furthermore, Father Fiorese had heard the rumor that the man was a pimp and that
he boasted of having "secret medicines." Clearly, the parish priest was not altogether sheltered from the sexual underworld of Venice. He may even have
heard the rumor, as specified in the denunciation, that Terrizzo, by claiming
that he could restore a girl's virginity, had induced "many poor women to
sacrifice the honor of their daughters."[13] Six years later, Father Fiorese would
initially suspect Maria Lozaro of being implicated in a sacrifice of that sort.
In the case of Giuseppe Terrizzo, the priest was merely an incidental witness, but in the case of Gaetano Franceschini, Father Fiorese was the prime
mover: making the denunciation, offering the very first testimony, and finally addressing the speculative question of Franceschini's intentions.

"For what reason truly did Franceschini seek out the girl?" the priest
was asked, and Father Fiorese outlined before the tribunal the alternative
possibilities for interpreting Franceschini's motives. "He told the mother
he was taking the girl as an adoptive daughter, and that would have been a
charitable act. He told his servant that it was to reinvigorate his advanced
age, but this motive seems troubling in view of his notoriously sensual

character." Especially inasmuch as there was talk about "other girls," the priest was compelled to suspect Franceschini of the "worst intentions."[14] Though Father Fiorese had been initially suspicious of both the housekeeper and the mother, and he had hesitated to intervene in a domestic matter, the priest finally came to the conclusion that Franceschini's true motive was sex with the child. The priest had made his denunciation and offered his testimony; the tribunal would now have to try to determine whether a crime had been committed, what sort of crime it was, and how it should be judged and punished according to the laws of the Venetian Republic.

The Blasphemy Tribunal

When Father Fiorese made his secret denunciation on September 2, 1785, it was probably deposited into the Lion's Mouth (*bocca del leone*) at the Doge's Palace. The Lion's Mouth was the totemic stone receptacle for such denunciations, and the Doge's Palace was the center of government and of justice, where Venetian tribunals conducted their investigations and held their trials. Montesquieu, when he wrote the *Spirit of the Laws* in 1748, considered as a hallmark of the Venetian system "the Lion's Mouth into which every informer may at all hours throw his written accusations"; it was the symbol of a secret justice that made arbitrary judicial despotism an inseparable element of Venetian political republicanism.[1] Not only was the identity of the informer kept secret but the criminal investigation was supposed to take place without the suspect's awareness, right up until the moment that the law might decide upon his arrest. Thereafter the accused would be confronted with testimonies against him but would never be told the identity of the witnesses who had testified. Gaetano Franceschini might have guessed, but would certainly not have been officially informed, that the Venetian state had begun to investigate his interest in young girls. Father Fiorese, when he made his denunciation, triggered the intricate mechanisms of the Venetian judicial system.

The Council of Ten was created in the fourteenth century to respond especially to plots and insurrections, crimes against the state—and this council became, over the centuries, one of the most powerful bodies in the Venetian government, concentrating much of the republican power of the patriciate in the hands of a limited few. In the eighteenth century, operating together with the three Inquisitors of State, the Council of Ten retained supreme judicial authority over Venetian patricians and maintained procedures of particular secrecy, but other tribunals also dealt with the recurring concerns of justice. The most important courts were those of the Quarantia Criminale (Council of Forty) and the Signori di Notte al Criminale (Lords of the Night). Father Fiorese's denunciation, how-

Text of denunciation by Father Fiorese: "Rassegno alle EEVV io P. Bortolo Fiorese Curato della Chiesa di Sant'Angelo e Servo Loro Umilissimo d'essermi ieri portato alla Casa del Signore Gaetano Franceschini abitante in questa Parrocchia e di aver levata da questa Casa in assenza del Padrone una Fanciulla di circa otto anni per nome Paulina Lozaro." (I submit to Your Excellencies, I Bortolo Fiorese, curate of the Church of Sant'Angelo and your most humble servant, that yesterday I went to the apartment of Signore Gaetano Franceschini, a resident of this parish, and removed from that apartment, in the absence of the master, a girl of about eight years, Paolina Lozaro by name.) The name, written in the denunciation as "Paulina," was then regularly given as "Paolina" (sometimes "Paola") in the records of the tribunal. Archivio di Stato di Venezia, Esecutori contro la Bestemmia, Busta 40, *Processi*, 1785, 1r.

ever, went to a very distinctive Venetian tribunal, the Esecutori contro la Bestemmia. As eighteenth-century Venetian law could not easily articulate or classify the criminal nature of Gaetano Franceschini's night in bed with an eight-year-old girl, the case ended up in the jurisdiction of the blasphemy tribunal.

The tribunal of the Bestemmia had been created in 1537 by the authority of the Council of Ten: "Since it is also the duty of men to have constantly in view the fear of God, upon which depends the particular and public interest of the state, without further delay it is proposed to take new and strong measures in this regard: to name by election from this Council three noblemen for one year, of perfect conscience, with the capacity of being reelected. . . . The three chosen will have the supreme power to inform against blasphemers of the holy name of God, the Virgin Mary, and the Celestial Court, to question them, to condemn them, and to punish them."[2] The Council of Ten thus authorized the founding of the Bestemmia, a new institutional addition to the interlocking and overlapping mechanisms of Venetian government, whereby different authorities attended to the diverse interests of the state. This particular interest, to assuage the anger of God by suppressing outbursts of blasphemy, was an unusual focus for a secular tribunal.

In 1537 the Venetian Renaissance was in its artistic prime. That was the year that Jacopo Sansovino began to build the classically inspired library building of the Biblioteca Marciana, opposite the Gothic facade of the Doge's Palace. In that year Titian was at work on his immense painting *The Presentation of the Virgin*, occupying today an entire wall in the Accademia, showing the Virgin Mary as a little girl in a halo of gold on the steps of the Temple in Jerusalem—though the crowd of Renaissance Venetians at the foot of the steps, and the pink building resembling the Doge's Palace in the background, suggests that the biblical scene must have taken place in Venice itself. If this was a moment of Venetian cultural confidence, however, it was also a time of some political insecurity. The establishment of the Bestemmia coincided with the outbreak of war against the Ottoman Empire, and in time of war the prosecution of blasphemy might be supposed to attract divine favor to further the interests of Venice against the sultan.

The new blasphemy court played an especially significant role in Venice's political opposition to papal Rome. At the beginning of the sixteenth century Venice had been almost brought to its knees by Pope Julius II, who excommunicated the Republic by papal interdict in 1509 and sponsored the allied armies of the League of Cambrai, which aimed to conquer and annex Venetian territories. At the beginning of the seventeenth century, in 1606, Venice was again challenged by a papal interdict, and once again fiercely resisted the presumptions of Rome to any sort of authority within the Venetian Republic. One crucial point of controversy was the jurisdiction of ecclesiastical courts, especially the Roman Inquisition, over Venetian subjects. The Roman Inquisition had been established in 1542 as the absolute arbiter of heresy in Roman Catholic Europe in the age of the Counter-Reformation. The Venetian Republic, however, could point to the tribunal of the Bestemmia as signifying that the Inquisition's judicial intervention was unnecessary in Venice, except for a strictly limited category of explicit heresies against Roman Catholicism that could be considered papal business. The Bestemmia thus became the political pretext for obstructing Roman attempts to monitor piety and impiety in Venetian society. Fra Paolo Sarpi, the patriotic theologian who rallied the Venetians to resist the interdict in 1606, insisted on the prerogatives of the state and its secular authority to judge crimes of blasphemy.[3]

By 1628, after less than a century of activity, Venetians already regarded the Bestemmia as a venerable organ of the Republic: "The crime of blasphemy is most serious for it may provoke the anger of Divine Majesty, and for that reason our most religious progenitors with pure zeal for the Lord God erected a magistracy with the title of Executors against Blasphemy."[4] The allusion to pious progenitors suggested that the Bestemmia, in less than a century, had already come to seem an essential and inseparable component of Venice's political constitution. Yet the truth is that by the seventeenth century the Bestemmia was already extending its jurisdiction far beyond the original vision of the founding Venetian progenitors. The multiplication of the tribunal's concerns pointed toward the peculiar evolution that would eventually, in the eighteenth century, bring a case of child abuse before the court of blasphemy.

Savonarola, preaching in Florence in the 1490s, regarded blasphemy against God's name as a depravity certain to incur divine wrath. He also, however, considered blasphemy to be closely related to certain other sinful activities, so he exhorted the Florentines in 1496 to expel from their midst "the gamblers, the blasphemers, the sodomites." Blasphemy was thus associated in the religious mentality with a variety of assorted sins, compulsively appealing to men and especially offensive to God, including at least one category of irregular sexual activity. In Venice the same association of evils was also evident. At Christmas in 1497 a preacher in the great basilica of San

Marco warned that plague in Venice was a consequence of "the blaspheming of God and the saints, the societies of sodomy, the numerous usurious contracts made at the Rialto, and above all the selling of justice and the policy of aiding the rich at the expense of the poor." In 1500 a letter was composed by an anonymous "servant of God" and addressed to the doge of Venice, warning that the Republic would not enjoy divine favor as long as it countenanced "injustices, blasphemies, the oppression of the poor."[5] In this same tense climate of religious anxiety, in 1516 the Ghetto was established as a restricted quarter for Venetian Jews, the Ghetto that would give its name to all the ghettos of Europe in the coming centuries. Such religious preoccupation also led to the creation of the Bestemmia in 1537 as a special blasphemy court, but the general fear of God's anger soon brought about the extension of jurisdiction to other sorts of sins and scandals.

After only two years of work, in 1539 the Bestemmia was declared so successful that "blasphemy had almost completely ceased." Such supposed success did not, however, lead to the new court's elimination, and, instead, the Council of Ten extended the competency of the Bestemmia from blasphemy to gambling. Over the course of the sixteenth century the court would become additionally occupied with scandal in sacred places, publishing without a license, the registration of foreigners, and the defloration of virgins. In the seventeenth century the executors would prosecute cases of serving meat during Lent, of beggars pretending to be pilgrims, of sexual relations between Christians and Jews, of improperly performed marriage ceremonies, and of scandalous behavior by priests and monks. There would also be some invigilation over prostitution, which, like gambling, was not strictly illegal, though either might involve criminal irregularity, public scandal, and even some incidental blasphemy. This last vice, of course, had certainly not disappeared, as men and women continued to express their insolence or outrage. A study of the cases before the Bestemmia in the mid-seventeenth century has counted around seven hundred cases of blasphemy over the course of a decade and a half, by far the largest category of cases presented for judgment. Particular arenas of city life could also be targeted as the special sites of blasphemy, as in 1632 when the Council of Ten noted that in the omnipresent *traghetti*, the little boats that ferried across the canals, Venetians were erupting into "horrendous blasphemies and other indecent, scandalous, base, and unworthy words." The Bestemmia was authorized to post proclamations at the stations of the *traghetti*, stipulating the penalties for blasphemy.[6] These could include monetary fines, banishment from

Venice, condemnation to the naval galleys, public shaming, imprisonment, mutilation of the tongue, and even capital punishment.

The executors who constituted the tribunal of the Bestemmia were chosen from among the men of the Venetian patriciate. The essence of Venetian republicanism was precisely that the patricians were both eligible by birth and obliged by civic responsibility to serve on the multifarious governing organs of the Venetian state. All Venetian nobles belonged to the Maggior Consiglio (Great Council), a total of thirteen hundred men in 1775, their families registered in the Libro d'Oro (Golden Book) of the patriciate.[7] It was from the members of the Great Council that the governing bodies of the Republic were chosen: the Senate, the Council of Forty, the Council of Ten, and the doge himself. The process of choosing involved the selection of nominating committees in the Great Council by a random lottery—the drawing of gold and silver balls—and then the election or rejection of the nominees according to cloth ballots whose silent deposit preserved the secrecy of the vote. In addition to balloting for the organs of political power, the Great Council chose from among the patriciate, that is, from among its own members, the most important administrative officials, whose brief terms of office necessitated constant elections and consequent rotations of service. A Venetian patrician might be called upon to serve in a variety of regularly changing positions of power and authority over the course of an active political career. Very probably he would, at some point, serve on one of the tribunals that constituted Venice's judicial system, including the tribunal of the Bestemmia that heard the case of Gaetano Franceschini.

Though the members of the Bestemmia were at first chosen from the Council of Ten, the selection later shifted to the Venetian Senate, thus creating a broader republican sponsorship. The number of executors, originally three, was increased to four, and a professional secretary exercised an important, ongoing responsibility for the work of the court; the elected executors rotated in and out of office from year to year, demonstrating their civic responsibility as patricians of the Republic. In fact, in the case against Franceschini new executors were actually chosen between the opening of the investigation in September and the conclusion of the trial in December, and only one of the four executors remained on the tribunal from beginning to end. The secretary would have provided crucial continuity, especially since the executors themselves were not necessarily present for the questioning of witnesses and might simply have read the transcript of the testimony. The membership of the Bestemmia in 1785 included such grand patrician family names as Valmarana, Contarini, Dolfin, and Morosini, famous through centuries of Venetian history. Their civic duty required that they immerse themselves in the unpleasant details of Franceschini's relations with Paolina Lozaro. Their judicial responsibility also placed upon them the charge of perfect secrecy in their investigations and deliberations; the Bestemmia maintained the same strictly secret procedures as the Council of Ten.

In the age of Enlightenment patrician republicanism in Venice was not immune to criticism, and supposed elements of "despotism" in Venetian government were regularly denounced, including secret justice. Furthermore, trials for blasphemy had already begun to seem irrational and archaic to enlightened minds of the eighteenth century. In 1761 a movement for political reform in Venice unsuccessfully sought to restrict the power of the Council of Ten. In 1764 the Milanese philosopher Cesare Beccaria published his manifesto of enlightened penal reform, *On Crimes and Punishments*, radically rejecting the judicial traditions of the ancien régime in Europe and making a modern case for humane and rational practice. Beccaria argued against both judicial torture and capital punishment but also offered a chapter against secret accusations. "Who can defend himself against calumny when it is armed with tyranny's strongest shield, secrecy?" he asked. "Can there be crimes, that is, public offenses, of which it is not in the interest of everyone that they be made a public example, that is, with a public judgment?" Though Beccaria protested that he was not discussing any government in particular, his readers certainly associated secret denunciations with Venice, and secret justice had been criticized there as recently as the political crisis of 1761. Beccaria, who published his work anonymously, was aware of the mistaken notion "that the book came from the pen of a Venetian subject involved in the opposition to the State Inquisitors in the recent troubles which took place in Venice."[8] For Venetians, as well as for foreigners like Montesquieu and Beccaria, one of the symbols of Venice's despotic or tyrannical character was the Lion's Mouth, where Father Fiorese probably deposited his denunciation in 1785.

Beccaria also had enlightened reservations about prosecuting crimes of speech, which notably included blasphemy: "When the crime is verbal, the credibility of witnesses is virtually nil, since the tone of voice, gestures, and everything that leads up to and away from the different ideas which attach to the same words, change and modify what a person says, so that it is almost impossible to repeat it in exactly the same way it was first said. Moreover, violent and uncommon actions, which are the real crimes, always leave a trace of themselves in the multitude of circumstances and effects which derive from them; but words remain only in the hearers' memory, which is generally unreliable and often imposed upon."[9] Such modern juridical reasoning posed a challenge to Venetian criminal law, but the prevailing politically conservative forces were not inclined to accept Beccaria's call for penal reform. The Council of Ten, characterized as "despotic" by enlightened critics, survived several challenges in the late eighteenth century to its power and prerogatives. Seeking to bolster its own political importance, the Council also reinforced the satellite institutions of its moral and legal authority, such as the Bestemmia.

In 1771 the "enormous audacious sacrilege" of blasphemy was proclaimed to be an epidemic crisis: "Today the excesses of the past have now returned, and that lively zeal with which upright people once had secret recourse to the law has cooled." This cooling perhaps corresponded to the growing prevalence of a casually enlightened attitude toward blasphemy, but the tribunal was not inclined to be casual about this "detestable habit of uttering blasphemies even in speeches, in tales, and in jokes." By proclamation of the Bestemmia, local officials, innkeepers, landlords, wine shop proprietors, and the agents of the *traghetti*, at the canal crossings, were all charged with making secret denunciations of any blasphemies that happened to meet their ears. They were furthermore supposed to listen for "obscene expressions," even if not explicitly blasphemous, that might "offend virtue and innocence."[10] This official encouragement of denunciations made it easier for someone like Father Fiorese to accuse Franceschini, who, even if he did not blaspheme, was suspected of obscene conduct offensive to virtue and innocence.

In addition to the Lion's Mouth at the Doge's Palace, the principal place for denunciations, the tribunal proposed to restore and refurbish additional receptacles in other quarters of the city, as well as on the islands of Murano and Burano. Venetians would be held legally responsible if they failed to denounce criminal conduct but would also be rewarded if their denunciations led to serious convictions. In this regard the Bestemmia was immune to the enlightened spirit of Beccaria's penal perspective. The proclamation of 1771, encouraging secret denunciations, was then republished in 1781, following a political crisis in 1780 when the Council of Ten once again prevailed over its critics. The guiding spirit of the conservative patrician hegemony was Pietro Barbarigo, who deplored the "universal inundation of pernicious books in every corner of the state," that is, the published blasphemies of the Enlightenment. In the 1780s the Venetian doge, the leading figure of the government, was Paolo Renier, formerly a man of enlightened values but a generally conservative doge between 1779 and 1789.[11] While the Inquisitors of State maintained their jurisdiction over the moral conduct of the patriciate, the Bestemmia became the organ through which the patriciate conservatively regulated the moral conduct of everyone else.

The Bestemmia thus received renewed encouragement to undertake investigations and prosecutions in the late eighteenth century, at a time when its mandate had moved far beyond the narrow compass of blasphemy to embrace a wide range of social and especially sexual improprieties. Blasphemy had become only a part of a more general judicial commitment pursued by the Bestemmia, a commitment that could also include investigating what happened in Franceschini's bed. Because the Roman Inquisition was responsible for blasphemy when it actually constituted religious heresy, the Bestemmia tended to focus on a purely secular sense of individual vice, judged according to its social perniciousness. At the same time, the agglomeration of competencies over various vices contributed to a unified conception of what it meant to be a disorderly and dangerous individual, beginning with the crime of blasphemy but extending to other forms of censurable behavior. Though many cases included a charge of blasphemy, with some shocking exclamations attributed to the subject under investigation, the court invariably looked beyond blasphemous words to other offensive aspects of disreputable living. Michel Foucault has observed that "in the classical period, indigence, laziness, vice, and madness mingled in an equal guilt within unreason."[12] In Venice, during the course of the eighteenth century, blasphemy became a marker for the more general perception of publicly pernicious and disruptive vice, as the tribunal investigated the vague but comprehensive charges of "bad living" (mala vita) and "scandal" (scandalo).

The case that brought Father Fiorese before the Bestemmia in 1779, that of the pimp Giuseppe Terrizzo who lived in the Campo Sant'Angelo, was not concerned with specific charges of blasphemy. Father Fiorese testified only very generally about the suspect's lack of piety: his failure to go to Mass, his failure to take communion. The denunciation of Terrizzo, for pimping and for purveying quack medicines to cure venereal disease and restore virginity, culminated in the charge that his activity constituted "universally the scandal of almost all Venice."[13] It was this generally scandalous aspect of his specifically sleazy pursuits that made his case a plausible one for the Bestemmia to investigate in the eighteenth century.

In other cases occurring in 1779, the tribunal addressed actual accusations of blasphemy. For instance, a priest on Murano testified against Bortolo Sigla, who said, "There is no God, and if there is, he must be with his whores." He was condemned as a blasphemer to seven years of military service in the Levant.[14] On Burano, a priest denounced the fisherman Giuseppe Constantini for uttering "blasphemies so horrible, so impious, and so frequent, that just thinking about them is horrifying to whoever professes the Christian religion." The worst of the blasphemous exclamations was considered too impious even to transcribe fully in the court record: *di sangue de quel dio por——, sia lo malad——, lo gho in c——*. Filling in the blanks, one may conclude that Constantini invoked "the blood of God, that pig, curse him, and shove it up his ass." Even with such dramatic blasphemies, however, the case against Constantini, which occupied the Bestemmia between 1779 and 1782, also addressed charges that he was generally violent, usually drunk, frequently gambling, and that he beat his wife and infected her with venereal disease. Taken together with his blasphemies, such conduct constituted "a scandalous way of living," and Constantini was condemned to eighteen months at the galley oars of the Venetian fleet.[15] Scandal, again, was the unifying category that summed up a variety of improprieties and brought the case before the Bestemmia.

In 1779 there also came before the Bestemmia a case that would have decisive cultural consequences concerning a young man destined for historic celebrity: Lorenzo Da Ponte, the future librettist of Mozart's masterpieces, just thirty years old when the secret denunciation to the Bestemmia was placed in the Lion's Mouth. He was a priest and a poet, leading the life of a libertine, celebrating Mass, and seducing married women. Da Ponte officiated at the church of San Luca, not far from Sant'Angelo; he rented a room in the neighborhood, began an affair with Angioletta Bellaudi in the house where she lived with her husband, and eventually ran off with her just as she was about to have a baby. They lived together under the fiction that Angioletta was his sister, but the neighbors were not deceived and called her "the priest's whore."[16] There was testimony before the Bestemmia to illuminate the circumstances of scandal and *mala vita*, while the fact that Da Ponte was born a Jew, and converted to Roman Catholicism before entering the priesthood, made his character appear even more suspect. The Bestemmia addressed an indictment to Da Ponte: "You were called from Judaism to the true Christian religion, and raised within it to the level of the priesthood, and with a libertine life you have wickedly profaned both the character of Christian and of priest."[17] A sexually active priest was always a source of scandal.

Da Ponte, however, had fled in anticipation of arrest and was therefore banished from Venice, which propelled him toward his artistic destiny. In the 1780s he was living in Vienna, where he collaborated with Mozart on *Le nozze di Figaro*, *Don Giovanni*, and *Cosi fan tutte*. By the time he wrote his memoirs in the 1820s, he had made his final migration to New York City, where he taught Italian at Columbia University and encouraged the performance of Italian opera. Rather than record the libertine details of his ancient affair with Angioletta, he attributed his downfall in Venice to political antagonisms, which had supposedly provoked a denunciation against him to the Bestemmia for "having eaten prosciutto on a Friday" and for "not having gone to church on several Sundays."[18] Da Ponte obviously regarded eating prosciutto on a Friday as a trivial infraction, both for a former Jew and a current Catholic, and in fact it was not the principal accusation against him. Eating meat on Fridays and skipping Mass on Sundays were, however, just the sorts of auxiliary issues that the Bestemmia did address in the eighteenth century, because such conduct was seen as symptomatic of a "scandalous way of living."

When, eventually, the time came for Franceschini to defend himself before the Bestemmia, he duly noted that, among all the witnesses who testified, "there was no one who introduced, who exposed, who represented me as an irreligious man, as a blasphemer."[19] Invoking the original purpose of the Bestemmia, as founded in 1537, Franceschini failed to appreciate how much its mission had been transformed by 1785. Blasphemy was now only one of the many manifestations of *mala vita* and scandalous conduct, and the tribunal took a broad view in investigating and prosecuting Venetians who disturbed the moral equilibrium of urban life. Whereas Foucault has noted the confused conception of different vices as mingled aspects of human unreason, Gaetano Cozzi has observed that, over the course of the eighteenth century, blasphemy was gradually "integrated into other kinds of accusations, to which the opinion of the judges and the public was more sensitive, like not having a profession or being idle, gambling, using violent and aggressive language toward your neighbor rather than toward God." The work of the Bestemmia became part of an amorphous reconception of criminality, encouraging the denunciation and apprehension of anyone scandalously disruptive of social order.[20]

The patrician executors were keenly sensitive to the general problems of *mala vita* and *scandalo* when, in 1785, they happened to find entangled in the judicial machinery of the tribunal a spectacularly scandalous case that challenged the conventional formulas for integrating the various social evils. Historically, there was some precedent for the tribunal's prosecution of men who deflowered virgins, but the case of Gaetano Franceschini would involve scandal of a different dimension, defying conventional categories of crime, and adumbrating the modern concept of child sexual abuse.

THREE

A Stroke of Providence

On Monday September 5, the Esecutori contro la Bestemmia heard the testimony of Maria Lozaro herself. Born Maria Barbota, she came from the small town of Aviano in Friuli and had been living in in the peripheral parish of Santa Maria Maggiore in Venice for ten years, working as a laundress. In the eighteenth century the church of Santa Maria Maggiore lay at the extremity of Venice, looking out at the lagoon, a sort of land's end, but the modern construction of docks at the Stazione Marittima has obstructed that vista while extending and transforming the city. The brick building of the church of Santa Maria Maggiore still stands—right next to a prison—in the neighborhood where Paolina Lozaro spent her childhood, but it is no longer a functioning church. Formerly a convent was connected to Santa Maria Maggiore, dating from the Renaissance, and in 1510, just before the creation of the Bestemmia, there was a scandal in the convent concerning the prioress, Sister Maria, and her relations with a priest, Father Francesco, from the church of San Stae on the Grand Canal.[1] He had no trouble finding his way to Santa Maria Maggiore, and neither did Gaetano Franceschini almost three centuries later; the neighborhood was out of the way but hardly isolated from the rest of the city.

Mattio played so late in litigating proceeding [handwritten annotation]

Maria Lozaro, summoned by the Bestemmia, would have crossed a large part of Venice to get from Santa Maria Maggiore to the Doge's Palace, where the tribunal awaited her. It was not she but Father Fiorese who had instigated proceedings against Franceschini, and the poor laundress must have felt considerable fear, not only at encountering the alien world of the ruling patriciate in the splendor of the Doge's Palace but also in wondering how the tribunal would judge her own role in the disaster that had befallen her daughter.

Maria Lozaro arrived at the Doge's Palace alone to meet the patrician tribunal, for though the court transcript mentioned that she had a husband, Mattio Lozaro, there was no indication that he was present, and he never gave testimony in the case. In fact, Mattio Lozaro remained so peculiarly invisible in the judicial affair that one might have been tempted to wonder whether there was any husband or father in this story at all. Possibly he moved back and forth between Friuli and Venice, depending upon the seasonal demand for labor, and would have often been apart from his wife and daughter. In the early September days of late summer he could have been working in the harvest in Friuli. When Mattio Lozaro very suddenly materialized in Venice at the conclusion of the case to play a small but striking part, his presence appeared all the more remarkable. In her dealings with

Doge's Palace, where the Bestemmia tribunal met in the eighteenth century.

Franceschini, and then in her encounter with the Bestemmia, Maria Lozaro seemed to have been fending very much for herself.

The story of Maria Lozaro, as she told it to the court, took its main features from the world of the Venetian urban poor, very remote from the patrician lives of the executors. Her poor neighborhood, however, was not out of reach of prosperous predators. Maria Lozaro herself described the advent of Franceschini.

> Last winter I used to see passing by, in my neighborhood of Santa Maria Maggiore, a well-dressed gentleman of a certain age, and what was his motive for coming I do not know. I do know, however, that during that winter my daughter, Paola, said to me that a gentleman had sought her out and wanted her to go into his service. I didn't pay attention to that, because since she only reached the age of eight in March, on the sixteenth, I believed the girl was wrong, or that whoever made the proposition was joking. But about a month ago, one morning, when my daughter was downstairs, I was called by that gentleman because he had tried to get to know my daughter, and he wanted her to go into his service if I agreed. I replied to him that she was too young and unable to do hard work, and he replied that he only wanted her to learn to read and write under the direction of his housekeeper and learn to do the work of a good housekeeper, since the one he had was rather old. So I said to him that if I were sure in trusting that she would be particularly brought up in the fear of God, I would give her to him.[2]

It was thus that Gaetano Franceschini entered into the lives of Maria Lozaro and her daughter, a gentleman who was immediately noticeable in their neighborhood by his nice clothing. He presented himself in the attractive role of an employer, a benefactor, in this case promising to train the eight-year-old Paola, or Paolina, to the calling of a higher domestic service, not mere labor but the sort of household management that required reading and writing. It would have been natural to regard such a stranger with suspicion, and Maria Lozaro invoked some religious concerns about her daughter's welfare. Perhaps her scruples frightened him away, because he did not return to resume their discussion for some time.

> I was not even thinking about him, until Thursday of the week before last when he returned, asking after the girl again, saying that she would be dressed and maintained entirely at his expense, and that she would be paid a silver ducat monthly, paid to me. I would go to see her every day and urge her to be good and obedient. I accepted the proposition, which I regarded as a stroke of Providence [*un tratto della Provvidenza*]. He told me that he would meet me the following Wednesday in the church of Sant'Angelo,

where his housekeeper would come to take the girl, and that together we would bring the girl to his house.[3]

Even after the arrangement had been revealed in a much harsher light, and even as she was telling her tale to the tribunal, Maria Lozaro could not forget that a silver ducat monthly had seemed to her, in her poverty, like a stroke of Providence. The story, as she told it, became a narrative out of traditional popular culture; that is, it became a kind of fairy tale. The characters included a poor mother, a young daughter, and a mysterious stranger who promised good fortune but secretly harbored evil intent. A devil's contract was concluded, the fate of the child bargained for a devil's ducat, and, as if in blasphemous defiance of God, the arrangement was to be settled in church. Now a kindly curate would enter Maria Lozaro's story: "I was called into the sacristy by a priest, who revealed himself to be the curate, and by the way he spoke to me, he revealed that he knew the purpose for which I had come to the church and told me that he was not fully persuaded that I should hand over my daughter."[4]

Maria Lozaro had come from the provinces, from Friuli, to the great metropolis, and her story peculiarly reframed the elements of a country fairy tale into those of a modern urban nightmare. There were even rustic woodsmen in this story, set in the middle of the city. When Maria Lozaro left Sant'Angelo to head for San Stefano, where Father Fiorese was supposed to meet her, she encountered two woodcutters of her acquaintance who lived in the neighborhood of Santa Margherita. "Knowing them, I stopped to have a few words with them, and meanwhile that gentlemen appeared with the housekeeper."[5] Suddenly Franceschini himself was on the scene.

The woodcutters went on their way, and Maria Lozaro, caught between two churches, was left with Franceschini and the housekeeper.

> They took my daughter by the hand, and led her away with them, and I followed them, not having the courage to resist, though not then fearing all that which I later learned, but only supposing that the reflections of the holy curate might concern bad treatment and nothing more. So having arrived at the house, I asked the gentleman to tell me his name and surname, but he did not want to tell me, saying that it was of no importance to me. I was there for some time in that house, curious to know what the curate had meant, and intending to return the following morning, but the gentleman told me not to return until the following Sunday on the pretext that the girl should become accustomed to not seeing me. I left, after he gave me a coin worth fifteen *soldi*.[6]

Such coins were the small change of eighteenth-century Venetian currency, silver not gold. There were coins of five, ten, fifteen, and thirty *soldi*, so Franceschini did not try to pacify Maria Lozaro with the smallest silver coin, but neither did he offer the largest. One example of a coin worth fifteen *soldi* from the 1780s, weighing 3.72 grams in silver, showed a kneeling image of the doge on one side and the winged lion of San Marco on the other.[7]

Maria Lozaro did not tell the tribunal, as she had told the curate, that Gaetano Franceschini wanted to make the girl his "adoptive daughter," perhaps wary that such a phrase would make her seem both credulous and complicit now that all was known. She insisted, however, on her own absolute blindness to the sexual danger of the situation, "not then fearing all that which I later learned." Father Fiorese had been initially suspicious of her, wondering whether she had perhaps really been ready to sell her daughter to Franceschini. The executors of the Bestemmia may have harbored similar suspicions. This was a mother who had, somewhat heedlessly, delivered her daughter into the hands of a man who would not even tell his name. A modern court would have certainly noted her neglect; an early modern tribunal would have wondered about her complicity.

At last, however, she was about to find out the old gentleman's name and game. For just downstairs from the apartment she ran into Father Fiorese, who was sitting and chatting in the coffeehouse. She explained to him what had happened with her daughter: "I told him what I had done. Then he told me that he had some inkling that the man might take her to sleep with him. You can imagine my agitation at such news."[8] Could a tribunal of prosperous Venetian patricians easily imagine the agitation of an impoverished Friulian laundress? Their response would have depended upon their susceptibility to the sentimental ideal of motherhood. The age of Enlightenment already recognized the force of a mother's love for her children, and eighteenth-century culture contributed to the emergence of the modern cult and mystique of motherhood—a cult that would fully flourish within the Victorian culture of the nineteenth century. A modern court would certainly recognize that maternal sentiment transcended the divisions of social class and economic circumstances and meant as much to a laundress as to a countess. The Venetian patricians of the eighteenth-century tribunal, however, might have had to stretch their male imaginations to sympathize with the maternal agitation of Maria Lozaro.

Father Fiorese told Maria Lozaro the name that she had not been able to learn from the gentleman himself: Gaetano Franceschini.

> I immediately returned to the house of this Franceschini to see if I could get my daughter out the door, to take her away with me. I would have climbed the stairs ten times, and the door to the street was open, but I could not manage to do it, because I lacked the courage to go into the house when the master was there. Meanwhile, as I was standing there and turning about, the neighboring coffeehouse proprietor appeared, and I told him the story, and he told me that I should try to get the girl away from there, since the man had the reputation [*concetto*] of being a beast [*bestia*] in matters of sex. And then the housekeeper came downstairs to get some wine, and I entreated her, but she replied that on her own responsibility she would not give the girl to me. Nevertheless, she was certain that the girl would have all possible protection and said that I should come back the next morning and she would have a complete report for me. However, I should take care not to expose her. She advised me that since the girl was quite young, there need not occur any certain evil [*certo male*]. So I departed, agitated.[9]

The housekeeper's reassurance about averting "certain evil"—meaning, probably, actual intercourse—could not have been completely reassuring, since Maria Lozaro had already heard from Father Fiorese that Franceschini might want to sleep with the girl and had learned that he had the sexual reputation of a "beast" among his neighbors. In this distressing situation there was someone to whom Maria Lozaro turned for advice and assistance, a woman named Elena Artico. She had employed Maria Lozaro as a wet nurse, creating a somewhat intimate relationship of patronage between the two women of disparate station, one a prosperous and respectable wife, the other an impoverished and dependent employee. Yet Maria Lozaro had nursed the child of Elena Artico and therefore regarded the wealthier woman as an "affectionate patroness."[10] Elena Artico, in turn, recognized a reciprocal obligation to Maria Lozaro, a sort of family obligation based on milk rather than blood. Even a poor Friulian laundress might have some connections to the higher levels of Venetian society, and on the morning of September 1, the morning after Maria Lozaro brought her child to Franceschini's apartment, the affectionate patroness went into action on behalf of her poor protégée.

Elena Artico (born Elena Gozzi) was a native Venetian living in the parish of Santa Maria Zobenigo, quite close to Sant'Angelo and San Stefano, that quarter of Venice contained in the first serpentine curve of the Grand Canal. She, too, was summoned to testify before the Bestemmia, and her testimony demonstrated how much more confident and unintimidated she was than the poor laundress whose cause she had undertaken to champion. "I will recount how I, compelled by the sentiments of virtue and religion, recently became involved. Last Wednesday morning around noon there came to me a certain Maria Lozaro, Furlana, whom I know because she nursed an infant of mine, and toward whom I am affectionately inclined for her virtue and Christian conduct." It made perfect sense to Elena Artico that Maria Lozaro would welcome Franceschini's initial proposition—"pressured circumstance obliged her not to neglect the opportunity"—but it was equally comprehensible that the mother might then have second thoughts, manifesting "agitation of the soul for fear that she had exposed her daughter to some sacrifice."[11]

Elena Artico threw herself into the mission of making local inquiries about Franceschini, and then, the next day, having established his dubious reputation, she appeared at his door. Maria Lozaro might have climbed the stairs ten times but did not. Elena Artico, with a friend, Cattarina Bartoli, to keep her company, had no such hesitations. The two women showed up when the master was out, but the child was there in the care of the housekeeper. Elena Artico did not like what she saw. "I found the child with her hair dressed. At the sight of me she began to cry, recognizing me and dirtying herself. I learned from her that she had slept the previous night with Franceschini, but I did not get any further with my inquiries. I tried to take her away with me, but the housekeeper who was there did not permit me for fear of the master."[12] The first attempt to rescue Paolina Lozaro thus foundered and failed.

Cattarina Bartoli (born Cattarina Minelli), who participated in that rescue expedition, lived herself in the neighborhood of Sant'Angelo. Her friend Elena Artico had sought her out with an urgent query that could best be answered by someone who belonged to that neighborhood. "Thursday morning she came to me out of breath, inquiring whether I had any knowledge of a certain Gaetano Franceschini, and if I knew his reputation," testified Cattarina Bartoli about her visit from Elena Artico. "I replied that I did not know him, but I knew the report of his bad reputation with regard to sex [la fama di un mal suo concetto rapporto al senso], as one seemed to hear commonly in conversation." It was rumored that Franceschini had such a bad reputation that when he was proposed for admission as an associate to a Venetian gambling casino, not exactly a moral institution, "everyone unanimously opposed him because of his character with regard to sex [tal di lui *carattere rapporto al senso*]."[13] Cattarina Bartoli was able not only to speak to his bad reputation in the neighborhood but also to suggest a more general notoriety in Venetian society. In fact, her language suggested the dynamics of reputation in eighteenth-century Venice, with common conversation as the medium that produced and defined such interlocking phenomena as *fama*, *concetto*, and *carattere*.

Cattarina Bartoli further recalled that she knew a former servant of Gaetano Franceschini and hastened to look up this woman in order to ask about her former master's character. This research yielded the information that Franceschini was "an extremely sensual man [*uomo sensualissimo*], that he entertained an infinite number of women in his house, that he had had another servant girl of about eleven years, and that he had sought to have yet another one but did not succeed because the parents found out about his character." When Cattarina Bartoli brought this report to Elena Artico, they both felt they now had reason enough to climb the stairs and try to rescue the child. Cattarina Bartoli also testified to her own glimpse of the girl on that first unsuccessful approach: "still dressed like a Furlana, but with silver buckles, and her head all powdered."[14] The remnants of folk Friulian costume—probably a colorful skirt worn with a white apron—might have seemed peculiar in conjunction with the newly powdered hair and shiny silver buckles, as if the child were being gradually made over to suit Franceschini's fancy.

After Paolina was finally removed from Franceschini's apartment, the child's original appearance was carefully restored. According to Elena Artico,

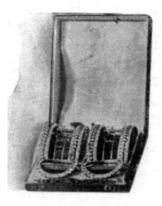

Silver buckles, eighteenth-century Venice.
From Pompeo Molmenti, *La storia di Venezia nella vita privata.*

"Since the girl's hair was dressed in the modern style [*acconciata moderna-mente*], completely powdered, and she was wearing a rather fine blouse that the master had her put on, her mother wanted to remove the powder and rearrange the hair according to their custom."[15] To the mother the hairstyle seemed alien, but to an upper-class Venetian like Elena Artico it looked merely modern, the powdered metropolitan urbanity represented in every eighteenth-century portrait. In fashionable families even little children, both boys and girls, might have powdered hair, in imitation of their stylish elders. Such a style only seemed incongruous on Paolina Lozaro because the little Friulian family was so distinctly unmodern in the context of contemporary Venice. After Paolina's stay in Franceschini's apartment, the powder appeared as a sort of travesty. According to the testimony of Maria Lozaro, "I found my daughter with her head all powdered and styled. I took her with me to the Artico house. I removed the powder and redid her hair according to our custom. I took her to Murano to the house of my brother. And that is what happened to me."[16]

So Maria Lozaro concluded her narration to the tribunal, having recovered her daughter, Paolina. The girl had been separated from her mother for only one night but already seemed somehow strange, altered, alienated from her previous self. The powdered hair appeared as the cosmetic manifestation of whatever more intimate contamination might have taken place in the master's bed. Paolina, powdered, appeared as a little lady, or perhaps a miniature courtesan. The first thing that Maria Lozaro did was to remake her daughter as a child, a Friulian child, with her hair combed according to country custom. Anyone who could imagine her maternal agitation the day before could also imagine her tremendous emotion the day after.

Some things, however, could not be left entirely to the imagination. The tribunal's question to Maria Lozaro was whether "anything sinister" occurred while the child was in Franceschini's house? She replied: "I could not find anything out from my daughter, because I was afraid to inquire, since I didn't want to cause her harm [*ponerla in malizia*]." Having herself placed the child in Franceschini's apartment, Maria Lozaro may not have really wanted to know exactly what occurred during the night. She refrained from asking her daughter questions about explicitly sexual matters and excused herself before the tribunal by pleading that such questions in themselves might have further harmed the girl, making her aware of what did or did not happen. The rescuers, however, had put some questions and later informed the mother, who now told the tribunal what little she knew. "They told me they had learned from the girl that she had been awake the whole night, because he had been tickling her and giving her pinches [*pizziconi*], and, in fact, in the Artico house, when her blouse was changed, I observed a light bruise on the side, but I don't know anything else about what happened to her, and I hope that nothing more than this occurred, thanks to her being removed from the turpitude of that wicked man [*della turpitudine di quel scellerato uomo*]."[17]

A word like "turpitude" from the mouth of the poor laundress might have given the impression that she had been purposefully coached by someone like her patroness or even the curate. There was something artfully dramatic in the righteous phrasing of her moral indignation: "the turpitude of that wicked man." Two years later in 1787 the Venetian librettist, Lorenzo Da Ponte, working with Mozart, would build the great ensemble at the end of the first act of *Don Giovanni* around the declamation: "Trema, trema, o scellerato!" (Tremble, tremble, oh wicked man!)[18]

The agitation of Maria Lozaro over what happened to her daughter did not generally rise to the level of operatic style, rhetorical elevation, and high moral principle. She was at once more direct and more desperate in her concern. Asked by the executors whether she proffered any claim upon the turpitudinous gentleman, she began an aria of moral outrage that immediately subsided into the more material distress of a laundress who had not had much time to do laundry during this very agitating period. "The betrayal [*tradimento*] practiced upon me keeps me in deepest grief and would merit the strongest instances against such a betrayal. I have lost so many days on this account, and I am made totally destitute by such an affair. Without making any solicitation I appeal for as much as the court may provide."[19]

The word "betrayal" was another piece of operatic diction, a charge to be brought against the seducer Don Giovanni in Da Ponte's libretto. In the mouth of Maria Lozaro, however, it betokened not just the betrayal of trust, inasmuch as she had entrusted her daughter to a wicked man who professed good intentions, but also the betrayal of her financial hopes for a silver ducat every month, the stroke of Providence. Instead, she had lost "so many days" that might have been spent doing laundry and earning money. Her anguished appeal to the court was for some financial compensation for herself, as much as the patrician executors might condescend to give.

Maria Lozaro concluded her testimony without being able to satisfy the tribunal on the crucial question of what had happened during the night between her daughter and Franceschini. The mother had heard about pinching and tickling, "but I don't know anything else about what happened to her, and I hope that nothing more than this occurred."[20] Maria Lozaro preferred not to question her daughter too closely, and the tribunal, in turn, did not press the laundress with further interrogation concerning the night in question. By contrast, two important, though speculative, questions were posed to Elena Artico, the middle-class wife and mother, as if she might be better able to assist the court in thinking through the challenging judicial circumstances.

The first question concerned the child: "For what motive truly did the girl begin crying at your appearance in the house of Franceschini?" Elena Artico was more tentative than usual in her response: "I do not know, but it seemed that she was embarrassed to be seen by me in that apartment, with her hair dressed like that, and all powdered." The second question concerned the gentleman: "What truly was the motive of Franceschini in taking that girl?" In reply to this, the witness seemed more sure of herself: "From all appearances it cannot be otherwise than for iniquity, because it is certain that at least he was causing harm to that girl."[21]

The court was interested in the child's emotions and the gentleman's motives because they were relevant to the purely judicial issue of what had happened and who was culpable. Yet these questions also had much broader implications, pointing toward the modern problems of how a child might be harmed by sexual relations with an adult and what sort of adult would behave in such a manner toward a child. The case of Gaetano Franceschini and Paolina Lozaro, from its earliest stages, aired those troubling concerns that later centuries would explore as trauma in child sexual abuse and psychopathology in adult sexuality. The participants in this eighteenth-century drama stood at the threshold of modern history, and the case was investigated in a spirit of critical interest that raised modern questions without yet being able to answer them in terms of psychological analysis and sociological classification.

The tribunal created in the sixteenth century to combat the evil of blasphemy and allay the wrath of God was hardly prepared to investigate the modern phenomenon of child sexual abuse. Since there were precedents for prosecuting the rape and defloration of virgins, the tribunal's first priority was to try to establish whether rape or defloration had occurred. The unspecific concerns of the court, however, were in some ways more important in this case; the mandate to investigate such vague categories as "bad living" and "scandal" encouraged the exploration of problems of criminality that could not be clearly defined or delineated.[22] Elena Artico believed that Franceschini was trying to cause "at least" unspecified "harm" (*malizia*)—that is, something short of defloration. Maria Lozaro herself could only barely articulate whether and to what extent her daughter had been harmed, and the court would find it correspondingly problematic to determine what crime had been committed in Franceschini's apartment.

FOUR

Sexual Criminals and Young Girls

Some forty years earlier, in 1747, a certain young man had been summoned to appear before the Bestemmia in Venice, and, as usual, the charge was not specified in the summons. This young man, a native Venetian, age twenty-two, about the same age that Gaetano Franceschini would have been at that time, was himself uncertain what the charge would be, not because he had led a blameless life but rather because he had already committed so many infractions against religion and morality that he hardly knew where to begin defending himself. A few weeks before, he had played a practical joke that involved sneaking into a cemetery in the middle of the night, digging up a corpse, cutting off an arm, and then using the severed limb to terrorize a middle-aged gentleman who had briefly been a rival for the favors of a servant girl. The next morning this humorous young man found that he was immediately suspected: "People said: 'It is you, only you could have dared to do that.'"[1] Yet it could not be proved against him, and the young man doubted that the Bestemmia had any real evidence to substantiate a charge of blasphemous desecration of the grave.

During the previous year in Venice he had spent his nights with a group of like-minded young men, usually drunk, playing practical jokes: mischievously setting gondolas adrift in the canals; blasphemously summoning priests to administer the last rites to men who were not ailing in the least but fast asleep in bed; or sacrilegiously breaking into churches, either to ring the bells in the middle of the night or to cut the cords so that the bells could not be rung in the morning. "The whole town complained about our nocturnal impertinences, and we laughed at the searches that were made to discover the disturbers of the public peace," commented the young man. At carnival in 1746, he was one of eight masked men who pretended to be officials of the Council of Ten in order to stage the arrest of a pretty young woman, the wife of a weaver, and then compel her to submit to sex with all of them in turn. The young man claimed that she was perfectly content to be thus used by them and pleasantly grateful when they escorted her home afterward: "We all had to laugh about her thanking us with the truest and best faith in the world." Nevertheless, her husband made a complaint to the Council of Ten, whose authority had been falsely invoked, and the Council offered a reward of five hundred ducats for information leading to the arrest of the criminals.[2] But this "nocturnal impertinence"—or gang rape, as we would call it today—was not the reason for the summons by the Bestemmia in 1747, as the young man soon discovered.

His name was Casanova. At the age of twenty-two he was already embarked upon his long career of sexual adventures and other risky endeavors that would keep him constantly on the move, all over Europe, one step ahead of the law. In 1785, Casanova was a sixty-year-old gentleman like Gaetano Franceschini. By then Casanova was living in Bohemia, where he would write his memoirs during the following decade, reliving his once exciting life. He still remembered in detail being summoned by the Bestemmia in 1747.

Having received the summons, Casanova nervously appealed to an older patrician acquaintance, Marco Barbaro, a man with powerful political connections, to find out what would be the charge. "It was a woman who demanded justice against me," Casanova learned, "because I had lured her daughter to the Giudecca, where I had abused her by force." Casanova was accused of having "violated" the girl, who was now in bed convalescing from his brutality.[3] As in the case of Gaetano Franceschini before the same tribunal, the accused was faced with a distraught mother and an abused daughter in a criminal case that was not explicitly about blasphemy but more generally about moral impropriety and scandalous outrage.

Casanova denied the violation but conceded the violence. He thought the case was being brought against him before the Bestemmia simply to cause him expense and embarrassment, and he indignantly drew up a declaration of innocence in his own defense. He quoted the declaration verbatim in his memoirs, as if he had conserved the document all his life to justify himself before posterity. For him the story began as an ordinary day in the life of a Venetian libertine.

On that day I saw the woman with her daughter. There was a wine shop on the same street where I found them, and I invited them to enter. The daughter refused my caresses, and the mother told me that the girl was a virgin and had reason not to let herself go without profiting by it. She permitted me to persuade myself with my hand, so I knew that this could be true, and I offered six *zecchini* to take the girl to the Giudecca after dinner. My offer was accepted, and this mother brought her daughter to the end of the Garden of the Cross. The mother received the six *zecchini*, and she went off. The fact is that the daughter, when I wanted to get to the matter, began to play at fencing with me, so that I always made the wrong move. At first this game made me laugh, but then growing tired of it, and becoming bored, I told her seriously to stop. She gently replied that it was not her fault if I was unable. Recognizing this trick, and having been stupid enough to pay in advance, I could not let myself become the dupe. At the end of an hour I put the girl into a posture such that it was impossible for her to play her game. And then she still managed to move.

"Why don't you stay the way I put you my pretty child [*ma belle enfant*]?"
"Because I don't want to do it in that fashion."
"You don't want to?"
"No."

Then without making the least fuss I took up the broomstick that was there, and I thrashed her. She cried like a pig, but we were by the lagoon where no one could get to us. I know, however, that I did not break either her arms or her legs and that the main marks of the blows can only be upon her buttocks. I forced her to get dressed, I made her get into a boat that was passing by chance, and I had her disembark at the fish market. The mother of this girl had six *zecchini*, and the daughter preserved her detestable flower. If I am guilty, it can only be of having beaten a daughter who is the infamous pupil of an even more infamous mother.[4]

This account, which strikes the modern sensibility as such a nasty one, seemed so plausibly exculpatory to Casanova that he not only composed it in his legal defense in the 1740s but unashamedly included it in his memoirs half a century later. Self-interest, of course, made him put the worst possible construction on the conduct of mother and daughter, seeing them as a team of confidence tricksters, cleverly playing upon the pangs of male lust to profit from the same inviolable virginity over and over again. This was, in fact, the worst construction that could have been placed upon the case of Maria Lozaro and her daughter in 1785, and the suspicions of Father Fiorese echoed Casanova's declaration that his offer of payment was purposefully solicited and eagerly received by the avaricious mother. The girl's resistance to sex did not make Casanova feel like a rapist but rather like the injured party in a breach of contract. Perhaps he found some redress of satisfaction in the pleasure of beating the girl on her buttocks, but he supposed that the magistrature would be able to ascertain, as he had done, that the girl was intact, had preserved her "detestable flower," and that no violation had occurred.

Unfortunately for Casanova, the Bestemmia was unimpressed by his declaration. He learned that the tribunal doubted the girl's virginity and that the mother denied having received any money. When in addition to the denunciation for sexual misconduct, Casanova was accused before the Bestemmia of cemetery desecration, another patrician protector, Mattio Bragadin, advised him not to fight the charges but just to get out of town. "I never departed from Venice with such great regret," Casanova later recalled, "for I had three or four ongoing engagements all dear to my heart, and I was having good luck at gambling." Such was his memoir's spirit of nostalgia for the rococo pleasures of the ancien régime, for the sort of gallant engagements that sometimes involved beating up young girls. In any event he was assured that the accusations against him would dissipate within a year at most: "In Venice everything can be accommodated when the town has forgotten the affair."[5] Casanova's historical reputation, ever since the first publication of his memoirs in the early nineteenth century, has been rather as a celebrated libertine lover than as a notorious sexual criminal. Yet his encounter with the Bestemmia demonstrated that his contemporaries could see him in either of those lights, and Venetian law inevitably had to consider the latter view of his character.

In the case of Gaetano Franceschini, the fact that the daughter of Maria Lozaro was a child, only eight years old, made the scandal particularly notable. What Casanova never mentioned in his memoirs, in spite of much circumstantial detail and a verbatim transcript of his exculpatory declaration, was the age of the girl whose virginity he purchased, whom he wrestled and pinned into position but could not penetrate, and whom he finally beat upon the buttocks in a mixed spirit of righteousness, indignation, and arousal. Writing in French, he referred to her as *la fille*, meaning both "daughter" and "girl," but in his sarcastic endearment he called her *ma belle enfant*, my pretty child. The girl could have been any age between eight and eighteen. Casanova's silence on this count may mean that he was embarrassed to admit her age or, more likely, that her age was a matter of indifference to him when he made the contract with her mother. Men who purchased the virginity of girls naturally expected them to be young, without necessarily worrying about how young they actually were. This case from the long libertine career of Casanova may serve as a point of departure for considering how Venetian law and society regarded the perpetrators and victims of sexual crimes, from the Renaissance to the Enlightenment, right up to 1785 when Franceschini was prosecuted.

Guido Ruggiero, studying the history of sex crime in Renaissance Venice, has noted that "adultery, fornication, rape, homosexuality, and other sexual acts labeled criminal threatened the stability and order of family and community" but were regulated inconsistently according to shifting boundaries between what was seen as illicit and what was prosecuted as illegal.[6] Cases of fornication and rape generally came before the Council of Forty, and though these were often regarded as minor crimes with minor penalties, Venetian tribunals regarded sex with children as particularly culpable. Rape was most harshly punished when the victim could be classified in Latin as *puella*, a prepubescent and therefore still unmarriageable girl, usually under twelve, but sometimes as old as fourteen.[7] According to historian Merry Wiesner in *Women and Gender in Early Modern Europe*, women in northwestern Europe might wait to marry until their twenties, but this was a very different marriage pattern from that of "upper-class women in early modern Italian cities, where the average age of marriage for men was over thirty and for women fifteen."[8]

Ruggiero's research suggests that in Venice a girl who had reached puberty was presumed to be marriageable; therefore, the rapist could cancel his crime by marrying his victim or providing her with a dowry, and this logic might even sometimes prevail for younger girls. In the case of ten-year-old Maria, a boatman's daughter who was raped in 1455, she was permitted to continue in a sexual relationship with her rapist when he promised to marry her; then, when he seemed to renege on his promise, the Council of Forty sentenced him to a year's imprisonment for fornication, unless he married the girl and provided a dowry of fifty ducats, which he promptly decided to do. In 1468 the rape of ten-year-old Marieta was punished by three months' imprisonment combined with a fine of two hundred ducats for her future dowry. In spite of the very young age of the victims, the resolution of these cases was not so different from that of the patrician Francesco Da Mosto, accused in 1469 of fornication with a teenage girl of the patrician Barbaro family; he was sentenced to supply her with a dowry of fifteen hundred ducats in compensation or marry her himself.[9]

An adoptive daughter (*figlia d'anima*) working as a servant in the hope of being eventually dowered as a daughter could be particularly vulnerable to becoming a sexual victim in her adoptive home. In 1467 a ten-year-old adoptive daughter was raped by her "father," who was sentenced to a year in prison as well as a fine to be invested toward her dowry.[10] It was the dangling of this desirable possibility, of her daughter's becoming the *figlia* *d'anima* of Gaetano Franceschini, that so powerfully motivated the maternal ambitions of Maria Lozaro in 1785.

Renaissance sex criminals were often judicially described as acting "in contempt of God" or under the influence of a "diabolical spirit." Such expressions could particularly apply to the incommensurate sexual assaults of adults upon children, as in 1422, when the rapist of an eight-year-old girl was supposed to have been "moved by a diabolical spirit."[11] Ruggiero suggests that there was an implicit category of "crimes against God" in Renaissance Venice, infractions that ranged from sex in sacred spaces, to sex between Christians and Jews, to sex with priests or with nuns. Men and women in ecclesiastical orders were themselves exempt from Venetian secular justice, but their sexual partners were not. In 1407 two men were prosecuted for doing with nuns "no less than they would do with public whores," in 1428 fifteen men were charged in a scandal surrounding the convent on Torcello, and in 1451 the patrician Giovanni Valier was described as "in contempt of God" for having sex with a patrician nun.[12] Casanova, himself a connoisseur of nuns, would have analogous adventures in the eighteenth century. Already in the Renaissance, however, the prosecution of sex crimes involved a significant sense of blasphemy, predating the establishment of the Bestemmia.

By the eighteenth century, the Bestemmia had taken over cases specifically concerning the defloration of virgins, a matter of public scandal for the community as well as criminal offense against the victims. Virgins might range in age but tended to be young, and at the youngest end of the spectrum they could be children like Paolina Lozaro. The defloration of very young virgins was considered especially culpable. Two legal treatises of the eighteenth century outlined the judicial norms for classifying and prosecuting this crime: *Della giurisprudenza criminale, teorica e pratica*

(Criminal Jurisprudence, Theoretical and Practical), by Benedetto Pasqualigo, published in Venice in 1731; and *Pratica criminale secondo le leggi della
Serenissima Repubblica di Venezia* (Practical Criminal Procedure according
to the Laws of the Serenissima Repubblica of Venice), by Lorenzo Priori,
published in Venice in 1738.[13] Pasqualigo began his discussion of sex crime
with a literary flourish by quoting Dante, from Canto V about the second
circle of hell, where carnal sinners suffer in the infernal winds:

> Nulla speranza li conforta mai,   No hope ever comforts them,
> Non che di posa, ma di minor pena.   Neither of rest, nor lesser punishment.

Pasqualigo's discussion proceeded from adultery through sodomy to rape.
He noted that in cases of violated virginity, sex was usually presumed to
occur without consent, that "even if in some appearance consenting, there
is ordinarily presumed to be suggestion and deception masked by artful flat-
teries and promises of matrimony on the part of the violator." Furthermore,
"if the woman is of servile condition, of weak and fearful spirit," then the
man may be supposed to have exercised pressure and made threats.[14]

The special case of children was not seen as an issue of consent, as it would
be in modern law, but rather as a matter of prepubescent physiological condition. Pasqualigo explained that the violent rape of a virgin was punishable,
in theory, by death, but even the attempt to corrupt a girl under the age of
ten—"not fit for carnal coupling"—merited the most extreme punishment.
The penalties for attempted rape, more generally, were left to the court's discretion: "according to the circumstances of the cases, of the age, of the custom, of the condition of the woman," and "whether she is noble or plebeian,
whether of audacious or reserved spirit, whether mistress or maidservant."
Priori's treatise was in complete agreement, noting that the prescribed death
penalty for the rape of a virgin could also be applied to the man "who deflowered or attempted to deflower a little virgin [*verginella*] of less than ten
years approximately, not fit to receive a man." Yet Priori also commented that
for merely attempted defloration, judges preferred not to apply the death
penalty but rather to condemn to the galley oars while imposing a fine for
the girl's future dowry.[15]

According to the law, as applicable to Casanova in the 1740s and Franceschini in the 1780s, the defloration of virgins was distinguished according
to age, because prepubescent girls were physiologically unready for intercourse. If consummated, the crime was considered the same for all ages,
but if unsuccessfully attempted, it was to be more severely punished when

the girl was under the age of ten. Yet in the court's discretionary calculus of culpability a range of factors had to be taken into account, and age was only one of them. In spite of Dante's medieval rigor, in the eighteenth century there was always hope of lesser punishment.

Maria Lozaro, if she were able to read, would have been terrified to learn from Pasqualigo that the death penalty applied to "fathers and mothers who prostitute their daughters." She would have felt all the more urgently the imperative of persuading the tribunal that she had no prior suspicion of Franceschini's intentions. Still, she might have taken some comfort, reading further, to discover that lesser culpability was attributed to parents who sold their daughters out of dire necessity, "miserably compelled to procure their nourishment by unworthy trafficking."[16] Venetian jurisprudence recognized that poverty inevitably influenced the moral conduct of parents and was prepared to take that into account as a mitigating factor when considering the punishment of impoverished mothers who supported themselves by selling their daughters for sex. The Bestemmia, investigating the scandals of Venetian society, had every reason to appreciate the relation between poverty and venality, as in the case of the pimp Giuseppe Terrizzo, accused in 1779 of inducing "many poor women to sacrifice the honor of their daughters."[17]

In the 1770s the Bestemmia considered the legal plea of four boatmen who operated the *traghetti* and hoped to be excused for their blasphemous exclamations along the canals and on the lagoon, since they were poor, hungry, and desperate to earn their daily bread. Since they were boatmen, however, the tribunal could not resist condemning them to the galleys.[18] Their blasphemies constituted one type of public scandal, but so also, in that same decade, did the cases of a venereally infected boatman who tried to rape a three-year-old girl and spent a year in prison, and a stonemason who raped a nine-year-old girl on her way home from school and fled from justice. A Greek tailor who was supposed to have deflowered and infected with syphilis a nine-year-old girl in his shop on the Rialto earned a sentence of six months in prison even though he demonstrated that the girl was actually eleven and he himself was not infected.[19] An artist from Bologna deflowered a thirteen-year-old girl and fled from Venice rather than marry her, and a sailor from Dalmatia deflowered a twenty-two-year-old virgin and then reneged on his promise of marriage.[20] In this single decade, the 1770s, the Bestemmia thus addressed the defloration of virgins, ranging in age from three to twenty-two, without dramatically differentiating, as jurisprudence might have indicated, those over and under the age of ten. Neither were these cases of sex crime sharply distinguished from the other unseemly scandals that claimed the attention of the tribunal.

The official proclamation of the Bestemmia in 1771, reissued in 1781, encouraged denunciations not only of blasphemy but also of "obscene expressions" that might "offend virtue and innocence."[21] Blasphemy and obscenity, like scandal and sex crime, were all linked together as the general concerns of the Bestemmia. In the 1780s the tribunal broadly monitored irreligious, immoral, and disorderly conduct in the urban neighborhoods of the metropolis, and the instigator of a case, the author of the secret denunciation, was often a parish priest like Father Fiorese. In 1784, for instance, a priest took the lead in rallying his neighborhood of San Simeone Grande near the Grand Canal against a loud young man, Alvise Loredan, who "obliges a whole quarter to have recourse to this tribunal, since the above-named Loredan is an execrating blasphemer who gives the greatest scandal in the neighborhood." The priest lived in the apartment just below Loredan, heard all his blasphemies, and heard him beating his pregnant wife as well. When the tribunal sent an officer to arrest him, Loredan jumped out a window and escaped for the moment, though he was eventually captured. The tribunal found Loredan to be the cause of "the most depraved scandal" and condemned him to three months in prison. In 1783 another priest testified against Antonio Gavardina, age twenty-three, who lived near the Rialto. Gavardina was unemployed, lived with a woman of "bad conduct," and blasphemed loudly, "with scandal to everyone and especially to the youth of the neighborhood." One witness was further scandalized at having seen him standing naked on the balcony of his apartment: "though since I was standing in the street I could not see whether he was wearing pants." Gavardina wore white pants and a red shirt when he came before the tribunal, confessed to blasphemy, and was condemned to a year in prison.[22] These cases confirm Cozzi's historical observation that blasphemy was being "integrated into other kinds of accusations," involving the general categories of *scandalo* and *mala vita*, which could also include obscenity and sex crime. Casanova departed from Venice in 1783, after a decade in which he had made his peace with the law by serving as a secret agent for the Inquisitors of State. In 1783 Franceschini moved from Vicenza to take up residence in Venice.

In 1784 the Bestemmia passed judgment on the interreligious romance between a Jewish man and a Christian woman, with five years in prison for him and three for her. A more typical case of that year, however, involved two men from Murano who, though they were not Jews, were nevertheless, in the eyes of the church sacristan, "of a custom not Christian, it being many years since they received the holy sacraments"; they uttered "horrendous blasphemies," causing "most serious scandal particularly when drunk." That same year Marco Menocchi, a boatman, was accused of causing "universal scandal" by living with "always varying and different women of his pleasure." Also in 1784 a pair of impoverished laundresses in the neighborhood of Santa Margherita were brought before the Bestemmia and charged as "most scandalous women" for their blasphemy, sexual impropriety, and loudly disruptive conduct. Some of their neighbors, at least, appreciated the extreme poverty of the women. "I can't say that she's scandalous," someone commented about one of the laundresses. "She has a loose tongue [*lingua lunga*], and I see that she dresses and eats badly."[23] This case was an interesting counterpoint to that of Franceschini the following year, because Maria Lozaro was herself a poor laundress, who, if her tongue had been a little bit looser, might well have found herself accused before the Bestemmia rather than testifying as a witness for the prosecution.

In the year of Franceschini's case, the tribunal also addressed such scandals as a Roman in Venice who trafficked in obscene songs; a ship's chaplain of the Venetian fleet who was supposedly selling condoms; and a young man renting a room from an old man with a young wife, displacing the husband in the matrimonial bed, strutting around the house without his pants, and blaspheming on all occasions. At the end of the decade, in 1789, the Bestemmia was busy with Bortolo Mergotti, a terrible blasphemer, who had supposedly been to bed with two Friulian sisters at the same time. In that year the tribunal also heard the case of Antonio Bernardini, known as *Morte* (Death), who was a polenta vendor near the Arsenal in the parish of San Martino. He treated his wife brutally, and he blasphemously told her that she should regard him as God. When she threatened him with the law, he supposedly "went into furies, exclaiming loudly, 'I shit on you, and on the government, and also on God.'" The tribunal condemned him: for "your abominable scandalous behavior" and "your most damnable habit of uttering the most horrid heretical blasphemies." Bernardini was given the choice between five years in the galleys and ten years in prison, of which he chose the latter.[24]

Over the course of the 1780s the Bestemmia confronted a rich variety of abominable behaviors and employed all the superlatives of evil to indict the most horrid and most wicked conduct of various Venetian subjects. Obscenity and sex crimes, including the defloration of virgins, were prosecuted together with other modes of scandalous conduct. The case against Casanova in 1747 was never fully articulated by the Bestemmia because of his timely flight, but the case of Gaetano Franceschini in 1785 challenged the tribunal's evolving perspective on scandal and criminality and provoked an investigation of unprecedented depth and complexity.

FIVE

The Housekeeper's Dilemma

Maria Bardini (born Maria Franchi), Franceschini's housekeeper, the woman in the silk shawl, was interrogated by the Bestemmia on Wednesday, September 7, exactly one week after the rendezvous in the church of Sant'Angelo. She began by explaining that she had only recently gone to work for Gaetano Franceschini, at the beginning of August 1785, and after eight days in his service she had received a proposition that she found troubling. A widow, Maria Bardini had two daughters being raised outside Venice, and her new master now suggested that she send for one, "that he would make her fortune, while keeping her at his table, and also in bed with him, because the warmth of youth would influence and revive him in his own advanced age, and that he would then think about making her condition secure."[1] Presumably he was promising a dowry, the one thing that secured a poor girl's condition in Venice, or anywhere else in eighteenth-century Europe. Maria Bardini had already told this story to Father Fiorese, and he had already told it to the tribunal, but she presented it again in her own testimony as the crucial background story to what followed with Paolina Lozaro.

The housekeeper herself was not tempted by her employer's proposition, especially because she already had a powerful patron engaged on behalf of her daughters. She tactfully explained to Franceschini—"not having the courage to refuse the proposition on the spot"—that her late husband had been a servant in the household of the patrician Erizzo family, and after her husband's death, that family agreed to provide charitably for the upbringing of the daughters. For that reason, the housekeeper explained to her master, she could not move either of her daughters to the city without first consulting the Erizzo family. Maria Bardini, born in Bologna, had been living in Venice for twenty-two years, and through her own service and that of her deceased husband she had managed to acquire connections even at the level of the patriciate. Indeed, the mention of the Erizzo family was enough to make Franceschini think better of his proposition, and he angrily warned his housekeeper against "gossiping" (*pettegolezzi*).[2] His concern about her indiscretion was, as it turned out, well founded.

The matter rested for the course of August in Venice, and then, at the end of the month, Franceschini gave her another assignment. She was to go to the church of Sant'Angelo the next morning and pick up a girl to bring back to the house. "Having understood this, I spent a night in the most frenzied thoughts, struggling between the need to maintain myself with my master and repugnance at cooperating in the sacrifice of an innocent [*al sacrifizio di un'innocente*]. I therefore determined in the morning to turn to a confessor whom I happened to find in that church." The confessor sent her to the curate in the sacristy, Father Fiorese. Franceschini then surprised her by appearing himself at the church, and she had to pretend that she had failed to identify the mother and daughter and even apologized to the master for being "stupid."[3]

> We all went back to the house together. He said to the mother to return to see the girl on the following Sunday, and then he went out. The mother was in distress [*affanni*] provoked by what the curate had told her, and she queried me about the security of her daughter. I was restrained from speaking for fear of the master, and because I did not trust in the secrecy of the Furlana, so I tried to protect myself with replies that, while not accusing the master, would still not fail to make her suspicious. Finally she left, but then she returned not long after, irresolute, not having the courage to take the girl away, nor the tranquillity to leave her.[4]

Testifying before the tribunal, Maria Bardini herself seemed rather irresolute about how to represent her own role. Well aware that she might appear to have been her master's procuress in this repugnant affair, she sought to convey to the judges that she had, at least, hinted to the mother, as well as spoken to the curate, about Franceschini's suspect proclivities. Like the mother, who testified to "the turpitude of that wicked man," the housekeeper was also able to strike an elevated rhetorical tone concerning "the sacrifice of an innocent."

Maria Lozaro finally left her daughter in the apartment, and Gaetano Franceschini eventually came home. Maria Bardini's perspective as the servant in attendance gave her an ideal vantage point for reporting on what transpired then.

> He ate at the table, together with the girl, and afterward he went to sleep, and took the girl with him, and put her in bed, but dressed. I stayed at attention listening for any cry, ready to rush in, but I heard nothing. When he got up, he ordered me for that evening to take in one of his shirts as best I could, for the use of the girl, and then to put her to sleep in his bed. Fear of the master made me obey. Though the other servant and I myself customarily went to bed early when we were not waiting up for the master, that evening we both stayed awake, but hidden, until the master went to bed, and we kept ourselves at attention to listen for any cry, determined to make noise if necessary and thus divert anything sinister, but after some time, hearing nothing, the other servant went to bed, and a little later I did too. When they were up the next morning I made all the most minute observations to see if anything had happened to either of them. In truth I could reassure myself that nothing had happened.[5]

Anyone paying careful attention to her testimony would have seen that if anything dramatic had occurred in the master's bed that night, anything that might have caused a cry, it would have to have happened in the interstice of the housekeeper's narrative, after the fateful nocturnal moment when she decided to go to sleep—"a little later I did too"—and before the resumption of routine domesticity, "when they were up the next morning." Maria Bardini needed to reassure herself and the tribunal that "nothing had happened" in order to diminish her own responsibility, but her testimony would also serve to defend Franceschini. The male servant, Giuseppe Masironi, who supposedly also listened outside the bedroom door, knew there was a "common rumor" that his master was "a most sensual man." Though Masironi had served in the house for seven months, he indignantly declared to the Bestemmia that he intended to quit his job: "I am already determined to remove myself as soon as an opportunity occurs, as my conscience does not permit me to serve a man of such custom."[6] Both servants were righteously disapproving when summoned to testify before the tribunal, but their duties had obviously obligated them to act as accomplices in their master's domestic adventures. Father Fiorese, from his first encounter with Maria Bardini in the church of Sant'Angelo, had noticed that she seemed frightened of her master, and during the following day and night, when the girl was in the apartment, the housekeeper was constrained by fear and dependency to serve her master in spite of her personal disapproval.

Maria Bardini had to perform a full range of female tasks during the brief but momentous visit of Paolina Lozaro. It was the housekeeper who wielded needle and thread to take in the master's shirt and improvise pajamas for the little girl. It was the housekeeper, furthermore, who powdered the girl's hair, a beautifying ritual that must have been learned in the service of elegant ladies rather than lecherous men. These duties Maria Bardini had to carry out even after having secretly betrayed the game to Father Fiorese in the church. In fact, she had to perform further domestic services at the order of Father Fiorese himself when he appeared that next morning to take the girl away. "The curate wanted me to remove the silver buckles that my master that morning had ordered to be placed upon the girl's shoes, and I also had by commission of the master dressed her hair in the modern fashion with powder, which turned out to be something ridiculous, the noble hairstyle together with the Friulian costume."[7] The housekeeper's own sense of style in the midst of this problematic encounter between the man she served and the child she powdered reflected the ambivalent role of a servant in eighteenth-century society. Through her husband's family Maria Bardini enjoyed the protection of the patrician Erizzo family and could knowledgeably discern what was noble and what was modern in a woman's appearance. At the same time, she lived in a condition of economic dependence and spiritual fear of her master. She had to do her master's bidding, even putting the girl in his bed, but Maria Bardini was sufficiently independent of spirit to betray him discreetly to the priest in the church. Indeed, it was she, more than anyone else, who brought about the tribunal's long investigation into his sexual proclivities.

In his study of servants in Renaissance Venice, the historian Dennis Romano has explored the ideal of domestic hierarchy that governed master-servant relations, and also the daily reality of service that undermined the expectations of loyalty and obedience. In the sixteenth century satisfied masters made special testamentary bequests to their servants, as the specified reward for loyal and faithful service, only to revoke those very same bequests by codicil as punishment for disloyalty and disobedience.[8] In the eighteenth century, as middle-class society mounted a challenge to noble privilege, and the philosophes of the Enlightenment disseminated the revolutionary values of social equality in Europe and America, the traditional deference of the servant was more and more often displaced by a spirit of presumption, impertinence, and independence.

In the opening scene of Carlo Goldoni's drama *I due gemelli veneziani* (The Two Venetian Twins), performed in Venice in 1748, the servant Columbina was supposed to be attending to the hair of her mistress Rosaura.

> ROSAURA. It seems to me, polite Signorina Columbina, it should be your duty to finish your mistress's hair before arranging your own.
>
> COLUMBINA. My duty? Signorina, for two hours I've been standing curling your hair, frizzling your hair, fluffing your hair. But you're never satisfied. And you keep pushing your fingers into your hair just to annoy me. So that I don't know what I've done and what I haven't.
>
> ROSAURA. How dare you! You've deliberately left my hair all anyhow simply to waste time on your own.
>
> COLUMBINA. I like that! I suppose I haven't hair on my head the same as you?
>
> ROSAURA. Yes, but I am the mistress and you are the servant.
>
> COLUMBINA. Thanks very much. There's no need to keep rubbing it in.[9]

Rosaura's traditional affirmation of hierarchy—"I am the mistress and you are the servant"—thus countered the insubordinate egalitarianism of Columbina. The character of Columbina originated in the *commedia dell'arte*, but her ideology reflected an enlightened emphasis on equality in the eighteenth century. The public of 1748 would have witnessed the resemblance of the two women, their divergent social status bridged by a mutual feminine vanity before the mirror.

The most impertinent servant of eighteenth-century drama was the celebrated figure of Figaro, first created for the Paris stage in 1775 by Pierre-Augustin Caron de Beaumarchais in *The Barber of Seville*. Beaumarchais brought Figaro back in 1784 in *The Marriage of Figaro*, which the Venetian Lorenzo Da Ponte made into an Italian libretto for Mozart in Vienna in 1786. The drama was driven by the sexual rivalry between servant and master, Figaro and the Count. When Figaro discovered that his own intended bride was being aggressively pursued by the Count, the servant prepared for battle and sang his defiance, in Mozart's melody and Da Ponte's words.

L'arte schermendo,	Parrying your skill,
L'arte adoprando,	Using my skill,
Di qua pungendo,	Stinging here,
Di là scherzando,	Joking there,
Tutte le macchine rovescerò.	All your plots I will overturn.

Se vuol ballare,	If you want to dance,
Signor Contino,	Little master Count,
Il chitarrino	My little guitar
Le suonerò.	I will play for you.[10]

The Frenchman Beaumarchais, the Austrian Mozart, and the Venetian Da Ponte could all invest their respective arts in sympathy for a servant who was ready to stand up to his master. Furthermore, the predatory master was no less engaged in this rivalry than the servant.

Vedrò, mentr'io sospiro,	Will I see, while I sigh,
Felice un servo mio?	My servant happy?
E un ben che invan desio	And that which I in vain desire
Ei posseder dovrà?	Shall he possess?[11]

That which the Count desired was Figaro's bride, the servant Susanna. This social landscape of *The Marriage of Figaro* did not have separate spheres for masters and servants but featured instead a tense struggle over prerogatives and presumptions in the decade of the 1780s, the decade that would end with the outbreak of the French Revolution.

When Giuseppe Masironi declared that he was ready to leave Franceschini's service, for reasons of conscience, he was surely saying what he thought the tribunal wanted to hear. Whatever his pangs of conscience, as a servant he would have had to accommodate his master's private pursuits, and as a manservant he probably had to assist even more indelicately than the female housekeeper. In 1787 Da Ponte and Mozart offered operatic recognition to the role played by men like Masironi when they created the character of Leporello, servant and supreme accomplice of a libertine master in *Don Giovanni*. When the curtain went up on the very first performance, in Prague, Leporello held the stage alone, standing guard while Don Giovanni, offstage, attempted to rape a nobleman's daughter.

Notte e giorno faticar	To labor night and day
Per chi nulla sa gradir;	For one who appreciates nothing;
Piova e vento sopportar,	To put up with rain and wind,
Mangiar male e mal dormir.	To eat badly and sleep badly.
Voglio far il gentiluomo,	I want to play the gentleman,
E non voglio più servir.	And I don't want to serve anymore.
Oh, che caro galantuomo!	Oh, what a fine gentleman!
Voi star dentro con la bella,	You stay inside with the beauty,
Ed io far la sentinella!	And I play the sentinel![12]

Masironi, waiting up with the housekeeper outside Franceschini's bedroom door, was supposedly concerned about the little girl in the master's bed, but it is all too easy to imagine him as the sentinel protecting his master's erotic adventures from any awkward intrusions. Indeed, Maria Bardini herself played the sentinel at the door the next day, when she at first prevented Elena Artico and Cattarina Bartoli from removing the girl from the premises.

Leporello labored as the servant while wanting to be the master and, famously, while keeping the catalogue of his master's sexual conquests. Like Giuseppe Masironi with Franceschini, Leporello sometimes threatened to leave Don Giovanni's service, as in the little duet at the beginning of the second act—"ed io non burlo, ma voglio andar" (and I'm not joking, I want to leave)—but for four gold coins the servant changed his mind. Later in the second act, when cornered by the virtuous enemies of Don Giovanni, Leporello excused himself—"il padron con prepotenza l'innocenza mi rubò" (the master with his power corrupted my innocence)—and at the finale, after Don Giovanni had been dragged down to hell, his servant sang, "io vado all'osteria a trovar padron miglior" (I am going to the inn to find a better master).[13] Yet Leporello had been Don Giovanni's perfect accomplice in pursuit of endless sexual conquests, and any master who was morally "better" would have certainly wasted the servant's talents for deception and connivance. The Venetian Lorenzo Da Ponte, who himself had been denounced to the Bestemmia in 1779, fully appreciated the role that a servant might play in his master's private life.

The historian Daniel Roche, writing the history of clothing and fashion in France in the eighteenth century, has shown that it was increasingly common for maids to acquire the discarded clothing of their mistresses and emulate their style, so it became correspondingly difficult to distinguish servants by their attire.[14] In *The Marriage of Figaro* the Countess and Susanna agreed to wear one another's clothes in order to deceive the Count; in *Don Giovanni* the master and servant also exchanged clothes and identities in order to facilitate Don Giovanni's seductions. When Maria Bardini appeared in the church of Sant'Angelo in her silk shawl, she indicated some consciousness of respectable fashion that could have come to her from her association with the patrician Erizzo family. Her costume might also have reflected the sense of personal worth that made her unwilling to be utterly complicit in her master's sexual scheming. Figaro's triumph over the Count, whose major misbehavior consisted of the sexual pursuit of his female servants, was performed as drama in Paris in

1784, and as opera in Vienna in 1786; in 1785 Maria Bardini brought about the downfall of Gaetano Franceschini in Venice. It was she, fatefully, who spoke to Father Fiorese in the church, and he, finally, who made the secret denunciation. She pretended to be "stupid," but it was she who played the tune on her guitar.

When Father Fiorese came to rescue the girl from Franceschini's apartment, Maria Bardini asked what she was supposed to say to her master when he returned. The priest suggested she say that there were four people who came for the girl: two gentlewomen, the mother, and himself. This was not exactly true, since the four had not come together, and the servant had already refused to turn the girl over to the two gentlewomen, Elena Artico and Cattarina Bartoli. In the spirit of Figaro, however, Maria Bardini entered conspiratorially into the priest's proposal to deceive her master. By the time Franceschini returned home, she was ready to deal with his agitation at finding that the girl was gone. "To his reproaches for having let her leave," said the servant, "I justified myself by saying to him that I had been alone."[15] He then warned her against "gossip" and told her to say nothing to anyone about what had happened. She, of course, had already told everything to everyone and must have given her promise of discretion with the knowledge that some sort of clock was probably ticking, that the resourceful priest, the two outraged gentlewomen, and even the miserable mother might well decide to appeal to the law against Gaetano Franceschini.

"And to whom might it be known whether the girl was in the bed with Franceschini?" The tribunal put this question to Father Fiorese on the very first day of the investigation, and he answered unhesitatingly: "That cannot be known except to the two servants of the house."[16] Servants were the crucial witnesses in cases of crimes that took place at home. Pasqualigo's *Criminal Jurisprudence* noted the special value of a servant's testimony in court but also recognized its unreliability. Servants lived together with their masters, like members of the family, and were sometimes "necessary, more than anyone else, for informing the court about the truth concerning nocturnal deeds of theft, rape, and adultery committed within the secrecy of the domestic walls." Yet the fact of domestic intimacy, complicity, and dependency meant that servants were generally not "witnesses of complete credibility."[17] Maria Bardini, before she testified, had to consider her own best interests, calculating the power and influence of her master, of the priest, of the tribunal, and of her patrician patrons in the Erizzo family. She also must have recognized that, whatever she reported about her master's scandalous private life, as lived within the secrecy of the domestic walls, she would risk betraying herself as complicitous.

Maria Bardini would have had to conceal from her master her secret summons to appear and testify before the Bestemmia, and she must have been nervous that he would come to suspect her disloyalty and indiscretion. She may have felt that the sooner he was arrested, the safer she would be. By the time she herself testified, the tribunal had been hearing testimony for a week, but in a system of secret justice Franceschini was not supposed to know that anything was happening, and the witnesses were all sworn to silence. However, in both the case of Casanova in 1747 and that of Da Ponte in 1779, there was a powerful friend, very close to the tribunal, who gave a timely warning to the suspects under investigation so that they could leave Venice and escape trial. In secret proceedings there was always the possibility of a leak. On Wednesday, Maria Bardini informed the Bestemmia that over the weekend Franceschini had been to Mestre

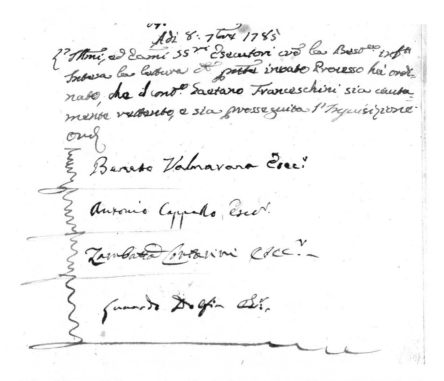

Order of Franceschini's arrest, signed by the four members of the Bestemmia tribunal. Archivio di Stato di Venezia, Esecutori contro la Bestemmia, Busta 40, *Processi*, 1785, 30r.

to make some arrangements for a boat, and that even now, as she spoke, a gondola was mysteriously waiting for him at the embankment near the house. "From these things I have begun to suspect that he is thinking about leaving," she told the tribunal.[18] On Thursday night, September 8, Gaetano Franceschini was arrested and imprisoned by order of the Esecutori contro la Bestemmia.[19]

PART TWO

Upstairs from the Coffeehouse

Adesso è in voga il caffè. (Now coffee is in fashion.)

—Carlo Goldoni, *La bottega del caffè*

SIX

The *Caffettiere* in His Coffeehouse

Franceschini lived upstairs from the coffeehouse in a four-story building on Calle della Cortesia, near the Campo Sant'Angelo, an ordinary Venetian neighborhood in the heart of the city. The coffeehouse was on the ground floor, and there were three floors of apartments above. At the top of the building was the residence of the coffeehouse proprietor and his family; below them was Franceschini's apartment, and below him was the widow of a Venetian patrician. Across the street from the coffeehouse, at street level, was the shop of a baker (*pistor*, in Venetian), so important for providing the neighborhood with its daily bread that the street was sometimes even known as the Calle del Pistor. Coffee was certainly a luxury in comparison to the necessity of bread, but the institution of the coffeehouse in eighteenth-century Venice was a new phenomenon, socially exciting and chemically addictive, the focus in every neighborhood of public community life. Jürgen Habermas has observed that the coffeehouse was, in fact, one of the crucial institutions for the creation of the public sphere in Europe in the eighteenth century.[1]

The coffeehouse on Calle della Cortesia offered the neighborhood the most fashionable form of modern courtesy [*cortesia*], the ritual of drinking coffee, and this was only one of two hundred coffeehouses all over Venice.

These locales first appeared in Europe in the seventeenth century and pro-liferated in the eighteenth century, becoming a celebrated part of Venetian public life. In 1750, at the Teatro Sant'Angelo, in this same neighborhood, the Venetian playwright Carlo Goldoni presented to the public what was to become one of his most famous comedies, *La bottega del caffè*, a drama of everyday life set entirely in a coffeehouse. Franceschini's case in 1785 was inevitably connected to the public life of the coffeehouse downstairs from his apartment.

Domenico Ravasin was the *caffettiere* who ran the coffeehouse on Calle della Cortesia and lived on the top floor of the building. Ravasin, a native Venetian, began his testimony by disclaiming any special knowledge about his neighbor Franceschini, pleading the constant demands of attending to the busy coffeehouse. It emerged, however, that he did know more than a little about what transpired in his neighbor's life and apartment.

> I cannot affirm anything with certainty relative to his behavior, because, standing in my coffeehouse, I do not see who comes and goes in his apart-ment. The universal concept of him is certainly that he is a man extremely devoted to women. But I don't think I have seen a woman go there more than once, except for a Furlana woman who sells ladles and spoons, and various Furlana women who pass by and look toward his apartment, but I don't know if they then go in, because, standing in my coffeehouse, I can't see. I will say that one day last winter I sent to him one of my men, Zuane Lorenzini, who was then working in the coffeehouse, and when he returned, he expressed himself to me in these precise terms: "The old pig, he has a whore with him who would make you vomit." And I will say that on Wednesday of last week a Furlana came to my place and said to me that he had brought home her daughter, and she asked my opinion whether the girl was safe, because the woman had come to feel some suspicion, and I replied that I couldn't tell her anything, but that if she had doubts, I advised her to go and take the girl away. The woman, however, was afraid.[2]

That woman, of course, was Maria Lozaro. She had come to the coffeehouse because her daughter was upstairs in Franceschini's apartment. Father Fiorese also remembered meeting her on that occasion. "Having retired nearby to the coffeehouse, to chat with someone," the priest testified, "I saw the Furlana approaching, agitated." Thus, the story of Gaetano Franceschini and Paolina Lozaro began to be discussed in the neighborhood coffeehouse.

Domenico Ravasin had a clear sense of where the proprietor of a coffee-house ought to be: "standing in my coffeehouse." That was his limited per-spective for peering into the private life of Gaetano Franceschini, and the

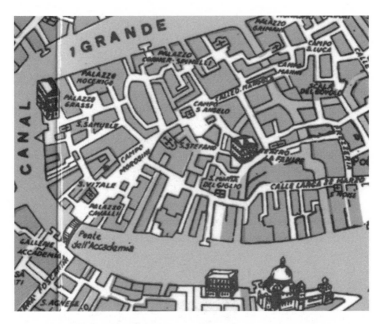

Map of Venice. Calle della Mandola (the street marked as Calle D. Mandola on the map) comes out of Campo Sant'Angelo (marked as Campo S. Angelo). Calle della Mandola, also remembered as Calle della Cortesia even today, was probably the location of Domenico Ravasin's coffeehouse and Franceschini's apartment. The Accademia bridge, represented here, was not built until the nineteenth century. The most prominent landmark in the vicinity of Campo Sant'Angelo, the Teatro La Fenice, Venice's celebrated opera house, was to be built very soon after the neighborhood events of 1785 and opened for performances in 1792. Adapted from a modern tourist map of Venice.

Street sign today for "Calle de la Cortesia" (as written in the Venetian style).

Calle della Mandola today (also known as Calle della Cortesia). The street opens into the Campo Sant'Angelo at the far end. Shops are at ground level with three floors above.

Shops (*botteghe*) at ground level with residences above in eighteenth-century Venice. From Pompeo Molmenti, *La storia di Venezia nella vita privata*.

testimony of what was directly witnessed was therefore accordingly limited. Standing in the coffeehouse, however, Ravasin found that the news of the neighborhood came to him. Maria Lozaro recalled in her testimony that "as I was standing there and turning about, the neighboring coffeehouse proprietor appeared, and I told him the story, and he told me that I should try to get the girl away from there, since the man had the reputation of being a beast in matters of sex." Ravasin not only knew Franceschini's reputation concerning women but could even quote verbatim for the tribunal a secondhand report on the presence of a woman in the upstairs apartment. What was Lorenzini—"one of my men," according to Ravasin—doing in Franceschini's apartment when there was a prostitute on the premises? Evidently, the coffeehouse delivered cups of coffee to local clients, at work, at home, in bed, wherever. The men who made the deliveries would then return to the coffeehouse with a few choice remarks about what they had seen on their route. Lorenzini himself would later be summoned by the Bestemmia to testify to what he had seen while delivering coffee.

The central role of the coffeehouse in eighteenth-century Venetian neighborhood life was dramatized by Goldoni in *La bottega del caffè*. When the curtain went up in 1750, the scene was the coffeehouse itself, on a Venetian street of small businesses—a barbershop, a casino, an inn—with the windows of urban apartments on the upper story of the stage set. The great Goldonian revolution in theatrical history produced the modern drama of urban public life, in which members of the theatrical public witnessed scenes from their own daily public routines, the drama of city spaces and urban neighbors. The public came in from the streets and found on the stage not Olympus, not Arcadia, but the same life of the streets that they had just left behind.[3] If, before the drama, they had stopped for a coffee in the neighborhood coffeehouse, somewhere around the Campo Sant'Angelo, they would have found a similar establishment on the stage of the Teatro Sant'Angelo.

Just as the Bestemmia recognized the testimonial importance of Domenico Ravasin, the *caffettiere*, as a central figure in neighborhood life, so Goldoni placed the character of the *caffettiere* at the center of the drama, named him Ridolfo, and portrayed him in the opening scene as he prepared his employees for a day in the life of a typical Venetian coffeehouse.

> RIDOLFO. Courage, boys, behave well. Be quick and ready to serve the customers with civility, with propriety. Because often the reputation of a shop depends upon the good manners of those who serve.

TRAPPOLA. Dear master, to tell the truth, this rising early has done nothing good for my health.

RIDOLFO. Yet it's necessary to get up early, necessary to serve everyone. Those who are going on a voyage arrive early. And workers, and boatmen, and sailors, these are all people who rise early in the morning.

TRAPPOLA. It's truly something that makes you collapse with laughter to see even the porters coming to drink their coffee.

RIDOLFO. Everyone tries to do what others are doing. Once alcohol was the thing, but now coffee is in fashion.

TRAPPOLA. And that lady, to whom I bring coffee every morning, almost always she asks me to buy her four *soldi* worth of firewood, and still she wants to drink her coffee.

RIDOLFO. Gluttony is a vice that never ends, and it's the vice that always increases the more a man ages.[4]

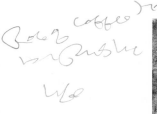

Goldoni's drama reflected the eighteenth-century moment when the public café was something new on the urban scene, and the social consumption of coffee constituted a revolutionary phenomenon in customs and refreshment. The coffeehouse played an important part in the dynamic currents of culture and society, from the philosophy of the Enlightenment to the

Carlo Goldoni. From Pompeo Molmenti, *La storia di Venezia nella vita privata.*

romance of libertinism, from contemporary medical debate to the gossip of urban sociability. Everyone drank coffee, fashionable elites as well as workers and boatmen. Because Gaetano Franceschini happened to live upstairs from a coffeehouse, the case against him was also notably conditioned by the compelling social implications of coffee.

The historian Fernand Braudel has traced the beverage revolution that brought coffee across the Mediterranean after its appearance in the Ottoman Empire in the sixteenth century. In 1585 the Venetian envoy in Istanbul, Gianfrancesco Morosini, reported on the custom of drinking coffee among the Turks: "Almost continually they remain seated and, in conversation, they are accustomed to drink publicly, in shops and in the streets, not only low people but also the most prominent, a black water, as hot as they can stand it, which is extracted from a seed that they call *kahvè*, to which they attribute the virtue of keeping a man awake." Venice, with its eastern Mediterranean island outposts and intricate Ottoman commercial relations, may have been the first port of arrival for coffee in Christian Europe. "Coffee reached Venice in about 1615," observed Braudel. "By 1643 the new drug was making its first appearance in Paris, and possibly by 1651 in London." In 1671 coffee was saluted in Lyon for a great variety of medicinal virtues: "It dries up all cold and damp humours, drives away wind, strengthens the liver, relieves dropsies by its purifying quality; sovereign equally for scabies and impurity of the blood, it revives the heart and its vital beat, relieves those who have stomach ache and have lost their appetite; it is equally good for those who have a cold in the head."[5] There would soon be critics who violently disagreed and would cite an equally long list of coffee's negative medical consequences, but either way, agreement was widespread that coffee was physiologically changing people's lives.

The social implications of this revolution in drinking were tied to the institution of the coffeehouse. In 1683 there was only one single Venetian coffeehouse under the arcades of the Procuratie Nuove in Piazza San Marco. By the middle of the eighteenth century, however, there were already two hundred coffeehouses in Venice. In Paris in the late seventeenth century, the French drank coffee at the Café Procope on the Rive Gauche and the Café de la Régence at the Palais Royal. In the eighteenth century, however, the number of cafés in Paris rose to six hundred, and instead of just importing coffee from the Middle East, France had begun to grow colonial coffee on Martinique, Guadaloupe, and Saint-Domingue (Haiti). Numerous though the cafés of Paris may have been, according to historian Brian Cowan,

English visitors had the impression that there were fewer than in London.[6] As medicine, as refreshment, as stimulant, as addiction, as fashion, and as vice, coffee had come to Europe to stay.

In Venice coffeehouses bore such regal names as The Empress of Russia, The King of France, The Queen of Hungary, and The Prince of Tuscany; mythological labels like Orpheus, Diana, and Aurora; or virtuously allegorical titles like Courage, Hope, Fortune, Peace, and Venice Triumphant, which was also already known as the Florian, as it still is today. The Florian, founded in 1720 under the sheltering arcades of Piazza San Marco, was frequented by Venetians like Goldoni and Casanova and would also attract such notable foreign tourists as Goethe and Byron. The nearby Aurora, by the Campanile of San Marco, was supposed to have served its coffee in fine porcelain cups, with such accompaniments as *rosolio* (sweet raisin liqueur), as well as sugared almonds and little biscuits brought out on silver plates.[7]

"Nobili al cafè." The *caffettiere* stands behind the counter. From Giovanni Grevembroch, *Gli abiti de veneziani*, eighteenth century. By permission of the Biblioteca del Museo Correr, Venice.

If such coffeehouses offered a certain luxury and pursued a posh clientele, more typical establishments like the one in Goldoni's play, and probably like the one in Franceschini's building, catered to a broad spectrum of the neighborhood population: workers, boatmen, sailors, porters, and parish priests. The price list from another neighborhood coffeehouse in Venice in the 1750s showed that a cup of coffee cost five *soldi*, and a cup of chocolate, fifteen.[8] In other words, Maria Lozaro, with her coin from Franceschini, worth fifteen *soldi*, could have afforded three cups of coffee, though only one luxurious cup of chocolate. There was something for everyone at the coffeehouse.

For Goldoni the setting of the coffeehouse enabled him to represent the drama of an entire Venetian neighborhood. For Gaetano Franceschini it was perhaps an unlucky circumstance to be leading a life of promiscuous sexual activity in a building where his neighbors inevitably congregated. Reports about his female visitors—old whores, young girls, and "various Furlana women who pass by and look toward his apartment"—were certain to circulate among the customers of the coffeehouse. On the other hand, it is possible that Franceschini considered the location of the coffeehouse as a personal convenience, not only for the coffee but also for the heterogeneous clientele; women who were too poor to pay for their firewood were perhaps just the women that he most wanted to meet, especially if they had young daughters.

Coffeehouses were, in fact, seen as problematic places of scandal and sex in Venice, and in the 1750s, the decade of Goldoni's drama, the Bestemmia ordered the closing of two establishments in the arcades of Piazza San Marco, a barbershop and a coffeehouse, "as scandalous places" visited even by priests.[9] In the 1760s there were Venetian attempts to legislate against the presence of women in coffeehouses because the stimulating atmosphere seemed to encourage libertine relations between the sexes. It proved impossible to enforce such a ban, and the proprietors, eager for business, were complicit in illegally serving women. The eighteenth-century poet Giorgio Baffo noted that impossibility in verse in Venetian dialect:

> Ma per quanto i voggia tegnir duro,
> ch'in bottega no vaga piu le done,
> gnente no i fara mai, ve l'asseguro.

> No matter how much one wants to hold firm,
> and keep women from going into the shop,
> nothing will ever make it happen, I assure you.[10]

Baffo implied that human nature was the obstacle to enforcement, and therefore the presence of women made coffeehouses into possible sites of sexual scandal.

The possibility of scandal in coffeehouses was aggravated by backrooms employed for unauthorized gambling, but also allegedly used for illicit sex. The Inquisitors of State in 1766 went so far as to "prescribe the demolition of certain indecent and scandalous rooms, profaned by the greed of the *caffettieri* and of wicked men." Women were not even absolutely necessary in the sexual indecencies associated with coffeehouses, and, in 1767, there was a report on the use of such "scandalous rooms" by Turks in the Piazza San Marco: "They sometimes go into the places that are above the coffeehouses and take with them also some youths in their company, and since the vice of the Turks is well known, one cannot but suspect some vile commerce in sodomy."[11] In this case, the Turkish associations of coffee may have aggravated the conviction that coffeehouses were a site of Turkish immorality. A letter to the *Gazzetta urbana veneta* in 1795 declared that "it is no longer decent to frequent the coffeehouses too much."[12]

Some *caffettieri* were actually arrested in 1767 for "transgressing the sage regulations against intolerable scandalous abuses" in the establishments around San Marco. In 1768 "there emerged from the deep and secret prisons the *caffettiere* Francesco," deemed "the least culpable in transgressing the sovereign precepts, among those who were arrested and punished some months ago."[13] Domenico Ravasin may well have felt nervous about testifying before the Bestemmia in 1785 concerning possible scandal upstairs from his coffeehouse.

Goldoni's drama presented coffee drinking as "a vice that never ends," and although the arrival of coffee in Europe had been originally accompanied by reports of its salubrious qualities, by the 1750s there was already a contrary medical literature stipulating the negative effects of this supposed vice. In 1755 Gian Jacopo Zannichelli published his *Osservazioni intorno all'abuso del caffè* (Observations concerning the Abuse of Coffee). "Few are those," remarked Zannichelli, "who, after having taken coffee in the evening hours, do not suffer from losing sleep on the subsequent night." Sleeplessness, however, was only the mildest of the negative consequences, and Zannichelli warned that excessive coffee drinking could lead to tremors, paralysis, apoplexy, emaciation, erysipelas, scurvy, scabies, herpes, pustules, fevers, heavy perspiration, excessive urination, loss of appetite, loss of blood, palpitations of the heart, sterility, convulsions, and even death.

Convulsions, he claimed, were becoming epidemic: "Now these same convulsions, and even sudden deaths, have become so frequent, because of the use of coffee in homes, and because the places where it is publicly sold have so strangely multiplied." Zannichelli recommended tea as a healthier alternative and urged the Venetian government to limit the number of coffeehouses as a public health measure.[14]

In 1759 the Venetian state seemed to follow Zannichelli's recommendation and established a statutory limit to the number of coffeehouses in the city. The regulation restricted the number of establishments to 206, affirming that in "occupying the best places of the city with luxury commerce, they restrict the practice of more useful and necessary arts."[15] Thus, the moral and medical implications of coffee were also complicated by economic considerations. In 1775 a French visitor to Venice, Ange Goudar, urged the Venetian government to intervene more drastically against the fashion for coffee, claiming that "the excess is so great that one takes more in a day in Venice than the Turks in Constantinople drink in a year." Goudar regarded the medical consequences as dire and thought that the Great Council should consider forbidding coffee altogether; short of that, he proposed that the *caffettiere* of each coffeehouse should limit his customers to a single daily cup of coffee.[16]

Zannichelli puzzled over the fashion for coffee in the 1750s, as he himself clearly found the drink distasteful.

> To me it has always appeared deserving of consideration how it happened that a beverage, not delightful to the eye, nor sweet to the palate, but, on the contrary, both despicable and disgusting in its bitterness and its sooty, murky color, should have by a sort of enchantment enthralled so many nations, notably the most polished and civilized in Europe. . . . It is quite true that our people, however, more prudent than the Orientals, add sugar by which, truly, the bitterness is tempered, and the coffee is rendered pleasing and agreeable to the most delicate persons. But this was the cause, if I am not mistaken, of the custom spreading more widely.[17]

For those who disapproved of the beverage, as Zannichelli certainly did, it appeared paradoxical that coffee should have been so enthusiastically adopted by the most "civilized" nations in Europe and that its triumph accompanied the rise of refinement and spread of civilization. Furthermore, though coffee was recognized as "Oriental" in its origins, it had clearly become the emblem of fashionable civilization in Europe. In Goldoni's Oriental harem drama of 1753, *La sposa persiana* (The Persian Bride), it was the

Persian characters who served coffee onstage and even discussed detailed instructions for preparation.

Usarlo indi conviene di fresco macinato,
In luogo caldo e asciutto con gelosia guardato.

It's suitable to use it freshly ground,
Jealously conserved in a hot and dry place.[18]

Yet Goldoni's drama of the Venetian coffeehouse in 1750 showed how well he knew that Europeans had already made coffee a pleasure and a vice of their own.

"The abuse of coffee," wrote Zannichelli in 1755, "has become more and more frequent and almost universal in our times, perhaps because for many it has become a noble pretext for passing the hours, indeed entire days, in idleness, without doing anything, fomenting in some cities the laziness and slothfulness that are, unfortunately, the predominant defects of this age."[19] This was not just medical but moral and spiritual disapproval. By the middle of the eighteenth century, however, there was also a clearly articulated contrary point of view, a moral and spiritual defense of coffeehouses. For these establishments offered not only coffee to their customers but the equally addictive pleasures of company and conversation. In 1761 Gasparo Gozzi, a leading Venetian journalist and the brother of the dramatist Carlo Gozzi, composed for *L'osservatore veneto* (The Venetian Observer) a tribute (*elogio*) to the coffeehouse as an innovative and salutary form of sociability. He considered the case of the solitary man, with no one to talk to, lapsing into pathological melancholy: "But if he goes out of his house and finds friends and acquaintances who reason about this and about that, they shake him up; and little by little his intellect is cleared, and the weight in his heart is lightened, and he returns healthy and happy in a short time. There cannot be a better convenience for those who need such assistance than the coffeehouses."[20] Gozzi seemed to speak from personal experience.

In fact, both of the Gozzi brothers frequented the Caffè dei Letterati (the coffeehouse of literary men), known also as the Caffè di Menegazzo. An informer for the Inquisitors of State reported that Casanova also drank coffee there and that he spoke up as an enthusiastic partisan of Goldoni's dramatic style.[21] Lorenzo Da Ponte in the 1770s thought this same coffeehouse provided the perfect retreat from a tumultuous romantic entanglement, "a most violent passion for one of the most beautiful but also the most capri-

cious ladies of the metropolis." Da Ponte explained: "In spite of all the jeal-
ousies and caprices of that woman, I kept to the good habit of going in the
evening to a certain coffeehouse, where the most civilized and learned men
of Venice gathered, and it was called on that account the Caffè dei Letterati.
I found myself there one evening, half masked, when a gondolier entered,
looked around, fixed his eyes on me, and indicated that I should leave."[22]
Da Ponte followed the gondolier to a gondola and found himself enjoying
an unanticipated rendezvous with an unknown woman. In fact, the boatman had brought the wrong man from the coffeehouse—but nevertheless,
this became the beginning of a libertine adventure.

For Gasparo Gozzi the coffeehouse was not only socially salutary but
voluptuously pleasant, and he recited its seductive comforts, democratically
available to any member of the public for the price of a cup of coffee. The
proprietors supposedly attended to every luxury:

> First of all, they try with ingenious and loving diligence to make the archi-
> tecture of the shop as pleasing as possible to the eye, to such an extent that,
> when approaching one of the shops, you don't seem to see a shop but rather
> a delightful spectacle of the theater with many beautiful views that present
> themselves to you with such recreation of the heart that you would not wish
> to see anything else. In one place the best painters have endeavored to repre-
> sent to you gardens, aviaries, waterfalls; in another the most diligent carvers
> of wood have labored over the most beautiful decorations, all gilded, with
> polished mirrors placed in the middle, so that while you remain seated, they
> show you and let you know the people who pass through the street; and
> without any discomfort, almost reclining if you like, you remain to enjoy the
> bustle of who comes and who goes. As for the seats, where would you find
> better ones? Don't you see how over here the cushioned chairs open their
> arms to you; over there, the long sofas? and in another place, if you don't want
> such grandeur, the most comfortable benches? Could you be better served in
> your own home, even if you had waiters, footmen, lackeys, and all kinds of
> household retainers? At your every word there is someone to boil the coffee or
> the chocolate, someone to present you with water, with baskets of pastries.[23]

Presumably the less fashionable coffeehouses, outside Piazza San Marco,
were less extravagantly enticing. Each *caffettiere*, however, must have had to
put some effort into providing some degree of luxury, and the ambience of
the coffeehouse on Calle della Cortesia must have been sufficiently attractive to make Father Fiorese want to take a seat and pass the time of day.

Yet Gozzi also recognized that the *caffettiere* was something other than a
benevolent host—primarily a businessman with an investment in Venetian

leisure. In 1760 in the *Gazzetta veneta*, Gozzi drily reported the local news of the day concerning a proprietor who worked in Piazza San Marco. "A certain *caffettiere* under the Procuratie Nuove, assisted by many in his enterprises, and embarrassed by debts for various reasons, repaid everyone by going away suddenly on Saturday and no one knows where." The *caffettiere* owed money to a Jewish merchant, who could not accept payment on Saturday, the Jewish Sabbath, and asked to be paid his sum on Sunday instead. "The *caffettiere* calculated that this would be enough for his journey, and, thus adding this new dishonor to his other shortcomings, he disappeared from Venice around noon."[24] In this manner, one of the statutory 206 coffeehouses went under, leaving a certain merchant of Venice dishonestly deprived of the ducats due him.

Domenico Ravasin, named by the tribunal as the son of Antonio, belonged to a family that practiced the trade of *caffettiere* in the coffeehouses of the neighborhood of Sant'Angelo. A government survey of the coffeehouses of Venice in 1761 revealed that there was one in Campo Sant'Angelo itself: Under the Sign of Prince Charles of Lorraine. The *caffettiere* of this grandly named establishment was listed as Antonio Ravasin. There was no sign or name, however, for a second and humbler coffeehouse in the neighborhood off the main square, identified simply as "located across from the baker and on the street that leads to the bridge of Sant'Angelo." This was almost certainly the coffeehouse of Calle della Cortesia, though today there is no bridge, since the relevant canal has been filled in. The *caffettiere* was listed as Battista Ravasin. Another government survey of 1781 showed that the coffeehouse in Campo Sant'Angelo was still being run by Antonio Ravasin, whereas the other, this time specified as "near the Ponte degli Assassini" (the Bridge of the Assassins), was now under the proprietorship of Iseppo Ravasin.[25] At some point in the following four years, the management of the latter establishment must have passed within the family to Antonio's son, Domenico Ravasin, for it was he who was summoned by the Bestemmia in 1785.

He testified then as the representative of a family with some standing in the coffee business. He might have worried that the investigation of Franceschini could compromise the respectability of his establishment and harm his income. In Goldoni's drama, the *caffettiere*, Ridolfo, issued a fervent defense of his own profession: "I earn the merit of doing good. I earn the friendship of people. I earn the marks of honor that I esteem above all things in the world."[26] Managing a coffeehouse became a matter of honor rather than an enterprise of commerce, and it was the honest *caffettiere* who, standing in for the dramatist himself, contrived the happy ending of the comedy.

> EUGENIO. You are a very decent and civil man. It's a pity that this is your profession. You deserve a better condition and greater fortune.
> RIDOLFO. I am content with what heaven allows me, and I would not trade my condition for others that have a better appearance but less substance. At my level I lack nothing. I have an honorable profession, a profession among the polite, dignified, and civil trades. A profession that, practiced with good manners and reputation, makes a man appreciated by all classes of people. A profession that is necessary to the dignity of the city, to the health of men, and to the honest entertainment of those who need to relax.[27]

Goldoni evidently perceived some relation between the honorable middle-class *caffettiere* and his own vocation as a playwright, providing honest entertainment and amusement to the Venetian public.

The *caffettiere* Domenico Ravasin may or may not have resembled this Goldonian ideal of virtuous proprietorship, but certainly, when he was standing in his coffeehouse, he stood at the center of his neighborhood community. He served coffee downstairs to Father Fiorese, he sent coffee upstairs to Franceschini, and he received the anxious inquiries of Maria Lozaro on the day that she delivered her daughter to the apartment above the coffeehouse. The great beverage revolution of the eighteenth century, bringing coffee to Europe, meant that the coffeehouse in Calle della Cortesia would constitute the fundamental crucible of testimony and opinion for investigating the case of Gaetano Franceschini and Paolina Lozaro.

SEVEN

Coffee and Gossip

Domenico Ravasin, standing in his coffeehouse, had learned from one of his employees about the prostitute in Franceschini's apartment, from Maria Lozaro about the delivery of the little girl, and from general neighborhood knowledge about the gentleman's "universal" reputation concerning women. Ravasin also learned a lot from his own wife: "My wife told me that the housekeeper in Franceschini's apartment told her that during the previous night he had taken the girl to sleep with him, and that the housekeeper, together with the male servant, remained at attention during the night, listening at the door, to hear whether anything significant occurred, ready in any case to knock on the door in order to derail any sinister happenings. And they did hear some crying, but after that quieted down, nothing happened at all."[1] Coffeehouses in eighteenth-century Venice were, conventionally, male preserves, and although Ravasin could obtain news of Franceschini from his male customers and male employees, even more intimate information could be obtained through female channels. Ravasin's wife, living on the top floor of the building, had no trouble obtaining details from Franceschini's servant on the floor just below. Through this chain of confidences, originating in Franceschini's apartment, spreading through the building, and then, presumably, further disseminated from the coffee-house, the whole neighborhood could have been vicariously listening at the door of Franceschini's bedroom.

Francesca Ravasin (born Francesca Trento), the wife of the coffeehouse proprietor, observed developments from inside the building, from the top floor. The residents of the building had a common entrance, and a common staircase ascended to all of the apartments. At the top of the stairs Francesca Ravasin presided over an internal balcony from which she commanded a view of everyone coming up and going down. Though her husband, work-ing on the ground floor, may have hesitantly testified that inside "I do not see who comes and goes," Francesca Ravasin, the mistress of the staircase, considered herself perfectly knowledgeable about the building's internal af-fairs. Neighborhood gossip seemed to rise to her aerie, and when asked about the "character and custom" of Franceschini, she had a lot to say.

> What I can say is that since he came to live here, a universal rumor [*fama*] has caused me to know that he is a sensual man and brutally inclined to-ward women; for this reason, although on the occasions of our meeting on the stairs he has politely greeted me, I reciprocated coldly and austerely, by which I achieved the desired effect that he greeted me nicely but did not presume the least intimacy or take the liberty of any inquiry. What I can say is that from an internal balcony of the building that looks out over the stair-case and also allows a view of the door that gives entrance into his house, or rather apartment, I have happened to see at various times women whose deportment seemed to suggest a bad life, knocking on his door and enter-ing. I also saw poor Furlana women going there with some little girls, some older and some younger [*di maggior e minor età*] , and sometimes I heard the servant tell them that the master was sleeping, and they departed. This prostitute quality of women who frequently went to his place could not help becoming scandalous to everyone, though people did not speak out about it publicly on account of the reserve that they all felt in speaking about it, concerning a person with the reputation of being rich.[2]

In her loquaciously forthcoming testimony Francesca Ravasin revealed a lively interest in whom she actually saw going up and down the staircase and also what she only imagined happening behind Franceschini's door. She was fascinated by the life of the gentleman himself with his libertine reputation and by the glimpses of other women from another level of Ve-netian society, the supposed objects of his brutal sensuality. Clearly, Signora Ravasin could even imagine herself as the object of lewd intimacies and in-appropriate liberties, which Franceschini might presume to undertake even in the semipublic space of the common staircase, and she congratulated herself on having forestalled his unwelcome advances by her own coldness of manner. She seemed to possess a vivid dramatic imagination, worthy of eighteenth-century Venetian theater, and the staircase was the stage of the ongoing drama, the internal balcony her private box, offering a privileged view that must have been the envy of her friends in the neighborhood, the broader audience. Gaetano Franceschini was unquestionably the star of the show, and were it not for the tragic involvement of an eight-year-old child, the drama of the staircase might have appeared to be a comedy: with its rich and lecherous old protagonist, the scandalous comings and goings of women of ill fame, and the prurient engagement of a certain respectable wife, avid for gossip.

Goldoni, in his own dramatic comedy of the Venetian coffeehouse, particularly emphasized that the caffeinated atmosphere was conducive to gossip. When the curtain went up in the Teatro Sant'Angelo in 1750, the audience saw onstage not only the coffeehouse but also the adjoining estab-lishments, such as the barber shop and the gambling casino, constituting a slice of Venetian neighborhood life. Above the barber shop was the window of the apartment of a dancer, a woman of questionable reputation.[3] The comic villain of the piece was a Neapolitan resident in Venice, Don Marzio, an inveterate gossip. Don Marzio passed his time in the coffeehouse, gos-siping maliciously, and he had something to say about the dancer who lived upstairs and about the Count who supposedly visited her.

> DON MARZIO. I know everything. I am informed about everything. I know when he goes there, and when he leaves. I know what he spends and what he eats. I know everything.
> EUGENIO. So the Count is the only one?
> DON MARZIO. Oh, there's a door in back.
> RIDOLFO (*with the coffee, to Eugenio*). Here it is, the third coffee.
> DON MARZIO. Ah! What do you say, Ridolfo? Don't I know everything about the dancer?
> RIDOLFO. I've told you before that I'm not getting involved.
> DON MARZIO. I am a great man for knowing things! Whoever wants to know what happens at the homes of all the female musicians and dancers should come to me.[4]

Goldoni implied that the passion for gossip was stimulated by coffee and flourished in the setting of the coffeehouse, wreaking havoc on marriages and ruining reputations. Francesca Ravasin, living upstairs from the coffeehouse and married to the *caffettiere*, could easily have been a character in Goldoni's drama.

While eighteenth-century Venetian coffeehouses were being created under the virtuous names of Peace, Hope, and Courage, they might just as plausibly have done business beneath the more ambivalent sign of Gossip. The association between gossip and coffee was established almost immediately with the creation of coffeehouses in Europe. When Lady Mary Wortley Montagu traveled from England to the Ottoman Empire in 1717, she visited the women's Turkish bath in Adrianople (Edirne today) and perversely wished that a male English artist could have been present to paint the scene. "I fancy it would have very much improved his art to see so many fine women naked in different postures, some in conversation, some working, others drinking coffee or sherbet, and many negligently lying on their cushions while their slaves (gen-

Goldoni's *La bottega del caffè*, suggesting how the world of the coffeehouse might become entangled with gossip and scandal. Frontispiece from Carlo Goldoni, *Raccolta completa delle commedie*, vol. 1 (Florence, 1827). Courtesy of the Fales Library and Special Collections, New York University.

erally pretty girls of seventeen or eighteen) were employed in braiding their hair in several pretty manners. In short, 'tis the women's coffeehouse, where all the news of the town is told, scandal invented, etc."[5] From this account of so much naked female flesh, there could hardly have been anything less like an English coffeehouse—or a Venetian coffeehouse for that matter—but Lady Mary insisted that the underlying essence and function of the institution was just the same, namely, gossip and scandal.

If the coffeehouse was a predominantly male world of gentlemen gossips like Don Marzio, there was nevertheless no question that gossip played a role in female sociability as well. Perhaps it was no coincidence that Goldoni followed up *La bottega del caffè* with *I pettegolezzi delle donne* (The Gossip of Women) in 1751. Composed in Venetian dialect to give a sense of social life among ordinary people, the comedy involved the destruction of a young woman's reputation through gossip about the circumstances of her birth, though Goldoni then brought about a happy ending. "What a lot of gossip!" exclaimed the heroine's admirer, when his doubts were finally dissipated. "On account of these gossips I have suffered a lot and have been almost in a state of despair," she replied, in the curtain speech. "The way to live well is to talk little and stay far from gossip, which above all other things causes the ruin of families."[6] In another play, *La casa nova* (The New House), performed in 1760, Goldoni further showed himself aware of how female gossip functioned between apartments on different floors of the same building, sometimes by means of balconies and always with the intermediary encouragement of servants.

Historian Joanne Ferraro has suggested the importance of gossip for Venetian judicial investigations of illicit sex.[7] In the case of Gaetano Franceschini, the gossiping male society of the coffeehouse, the domain of the *caffettiere*, and the gossiping female company dominated by the wife of the *caffettiere*, perched upstairs at her internal balcony, produced all the information necessary for the prosecution of criminal vice. Indeed, personal gossip was transformed into legal testimony, demonstrating the permeable boundaries between private and public life in eighteenth-century Venice. Francesca Ravasin gave her testimony before the Bestemmia without concealing the conversational gambits by which she had acquired her information about Paolina Lozaro.

> So it happened in these recent days, I can't remember which day precisely, that I was going down the stairs after lunch, and I met his housekeeper who had entered his service some days before. And when I greeted her, she said,

with reference to some point or other, that she wanted to leave his service, and she seemed to be very disgusted. She had with her a Furlana girl who seemed to be about seven or eight, whom I had seen arriving that morning. So I said, concerning that matter, that then he would be well off with this chambermaid, and I pointed to the little Furlanetta, and the woman remarked that it was just on that account that she was going away. Then in the morning at the entrance to my husband's coffeehouse I met another woman—I don't know her name or where she lives—who usually does the daily menial work in that apartment, and she told me that Franceschini had kept the girl with him in bed during the previous night. And that the housekeeper and the other servant had stayed at attention during the night, and they had decided to knock on the door if they heard any significant noise, and thus to avoid any sinister effect. And that they had heard the girl crying out something, but they were able to reassure themselves that no decisive misfortune had happened to that girl. And here that woman went on to declaim against Franceschini, and I, shrugging my shoulders as I customarily do, continued on my way.[8]

Francesca Ravasin suggested that it was beneath her dignity to gossip with servants, but the tribunal had surely already recognized her proprietary relation to the neighborhood news, as investigated from the internal balcony, on the staircase, and at the entrance to the coffeehouse. No doubt, continuing on her way meant repeating the story to everyone she met, and she even had a certain storyteller's sense for accenting the sentimental details. Paolina Lozaro, the Furlana, was rendered even more appealingly girlish with an Italian diminutive: the Furlanetta.

Francesca Ravasin also worried about Franceschini making advances toward her own servant girl, Cattarina Callegari, who was always going up and down the staircase between the Ravasin apartment and the coffeehouse. One day Franceschini actually stopped the girl and asked for her help in finding a servant girl for himself. Francesca Ravasin was outraged, or perhaps thrilled, to receive a full report on the encounter. She forbade the girl to have anything to do with Franceschini: "And I commanded her also not ever to enter that apartment, and to be reserved and uncivil with Franceschini. And furthermore, because I was in fear of him in this regard, whenever it happened that I sent the girl downstairs, I stayed on the internal balcony that I mentioned, which looked out over the staircase, so that I could reassure myself that she was observing my commands."[9] A measure of surveillance was, thus, supposed to guarantee the girl's protection from entrapment and sexual predation. Yet surely there was an element of dramatic prurience, even of baiting the trap, when Francesca Ravasin sent her own servant girl down the staircase, on some errand or other, while peering over the internal balcony to watch intently in case of an indecent encounter.

Of course the Bestemmia summoned Cattarina Callegari, the servant girl herself. She recalled her encounter with Franceschini on the staircase some five months before. "He asked me if I wanted to go into his service instead of staying with the *caffettiere*. I replied that since I had gone into that service, I would not be persuaded to abandon it. He then asked whether I knew any other girls like me, around thirteen years old, to place in his service, and I answered no. When I returned to the apartment, I told this to my mistress, who commanded me to keep myself reserved with him, as I did." Cattarina Callegari, despite her young age, was observant enough to notice "some women who sell ladles and spoons, with some girls," around Franceschini's apartment, and attentive enough to have heard about his reputation: "I have heard everyone saying that he was an old pig [*vecchio porco*] and a scoundrel [*baron*]." In her account of herself she mentioned that she had been working for the family of the *caffettiere* "until yesterday" and now was living with her mother again.[10] In other words, either the servant girl had been fired or she had quit, just at the time of the neighborhood uproar over Franceschini. It is possible that Francesca Ravasin had heard something disturbing about the behavior of her servant, or the servant, perhaps in consultation with her mother, had decided that service seemed suddenly dangerous for a young girl.

In his testimony Domenico Ravasin mentioned sending one of his men, Zuane Lorenzini, upstairs to deliver a cup of coffee to the apartment of Gaetano Franceschini during the previous winter. Lorenzini had formerly worked for Ravasin as *uomo da caffè* (a man of the coffeehouse), but by the end of the summer, he was no longer employed there. The tribunal located Lorenzini and summoned him to appear on September 14; though he had probably served many cups of coffee to many people in the meantime, he seemed to have no trouble remembering Franceschini.

> TRIBUNAL. Do you know a certain Gaetano Franceschini?
> LORENZINI. I know him very well [*benissimo*], because last winter he came to live in an apartment above the coffeehouse in Calle della Cortesia in Sant'Angelo, and I worked there as a man of the coffeehouse.
> TRIBUNAL. Did you ever go to Franceschini's apartment?
> LORENZINI. I was there several times to bring him coffee.
> TRIBUNAL. In these encounters did you see any observable person?
> LORENZINI. Never, but I will say that more than once, going to bring him coffee, when I was in the hall the servant took the tray and brought to his room two coffees that he had ordered, and in the meantime, while I

waited in the hall, the housekeeper told me once that he had a whore [*puttana*] in bed with him, and that whenever they ordered two coffees from me, he had such a person with him, because at other times he had me go into the room to bring him only one coffee, and I conjectured all the more inasmuch as he had a universal reputation for being, as people said, a pig with regard to women. But I never happened to see any women there.[11]

Lorenzini, before the Bestemmia, could not claim under oath to have actually seen the women in the bedroom, but he almost suggested that he had—"the old pig, he has a whore with him who would make you vomit"—when gossiping in the coffeehouse.

The testimony of Lorenzini suggested possible intersections between the private life of the bedroom and the gossiping public life of the coffeehouse with its convenient but invasive system of home deliveries. The *uomo da caffè*, bringing coffee to the customer, was able to observe and report upon matters of private impropriety, notably sex, which could then become the subject of gossip in the coffeehouse. Indeed, coffee and sex could be considered complementary pleasures. Franceschini, with a woman in bed, did not hesitate to order out for coffee. Lorenzini, with two coffee cups on his tray, did not hesitate to envision two customers in bed.

For these reasons, the proprietors and service personnel of the coffeehouses were familiar witnesses before the Bestemmia. In another case that came before the tribunal in 1785, when a young wife with an old husband was accused of behaving scandalously with a young man, the local *caffettiere*, Iseppo Stivanello, brought coffee to the house and could testify that the adulterous pair "sat close to each other" while drinking their coffee.[12]

The coffeehouse at Calle della Cortesia intersected with other social and commercial spheres, including the shadowy world of procuring and prostitution. Lorenzini, as *uomo da caffè*, did not actually see with his own eyes any women in Franceschini's apartment but could testify to numerous suspicious characters who appeared in the vicinity of the coffeehouse. He claimed to have seen frequently the woman who sold ladles and spoons—"with a girl of young age, that is, around five years." There was also a mysterious man who once appeared outside the coffeehouse, looking for Franceschini, and Lorenzini thought that he could date this appearance back to the last Sunday of carnival during the previous winter.[13]

I will say that one morning early, when I was opening the coffeehouse, I was approached by a man who seemed to be around forty years old, and he told me that Franceschini had asked him for a girl, I don't know of what age, to take on as an adoptive daughter, and so this man was waiting there to speak with him, but did not know what to do, and so he asked me for advice. Because of the ill fame [*mala fama*] of Franceschini I insinuated to him not to bring a girl, telling him about the man's reputation [*concetto*]. Nevertheless, he told me he wanted to wait, and I saw him around there for about two hours and don't know whether or not they spoke.[14]

Lorenzini could not identify the stranger but thought that he must have been born, of all places, in Friuli. It was an ethnographic identification that Lorenzini could make with some confidence since he himself came from Friuli, though he had been living in Venice for ten years, now resident in the nearby parish of San Lio, not far from the Rialto.[15] In and around the Venetian coffeehouse there appeared a motley crew of Friulian immigrants, including the woman who sold ladles and spoons, the mysterious male procurer of adoptive daughters, the *uomo da caffè* Zuane Lorenzini, and the laundress Maria Lozaro. When the festive spirit of the Venetian carnival put Franceschini in mind of adoptive daughters, he made contact with an underworld of venal immigrant Friulians.

The Venetian carnival was the most famous in Europe in the eighteenth century, and foreign tourists came to Venice to marvel and participate. It was a long winter carnival, from Christmas to Lent, with some carnival activities beginning as early as the autumn; those activities included gambling, dancing, theater, acrobatics, and fireworks. Historian James Johnson has analyzed the complex significance of carnival masking, which encouraged a greater liberty in celebrating carnival—"the joyous production of a community in celebration of itself"—without actually challenging fundamental Venetian social values.[16]

Carnival could, on occasion, also provide cover for sexual adventures and even criminal activities; it was at the carnival of 1746 when Casanova and his friends, in masks, pretended to be agents of the Council of Ten and brazenly carried off the young woman who had aroused their interest. So overriding were the claims of the carnival that when Doge Paolo Renier died in February 1789, the public announcement of his death was postponed until the coming of Lent so as not to impinge upon the festive season. The last weekend of carnival traditionally witnessed a climax of revelry and provided the perfect cover for someone like Franceschini to pursue his personal agenda of sexual opportunities. It was just then—the last Sunday of carnival—that the unidentified gentleman was waiting outside the coffeehouse to speak with Franceschini about delivering a young girl.[17]

The Bestemmia was definitely interested in learning more about the Friulian man who had been waiting for Franceschini during carnival. The tribunal summoned Anzolo Marason, who worked in the bakery across from the coffeehouse; he too was born in Friuli, had been living in Venice for fifteen years, and like Lorenzini, was resident in the parish of San Lio. Marason was questioned about Franceschini and the Friulian stranger: "Do you know whether during the last days of the carnival there was a person waiting to speak with the said gentleman?" Marason insisted he knew nothing about it, and though he conceded that Franceschini sometimes came into the bakery to make purchases, there were no overheard or remembered conversations to report to the Bestemmia.[18] The bakery was an essential establishment in the neighborhood, an obligatory stop for all the neighbors, the source of everyone's daily bread. For bread was the single most important staple of an eighteenth-century diet, filling the stomachs of even the most impoverished Venetians. Coffee, by comparison, was a luxury: chemically addictive, morally controversial, and by no means nutritionally necessary.

The bakery must have had many daily customers, but it was not a center of conversation and gossip. Marason's work in the bakery did not involve dealing with customers, so he could not even claim to know anything about Franceschini's reputation. "About these things I don't know and cannot know anything, because my work is with the flour, so I was staying always either in the flour room or else asleep, and I saw nothing of what went on outside that place."[19] Bastian Todesco, who both lived and worked in the bakery, testified more readily to the comings and goings of various women across the street: "I saw going into the entrance of that house some women of every aspect, some girls, some Furlana women, among whom frequently was one who sold ladles and spoons, with some girls, but since the entrance is common to the three apartments, I do not know where those women then went."[20]

The baker himself, Bernardo Manella, made the same point about the common entrance across the street. Asked by the tribunal "whether he had occasion to see people, and especially girls, going to Franceschini's place," Manella objected that he was a busy man. "First of all, occupied as I am with my profession, I do not observe who comes and goes through that door. And besides, since it's a shared entrance for the coffeehouse as well as the three apartments, I would not have known where such people were intending to go even if I could have seen them enter."[21] The baker and his employees were limited to the view from across the street; the coffeehouse offered a more advantageous position for observation.

In addition to Zuane Lorenzini, Ravasin employed a boy [*garzon*], Giacomo Bassagia, who actually lived as a servant with the Ravasin family. Like Lorenzini, Bassagia sometimes delivered coffee directly to Franceschini in his apartment: "When I went there, the servant took the tray from me, and I did not see if Franceschini was alone or in company. Sometimes I brought two coffees, sometimes only one, but I do not know who then drank the other coffee when I brought two." The coffee boy spoke to the tribunal about a Furlana who visited Franceschini frequently with girls [*puttelle*]. There was also a man "who seemed to be a peasant" and waited around the coffeehouse for Franceschini at the time of the carnival.[22]

Most memorable among the visitors to the apartment, however, was a certain Frenchwoman, familiar to Bassagia because she also lived in the neighborhood, in Corte Barbarigo of Sant'Angelo, and he sometimes brought coffee to her. "She is a woman who seems to be bad, because, when I go to bring her coffee, I always see her with one person or another in her house . . . and once, on the occasion of my bringing her coffee, she asked me whether Franceschini was a prosperous man, whether he had money and income."[23] The coffee boy, as opposed to the bakery workers, was in an excellent position to piece together the puzzle of worldly relations in this Venetian neighborhood. The Frenchwoman, just like Franceschini, ordered out for coffee when there were visitors at home, even if the circumstances were personally compromising.

The accumulated testimony about the presence of suspect characters—about the woman who sold ladles and spoons, about the man who could provide adoptive daughters during carnival—made the coffeehouse on Calle della Cortesia appear to be a somewhat unsavory locale. These characters might have been lurking around the coffeehouse only for the sake of Franceschini, but it is also possible that the coffeehouse itself offered them the opportunity to encounter other customers for their wares. Prostitutes were sometimes a presence on the margins of male coffeehouse society as it developed in eighteenth-century Venice under the arcades of Piazza San Marco. In 1754 the Venetian government received a report concerning a prostitute from Mantua, living in Venice, who was spending her evenings under the arcades of the Procuratie Nuove, even at the Florian. Dressed "in licentious costume," she enjoyed "the admiration of the entire piazza."[24] Giorgio Baffo played upon an association between coffee and prostitution when he composed a

verse in Venetian dialect that made an allusive comparison between the coffee
cups in a public coffeehouse and the female genitals of a public prostitute.

> Mi digo: sentì, cari paregini,
> co andè al caffè bevè pur in la tazza,
> dove che beve zente d'ogni razza.

> I say: listen, dear gentlemen,
> when you go to the coffeehouse, you drink from the same cup,
> where people of every race are drinking up.[25]

This obscene analogy between the taste of coffee and the savoring of sex probably made sensual sense to Franceschini when he was entertaining a woman
in his bedroom and ordered two cups of coffee to be brought upstairs.

In 1785 the tribunal of the Bestemmia did not hesitate to take advantage
of the gossip surrounding the coffeehouse in order to penetrate into the
private life of Franceschini. The deliveries made by the coffee man Zuane
Lorenzini and the coffee boy Giacomo Bassagia brought the investigation
inside the common entrance of the building on Calle della Cortesia and
upstairs into Franceschini's apartment. It was Gaetano Franceschini's own
taste for coffee, perhaps the most conventional of his Venetian vices, that
helped bring about his downfall. The establishment downstairs must have
been useful to Franceschini for making contact with networks of procure-
ment and prostitution, discreetly attuned to the male company of the coffeehouse. At the same time, however, the gossip on the premises meant
that his private life was constantly at risk of the sort of public discovery that
would eventually facilitate judicial prosecution.

"I know everything. I am informed about everything," boasted Goldoni's
Don Marzio, and this was partly because he was a fixture in the coffeehouse.
"Whoever wants to know what happens at the homes of all the female mu-
sicians and dancers should come to me." The Bestemmia in 1785 might have
taken him at his word and did indeed value the coffeehouse on Calle della
Cortesia as a repository of knowledge. Furthermore, the accumulation of
information and knowledge at the coffeehouse was capable of producing
not only the gossip that the Bestemmia processed as testimony but also
the articulation and discussion of social issues in the neighborhood. In this
regard, gossiping in the coffeehouse about the private life of Franceschini
could also become a substantive matter of the public sphere.

According to Gasparo Gozzi, any Venetian who spent his day at the coffeehouse would inevitably learn all sorts of things from the conversation

over coffee: "He will get information about the customs of all peoples and of all the nations of the world, of the art of war—sieges, battles, marches, retreats—and above all his tongue will become skillful at articulating with facility all things, due to the experience of often repeating names from foreign countries, names full of consonants, that give the greatest labor to the throat and destroy the uvula of the palate in anyone who has not heard and repeated them several times in a coffeehouse."[26] Gozzi appreciated, albeit with ironic inflection, that coffeehouses could stimulate the curious intellect with a curriculum of worldliness. The testimony received by the Bestemmia suggests that in 1785, in the coffeehouse in Calle della Cortesia, tongues may have been talking in unfamiliar fashion and unaccustomed detail about the phenomenon of sex between adults and children.

 The coffeehouses of eighteenth-century Europe were recognized even then as important institutions of the Enlightenment, precisely because of the discussion that they stimulated and encouraged among their customers. Looking back in historical retrospect, Jürgen Habermas argued that the eighteenth century witnessed the emergence of an entirely new form of public life, an arena of society independent of government power and at the same time distinct from the private world of home and family. The institutions of the public sphere were the sites of critical discussion concerning politics and culture and, therefore, the crucible of modern independent public opinion. Habermas noted salons in France and coffeehouses in Britain as "centers of criticism—literary at first, then also political—in which began to emerge, between aristocratic society and bourgeois intellectuals a certain parity of the educated." In London at the beginning of the century Richard Steele and Joseph Addison, publishing the *Tatler* and the *Spectator*, saw the coffeehouses of the city as the social base of their intellectual enterprise. Newspapers were made available to coffeehouse patrons, who thus became the reading public, prepared to discuss the issues of the day. In Venice the *Gazzetta veneta* was sold in coffeehouses, including the Florian.[27]

In England Addison grandly declared that "it was said of Socrates, that he brought Philosophy down from Heaven, to inhabit among Men, and I shall be ambitious to have it said of me, that I have brought Philosophy out of the Closets and Libraries, Schools and Colleges, to dwell in Clubs and Assemblies, at Tea-tables, and in Coffee-Houses." British historian John Brewer notes that in the eighteenth century the London stock market emerged from Jonathan's Coffee House in Exchange Alley, and London shipping and insurance developed at Lloyd's Coffee House. Business and intellectual life in London advanced together under the auspices of the coffeehouse, according to Brewer: "The coffeehouse was the precursor of the modern office, but once you were there you were as likely to talk about matters of general interest—the latest play, sexual scandal, or political quarrel—as carry on business."[28] James Boswell came to London as a young man in 1762 and eagerly sought stimulation in Child's Coffee House. "It is quite a place to my mind," he remarked in his diary, "dusky, comfortable, and warm, with a society of citizens and physicians who talk politics very fully and are very sagacious and sometimes jocular."[29] The coffeehouse was one site for the articulation of what was coming to be called public opinion.

In France, an absolute monarchy, the spirit of criticism that was enthusiastically cultivated by the philosophes tended to take refuge in the somewhat more private setting of the salons rather than the fully public coffeehouses. Nevertheless, the philosophes of the Enlightenment appeared at the Procope and the Régence, including Diderot, D'Alembert, Rousseau, and Voltaire; it was the beginning of a tradition that would, in the twentieth century, associate such intellectual celebrities as Jean-Paul Sartre and Simone de Beauvoir with the Café de Flore and Les Deux Magots. In eighteenth-century Milan, under Habsburg rule, coffee was synonymous with enlightenment, for the city's philosophical journal of the 1760s was called simply *Il caffè*, and its publishers, the brothers Pietro and Alessandro Verri, celebrated coffee as their intellectual stimulant. "Coffee," wrote Pietro Verri, "cheers the spirit, awakens the mind, is diuretic for some, keeps away sleep for many, and it is particularly useful to people who do not move around much, and who cultivate the sciences." Cesare Beccaria, the author of *Crimes and Punishments*, which made such an impression in Venice, belonged to the circle of *Il caffè* in Milan.[30] In republican Venice, with its large civic patriciate—and in spite of the limitations on free speech implicit in the very existence of a tribunal like the Bestemmia—political discussion easily escaped the official confines of government bodies into the emerging institutions of the public sphere, such as the 206 coffeehouses.

Though Goldoni would not have presumed to introduce topical political discussion into his coffeehouse on the stage of the Teatro Sant'Angelo, he humorously depicted the sharp expression of opinions, as the customers in the drama discussed world affairs over cups of coffee:

DON MARZIO. Did you know that the Muscovite troops have gone to their winter quarters?
LEANDRO. They have done well. The season required it.

DON MARZIO. No Signor. They have done badly. They should not have
abandoned the place they had occupied. . . .
LEANDRO. So then, what should they have done?
DON MARZIO. Let me see the map, and then I will tell you exactly where
they should have gone.[31]

Goldoni meant to mock Don Marzio, a Neapolitan in Venice, for the indiscreet chatter that he practiced in the coffeehouse, presumptuously pro-
nouncing upon the deployment of remote armies. This was, however, a
plausible representation of the emerging public sphere, in which people
all over Europe expressed opinions about the conduct of political affairs.
The coffeehouse was precisely the forum in which such opinions were proposed and debated. James Johnson has suggested that the wearing of masks
in Venetian coffeehouses further encouraged free conversation, especially
across social classes, such that "cafés provided the setting for the population
to recognize itself as a public."[32]

An anonymous letter to the *Gazzetta urbana veneta* in 1792 complained
about "idle people" who publicly cultivated controversial opinions: "Instead of addressing subjects about which they know nothing, instead of
speaking in political, military, and judicial capacities about the great events
of the world, why don't they think about better regulating their families, or-
ganizing their enterprises, and educating their children? I know a quantity
of people who set up their professorial chairs in the coffeehouses and night
spots to dictate laws to Europe." The letter writer was reacting against the
forms of public life and public opinion that he perceived in the world of
the coffeehouses. Another letter to the *Gazzetta*, in 1795, expressed a sense
of conservative outrage. "How many coffeehouses there are in every city
today! They are usually the refuge of the idle, of the gossips, the asylum
of the indigent. . . . In some they hold an academic tribunal; they judge
authors and theatrical pieces, and assign them a rank and value. There are
formed cabals for and against the authors and professors." Even worse was
the "chatter" (*cicaleccio*) that came from coffee drinkers discussing the news
of the day as reported in the gazettes.[33] This was a society on the brink of
modernity, reading the newspapers, discussing the news, and presuming to
formulate critical opinions about authors and ideas.

The "chatter" of the coffeehouses clearly included both gossip about people's private affairs and discussion concerning public affairs, but these were
often intermingled and not always easy to differentiate. If the conversation
at the coffeehouse on Calle della Cortesia concerned Franceschini's rela-

tions with women and girls, that was gossip, to be sure. If the conversation, however, took a turn toward the general, reflecting on the issue of sexual relations between adults and children, that could be considered something more like public opinion. Finally, if the customers over coffee discussed the role of Venetian law and government in investigating, judging, and punishing sexual relations between adults and children, that would have indisputably constituted participation in the public sphere. The Bestemmia took advantage of neighborhood gossip to further its own investigation of Franceschini. Yet each time a witness was summoned to testify, each time gossip was solicited by the judicial apparatus of the state, the chatter of the neighborhood was registered as a matter of public significance. The Bestemmia in particular, with its mandate to investigate scandal, was inevitably implicated in matters of gossip, for scandal emerged as the public manifestation of private gossip.

For Francesca Ravasin, watching from the top of the stairs, gossip was also a matter of public import because it constituted a form of public entertainment. She observed the doings at Franceschini's door with all the rapt attention of a spectator at the theater: "I will also say that I forgot to mention that on the morning of the day when Franceschini was arrested in the evening, I saw coming to his place a woman who seemed foreign, with a trunk and a hatbox, and she remained in his apartment. Actually it was, to tell the truth, the cause of jokes [*motivo di scherzo*], people hearing that this woman was visiting him and could not even spend one night with him because of his arrest."[34] The mysteriously foreign woman, with her theatrical props of trunk and hatbox, was naturally assumed to be of "prostitute quality," like all of Franceschini's female visitors. Yet the joking that her visit provoked on the day of his arrest—that is, a week after the neighborhood already knew all about Paolina Lozaro and her night in Franceschini's bed—strikingly reveals the distance that separated eighteenth-century Venice from a modern moral sensibility. Though the case did involve intimations of shock and horror at Franceschini's conduct with the child, the neighbors were also quite capable of enjoying the drama as comedy.

When Francesca Ravasin was asked by the tribunal about Father Fiorese's intervention to remove the little girl from the building, that respectable woman replied, "I suppose that the curate removed her, as people customarily say, because of the scruple of conscience."[35] She seemed to recite the phrase "scruple of conscience" as if she were herself putting quotation marks around it, quoting a conventional phrase ("as people customarily say") with the rhetorical flourish of pious morality. Francesca Ravasin remained entirely righteous even as she acknowledged her role as the neighborhood gossip.

In Goldoni's drama of the coffeehouse, the gossip Don Marzio was finally denounced by the entire community for his indiscreet chatter, and he felt he had no choice but to leave Venice altogether: "Everyone insults me; everyone abuses me. No one wants me here; everyone chases me out. Ah, yes, they are right. My tongue, sooner or later, had to lead me to some great precipice. It has brought me infamy, which is the worst of evils. There is no point in justifying myself here. I have lost credit and will never regain it. I will go away from this city."[36] The curtain fell at the conclusion of this speech, thus resolving the comedy by restoring the moral order of the coffeehouse and the city of Venice, the former made into a sort of microcosm of the latter.

Yet the arrest of Franceschini in 1785, upstairs from the coffeehouse, and the testimony before the tribunal concerning his sexual activities, suggested that gossip could actually have salutary consequences for the moral order of the community, revealing the private presence of pernicious vices. The Bestemmia, pursuing secret justice in a closed trial, discovered that the private evils of Gaetano Franceschini were already matters of public fascination, discussion, and even entertainment in the neighborhood of Sant'Angelo.

The *caffettiere* Domenico Ravasin, standing in his coffeehouse, occupied a focal position in the community network of information and discussion, concerning both public affairs and personal gossip. The "chatter" of the coffeehouse was the audible buzz of modern urban society in the making. Inasmuch as the encounter between Gaetano Franceschini and Paolina Lozaro received public attention through the gossip in the coffeehouse, and official attention with the case before the Bestemmia, coffee did indeed play its part as a stimulant to critical reflection on urban affairs. In an unprecedented development, the issue of sex between adults and children became a matter of public discussion in Venice in 1785.

EIGHT

Friulians in Venice

Domenico Ravasin, the *caffettiere*, was a native Venetian, but all around his coffeehouse he was aware of the presence of Friulian immigrants. Ravasin's own employee Zuane Lorenzini was Friulian, as was Anzolo Marason, the man who worked for the baker across the street. The mysterious woman who sold ladles and spoons, noted by several witnesses as a presence around the coffeehouse, was from Friuli. The mysterious man who had heard that Franceschini required an adoptive daughter and had appeared at the coffeehouse during carnival was from Friuli. Domenico Ravasin had no doubt about the ethnic character of the women who walked past the coffeehouse looking up at Franceschini's window: "a Furlana woman who sells ladles and spoons and various Furlana women who pass by." Francesca Ravasin had the same impression: "I also saw poor Furlana women going there with some little girls, some older and some younger." Age seemed to make less of an impression than ethnicity, the Friulian character of the females, young and old, who came to visit Franceschini. Ultimately, of course, the case against Franceschini would be based on his encounter with the Furlana Maria Lozaro and her daughter, Paolina, the Furlanetta.

The case of Paolina Lozaro and Gaetano Franceschini was a tale of Friulian immigrants in Venice. He successfully lured the Friulian mother and daughter from the neighborhood of Santa Maria Maggiore, on the other side of Venice, to his apartment in the neighborhood of Sant'Angelo. This crosstown urban displacement, however, occurred in the context of a much broader movement of migration, bringing great numbers of Friulians from their native province north of the Adriatic to the metropolis of Venice. Like many poor immigrant populations to great cities, in many other times and places, the Friulians in Venice were vulnerable to exploitation, and Franceschini's manipulation of the mother and molestation of the child may be partly understood in the social context that brought so many provincial subjects to the imperial capital, hoping for a stroke of Providence that would rescue them from economic desperation.

The Bestemmia, while taking testimony from those who knew Franceschini in the neighborhood of Sant'Angelo, was simultaneously summoning the Friulian neighbors of Maria Lozaro from the quarter of Santa Maria Maggiore. The residents of that quarter were able to describe the circumstances of the first encounter between Maria Lozaro and Gaetano Franceschini and to help the tribunal understand how Paolina Lozaro ended up in Franceschini's apartment.

On September 12, Maddalena Schiavon was summoned to testify, and though most witnesses were being asked whether they knew Gaetano Franceschini, she was asked if she knew Maria Lozaro. "I know her because she is from my hometown [*del mio stesso paese*], and I live with her here in Venice," the witness replied.[1] Both women came from the same little town of Aviano in Friuli. (In fact, the word *paese* can mean both native country and native town.) The Friuli region joined the Italian and Slavic coasts of the Adriatic, and Maddalena Schiavon reflected some Slavic affiliation in the name of her husband, Schiavon, meaning "Slav." The Friulians appeared ethnographically distinct to native Venetians and conversed with one another in Friulian. Gaetano Franceschini was a native of Vicenza, one of the principal Italian cities of Venice's mainland state. When he wandered into the outlying parish of Santa Maria Maggiore, among the Friulian immigrants, this was not just an excursion into other Venetian neighborhoods but an encounter among the different divisions of Venice's Adriatic empire.

Franceschini made the acquaintance of Maddalena Schiavon, as she recalled, because he was interested in her young daughter.

> About a month ago, I don't remember the day precisely, it was in the evening and I found myself on the embankment of Santa Maria Maggiore with my daughter, seven years old, and a boy of mine. There passed by a gentleman

who, observing my little girl, said to me that if she were a little older, he would want to place her under the direction of a chambermaid and to make her a little lady [*signoretta*], as they say. Then he took out of his pocket a purse and gave a coin to each of my children. A little way off was the daughter of Maria Lozaro, about eight years old, named Paolina, who, seeing him give the coins to my children, ran over to demand one for herself. When he saw her, he said, "Oh, this one, this one," and touched her on both cheeks and asked her if she wanted to go and serve him. She replied that she did, and meanwhile her mother arrived; and when the inquiry was put to her, she replied that if he acted so that the child might be well brought up in the fear of God, then she would give the child to him; and he left, saying that he would speak with his housekeeper and would then return and give an answer. Maybe seven or eight days later, I came home and Maria said to me that the gentleman had been there, whose name she never knew, and that she was supposed to take the girl on the following Wednesday to the church of Sant'Angelo.[2]

Maddalena Schiavon recalled that Maria Lozaro's only hesitation about the gentleman's proposal was some concern that the child would not receive as pious an upbringing in his home as in her own; her readiness to surrender the child did not seem at all unreasonable to another Friulian mother, even afterward, knowing something of the outcome. Maddalena Schiavon, whose Friulian immigrant story was so similar to that of Maria Lozaro, registered the gentleman's interest with all the composure of one who might have made a similar arrangement for her own child, as indeed she almost did. It was Franceschini who felt that the seven-year-old girl was still a little too young to enter his very special service, while the eight-year-old—"Oh, this one, this one"—appeared just old enough. Maddalena Schiavon and Maria Lozaro were godmothers to one another's children, and the ensuing tragedy touched them both in their extended Friulian family. No one would understand so well as Maddalena Schiavon the peculiar emotional chemistry that motivated the impoverished mother, Maria Lozaro, the psychological balance of need and greed, naiveté and ambition, piety and calculation, maternal love and personal desperation. They brought to Venice the very same Friulian provincial perspective.

Friuli was an independent ecclesiastical principality in the late Middle Ages, ruled by the Roman Catholic patriarch of Aquileia. Under the ultimate sovereignty of the Holy Roman Empire, the Adriatic patriarchs presided over a Friulian culture marked by elements of Byzantine style, and a population whose Romance language, Furlan, showed traces of the region's Celtic origins. The Roman town of Aquileia predated Venice, and refugees from towns like Aquileia, retreating before the Huns in the fifth century and the Lombards in the sixth century, contributed to the establishment of urban society on the Venetian lagoon. Venice, however, conquered and annexed Friuli at the beginning of the fifteenth century, in the same great movement of expansion that established Venetian rule to the west on the Terraferma of mainland Italy and, to the east, along the Dalmatian coast of the Adriatic. In 1419 Venetian armies conquered Aviano, the hometown of Maria Lozaro, and, more important, in 1420 they took the major Friulian stronghold of Udine. Friuli was ultimately partitioned between the Republic of Venice and the Habsburg monarchy.

The province became a part of the national Italian state after the unification of Italy in the 1860s. Within Italy, Friuli acquired regional autonomy

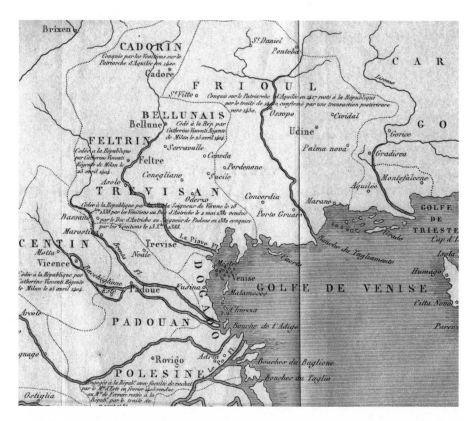

Map of the Republic of Venice with Friuli (Frioul) shown to the north of the Adriatic Gulf of Venice (Golfe de Venise). From P. Daru, *Histoire de la République de Venise* (Paris, 1853).

in 1963. A modern Friulian movement encouraged the provincial culture and even articulated a separatist agenda. The *History of Friuli* by Gian Carlo Menis, written in the 1960s, interpreted the Venetian conquest of 1420 as a matter of imperialism, "the political humiliation of Friuli and its annexation to the Venetian Republic," and told a story of cultural survival in the face of foreign political domination.[3]

Historian Edward Muir, writing about a Friulian massacre during carnival in Udine in the sixteenth century, has described the cultural chasm that separated Friuli from Venice: "on the one hand, a population whose rural poverty and linguistic isolation underlay a feudal and archaic culture and, on the other, a sophisticated, capitalist, imperialist city-republic that had become the paragon of Renaissance civic culture."[4] By the eighteenth century Friuli was already notably involved in the sphere of Venetian culture, and the greatest Venetian artist of the century, Giambattista Tiepolo, achieved his first brilliant success with frescoes in the cathedral and archepiscopal palace at Udine in the 1720s. He painted biblical scenes: the family tales of the Old Testament, with winged angels appearing to Abraham and Sarah, and a dazzling angelic savior descending to prevent Abraham from sacrificing Isaac. Tiepolo returned to Friuli in 1759 to paint the Assumption of the Virgin Mary in the cathedral of Udine, right around the time that Maria Lozaro was born not far away in the town of Aviano. Venetian high culture imperially triumphed over provincial Friuli, but Friulian popular culture persisted in local language, customs, costumes, and folk tales. In the early twentieth century, the Friulian writer Dolfo Zorzut was still able to collect and publish, in the Friulian language, folk tales that survived in popular culture. Later, Pier Paolo Pasolini was fascinated by Friulian language and culture, and Italo Calvino included in his collection of Italian folk tales several Friulian specimens previously published by Zorzut. A series of tales, *Jesus and St. Peter in Friuli*, evoked the harsh poverty of the province.

In 1976, the year that Friuli was devastated by a tremendous earthquake, with more than a thousand dead, the Italian historian Carlo Ginzburg published his pioneering work of microhistory, *The Cheese and the Worms*. The subject was a sixteenth-century Friulian miller, Menocchio, who was tried for heresy by the Inquisition and burned at the stake in 1599. Ginzburg discerned in Menocchio's unusual ideas about the world the traces of an authentic popular culture, which the Roman Catholic Counter-Reformation interpreted as heretical and sought to eradicate. Since 1976 an entire generation of historians has taken Menocchio's Friulian perspective as a point of departure for thinking through the structure and significance of popular culture in relation to elite culture.

Menocchio lived in the little town of Montereale, but Ginzburg speculated that he must have received his limited formal education from schools either in nearby Pordenone or in Aviano. Ginzburg stressed the remoteness of someone like Menocchio, immersed in peasant popular culture, from the elite metropolitan world of Venice, the capital from which Friuli was ruled. "It also seems to me," commented Menocchio, "that these Venetian lords harbor thieves in that city, so that when a person goes there to buy something, and asks, 'How much do you want for these things?' they reply a ducat, even if they are only worth three *marcelli*." Ginzburg emphasized this Friulian resentment of the metropolis, noting that "the jump from Montereale or Aviano to a great city like Venice was a big one."[5] That was precisely the jump that Maria Lozaro would make, from Aviano to Venice, two centuries later, and small coins would also be of large significance for her.

In another book, *Night Battles*, Ginzburg explored a different aspect of Friulian popular culture: the night battles in which men imagined that they were fighting against witches. Armed with fennel stalks, these Friulian fighters for good, known as *benandanti*, waged war on behalf of the fertility of their fields for the sake of a better harvest. Ginzburg saw the witch beliefs in Adriatic Friuli as an ancient survival of popular culture, and he compared them to the contemporary werewolf beliefs in Baltic Livonia. "Obviously what we have here is a single agrarian cult, which, to judge from these remnants surviving in places as distant from one another as were Livonia and the Friuli, must have been diffused in an earlier period over a much vaster area, perhaps the whole of central Europe."[6] Friuli thus served as a window into the little-known past of supernatural belief and magical practice, the disappearing popular culture of ancient Europe

Ginzburg told the story of an eight-year-old girl, Angiola, a little Furlana, who innocently described attending a witches' sabbath in 1668. Her mother invited her to come along: "Would you like to come with me to nuptials where you will eat sweets, where there are handsome gentlemen and ladies dancing, and the tallest of these gentlemen plays the violin so softly as to put one to sleep, and said he wanted to give me a beautiful ring?" Angiola ate candy while her mother went upstairs with the tall gentleman. At one point the girl herself was approached with interest by a young man. Then the tall gentleman said, "What do you want with her?" and the young man replied, "I want her for my lover, if you will give her to me." According to the girl, "He kissed me and fondled me, and my mother was there too, laughing, and then we went out again to the ball."[7] In 1668 an eight-year-old Friulian girl might have experienced some sort of sexual initiation, with her mother's approval, in the context of traditional rituals and popular culture. In 1785 the sexual initiation of Paolina Lozaro took place in the metropolis of Venice under conditions of exploitation and abuse that were already recognizably modern.

Gaetano Franceschini, visiting the neighborhood of Santa Maria Maggiore, pretended to be looking for a young servant and even piously asked the immigrant mother, Maria Lozaro, whether she could provide a character reference for her daughter. A neighbor, Cattarina Burubù, served as the reference, as she later testified before the tribunal. "In the final days of last month a certain Maria Lozaro who lives near me called upon me, indicating to me a gentleman who was with her," recounted the neighbor. "She invited me to certify for that gentleman the good character and custom of her daughter, as I did. For in truth, I cannot but certify to the virtue and good custom of that family, living near me. Afterward, I heard as a rumor, and from Maria herself, that she had conducted the girl, a few days later, to the home of that gentleman, having waited for him in the church of Sant'Angelo."[8] It seemed perfectly natural to Cattarina Burubù that the rich gentleman should seek a reference of moral character for the poor Friulian child, rather than the other way around.

Maria Beloisi, a boatman's wife, also lived in Santa Maria Maggiore and was asked by the Bestemmia whether she knew Maria and Paolina Lozaro. "I know them both, because they live near me," she replied. "They are Friulian, and the mother does laundry." The boatman's wife could date the first appearance of Franceschini with reference to the traditional Roman Catholic calendar of saints' days. "Some days after the solemnities of San Rocco, I don't remember precisely which day, I was standing on my balcony, and I saw a rather tall gentleman of some age who had stopped to chat with Maria Lozaro, and there was another Furlana who lived with them, and her two children. I did not hear what they chatted about." A few days later, however, Maria Lozaro came to visit Maria Beloisi, and the former "demonstrated total exaltation, hoping to have found her fortune."[9] From her external balcony in the neighborhood of Santa Maria Maggiore, Maria Beloisi witnessed the very beginnings of this episode, just as Francesca Ravasin, from her internal balcony in the neighborhood of Sant'Angelo, tracked the tragedy to its conclusion.

Maria Lozaro had told the tribunal that when she stepped out of the church of Sant'Angelo, having been warned away by Father Fiorese, she happened to encounter two woodcutters she knew; while she was talking to them, Gaetano Franceschini suddenly appeared. The Bestemmia succeeded in locating one of the woodcutters, Zuane Meniuto, who, unsurprisingly, turned out to be Friulian by origin and had lived in Venice for the last four years. At this time he resided in the parish of Santa Margherita, but previously he had lived in Santa Maria Maggiore, and it was there that he had known Maria Lozaro among the other Friulians of the community. "I employed her as a laundress," he reported, "for that was her profession." They met again in the Campo Sant'Angelo on the last day of August: "She told me that she was there because she was going to put into service her daughter, whom she had with her, and as soon as she said those words, a gentleman suddenly appeared and asked what she was doing." Franceschini was perhaps also worried about what she was saying to the woodcutters, who might—and eventually did—become witnesses of the day's events. His sudden appearance, however, put an end to the Friulian conversation, and Meniuto had nothing else to tell the tribunal. He did account for his fellow woodcutter, "my companion, who has now returned to his hometown [*al suo paese*]."[10] Meniuto did not specify the town, but it seems very likely that the companion who chatted that day with the Friulian laundress and the Friulian woodcutter was himself Friulian, a part of that same immigrant community whose members recognized one another in the alien metropolis of Venice. One might even read a hint of hometown nostalgia into Zuane Meniuto's simple accounting for his companion, a suggestion of the longing that Friulians in Venice might have felt for the native province that they had left behind. To be sure, the case of Maria Lozaro powerfully dramatized the dangers of metropolitan life for the poor provincials who migrated there in the hope of earning a living and raising their children.

Fernand Braudel, in his epic history of the Mediterranean, described the Mediterranean immigration in the sixteenth century, by land and by sea, that made a great port like Venice into a multiethnic metropolis. Braudel commented specifically on the economic role of the Friulians in Venice: "The people of Friuli—the *Furlani*—were good recruits for domestic and heavy labour." Venice's commercial success encouraged the emergence of an immigrant underclass while also attracting foreign merchants. Braudel described the urban population of Venice in all its complexity: "The Venetian empire and the surrounding regions also provided a crop of immigrants:

Albanians, quick to quarrel, dangerously jealous; Greeks, honourable merchants of the 'Greek nation' or poor devils who prostituted wives and daughters to overcome the initial difficulties of settling in the town, and who developed a taste for this easy living; Morlacchi from the Dinaric mountains [of Dalmatia]. . . . Venice became even more Oriental with the arrival of the Persians and Armenians, of Turks too."[11] In addition to Friulians, Albanians, Greeks, Slavs, Armenians, and Turks, there was a significant Jewish community. Since 1516 the Jews of Venice had been confined to the Ghetto, technically an island that was separated from the rest of the city by canals. In spite of that spatial confinement the community grew larger in the sixteenth century, welcoming Jews who had been expelled from Spain and flourishing in the world of Venetian commerce. By the end of the sixteenth century the Jews of Venice were sufficiently well known for Shakespeare, in England, to compose *The Merchant of Venice*.

Both foreign merchants and immigrant workers formed distinctive communities within early modern Venice. The Fondaco dei Tedeschi was the headquarters of the German merchants in the sixteenth century, and the Fondaco dei Turchi was built for the Turkish merchants in the seventeenth century. The church of San Giorgio dei Greci offered religious services for Orthodox Greeks in Venice, while Greek community life involved a confraternity, known as the *scuola* of Saint Nicholas. The nearby *scuola* of the Dalmatian Slavs was affiliated with the church of San Giorgio degli Schiavoni. In the early sixteenth century Vittore Carpaccio painted the frescoes of the *scuola*, representing the favored saints of the Dalmatians. In the eighteenth century, the confraternity provided dowries for impoverished Dalmatian maidens, perhaps aware of the dangers that might menace undowered girls from immigrant communities.[12]

Writing about working women in early modern Venice, Monica Chojnacka has emphasized the important presence of immigrant women and described the ethnic pockets that they created within urban neighborhoods, as in the case of Friulians living in the Castello quarter: "In the Corte da Ca' Baffo, Antonio from the Friuli lived two doors away from Lucia, a Friulian widow with her four children. Next door, another Friulian, Pietro, and his wife shared their home with an orphan named Iseppo. After Pietro's family came his compatriot Lundardo with his wife, children, and sister. A few streets away lived a group of three Friulian women in the home of Menega de Squaldo. Next door was the widowed Valentina, another Friulian."[13] There was a similar pocket of Friulian neighborhood life along the embankment in Santa Maria Maggiore, where Maria Lozaro and Maddalena Schiavon lived and raised their children. Some Friulian women did laundry; others sold ladles and spoons.

"About these Friulian women who sell ladles and spoons, was there more than one who went to see Franceschini?" It was a simple question, but one that Francesca Ravasin somehow hesitated to answer. "This I cannot precisely say, because standing at the balcony, I saw well the figure but did not distinguish precisely the face. The figures of such women are so similar to one another that it is not easy to distinguish them without a determination to recognize them, which I did not have, as I gave no reflection to the matter."[14] Like the picturesque human types of Venetian rococo genre painting, like the stock characters of eighteenth-century Venetian stage comedy, the Furlana women appeared simply as a recognizable ethnographic type within the Venetian neighborhood.

Though Francesca Ravasin could barely distinguish these Furlana women as individuals, Venetians seemed to have no trouble identifying such women generically as Friulian. Such an identity could have been confirmed by overhearing unintelligible snatches of conversation in the Friulian language, and costume must also have been a crucial factor in recognizing a Furlana. Maria Bardini, Franceschini's servant, had arranged Paolina Lozaro's hair "in the modern fashion with powder" and thought the effect was incongruously ridiculous when combined with "the Friulian costume." Cattarina Bartoli, participating in the rescue party, found the child "still dressed like a Furlana, but with silver buckles, and her head all powdered." Thus, both Maria Bardini and Cattarina Bartoli had a clear conception of what it meant to dress recognizably as a Furlana in Venice.

In the late eighteenth century Giovanni Grevembroch, a Venetian artist of Flemish descent, created a series of volumes that offered a comprehensive survey of Venetian costumes: from the doge, the admiral, and the merchant, to the glass artisan of Murano, the gondolier on the canal, and the prostitute in the bordello. The dramatic foreign accents of costume were evident in the images of the Greek merchant in sober black with a blue beret, the Armenian merchant in a scarlet cloak with a fur cap, and the turbaned Arab merchant in a striped robe with red slippers. Women's dress was represented as no less diverse: a Greek woman in black with a white kerchief, a Slavic woman from the Adriatic island of Cres in an amber robe trimmed with blue velvet.

Then came the Furlana. In Grevembroch's depiction she wears a dress of indigo blue, open at the top to reveal a scarlet bodice, with sleeves of golden yellow: the colorful Furlana. She has a white apron, with a strip of lacework along the bottom. There are white lapels at the shoulders and a white kerchief on her head. Around her neck are red beads, and her stockings are also red; in her hands she holds a spindle with red thread, suggesting that she works with her hands, and even, perhaps, that she makes her own clothes.[15] Grevembroch presented his Furlana with folkloric attention to the colorful details and trimmings of her costume, and perhaps Paolina Lozaro wore a miniature version of this outfit, immediately recognizable as the costume of a Furlana. Indeed, it would have looked peculiar with stylishly powdered hair, emphasizing the contrast between folklore and fashion.

The text that accompanied the image in Grevembroch's collection sought to explain the presence of the Friulians in the metropolis. It began by noting paradoxically that the sterility of the agricultural land in Friuli, the cause of provincial poverty, contrasted with the exceptional fecundity of Friulian women. Thus, they biologically overpopulated the province, inevitably pro-

Furlana. "They are counted in the thousands here, one better than the next, not regretting the delay in returning to their homeland until they have improved their condition." From Giovanni Grevembroch, *Gli abiti de veneziani.* By permission of the Biblioteca del Museo Correr, Venice.

ducing an immigrant outflow of population to the capital. The fecundity of the Furlana also made her an ideal wet nurse, once arrived in Venice, and, in fact, Maria Lozaro gave satisfaction in that role for the child of Elena Artico, who then became the "affectionate patroness" of the poor Furlana. Grevembroch explained that poverty sometimes induced the Furlana to leave her husband in Friuli and come to Venice to work as a wet nurse. "They are counted in the thousands here, one better than the next, not regretting the delay in returning to their homeland [al patrio Nido] until they have improved their condition. Besides, even the men of this country are worth a lot in Venice, especially in the job of porters, and in all those tasks which cannot be undertaken without great labor. The women have the opportunity every day to speak their own language, to have news of their husbands, and to accustom themselves and render tolerable the cause that inspired them to pass from the rustic village to an august metropolis."[16] Such circumstances might explain Maria Lozaro's life as a seemingly single mother in Venice, married, but with no husband in evidence, neither intervening to protect his daughter from Franceschini nor testifying before the Bestemmia after the fact. He must have remained in Friuli while Maria Lozaro worked in Venice and raised their daughter, Paolina.

Grevembroch recognized such an immigrant life as sometimes lonely and difficult but justified by the compelling purpose of escaping from provincial poverty. The first step, however, involved an immersion into urban poverty while searching for urban opportunity, without the consolations of family and homeland. Grevembroch actually dedicated his image of the Furlana to a particular Furlana of his acquaintance, Maria Pasotta, "who dowered three daughters in Venice through the incredible transport of water from public wells to private houses."[17] Thus, the hardest labor was vindicated by the highest aim of achieving a kind of family security in the next generation, three dowries for three Friulian daughters. The possibility of a dowry probably played a large part in Maria Lozaro's "exaltation" at the thought that Gaetano Franceschini might ultimately adopt her daughter.

Just preceding the ethnic images of the Slavic and Friulian women, Grevembroch included a professional picture to represent a category of female laborer called Massara, described as "servants of the third rank," who were employed in "the hardest labors of the house, from which they cannot rest in even a moment of idleness." The picture of the Massara showed a woman in the same blue dress and red bodice as the Furlana, hard at work, with a big wooden tub of laundry. An empty bucket suggested that the

Massara had been carrying water from the well to fill the tub. The text confirmed that she was, most likely, a Furlana: "Few of the Venetian plebeians are resigned to this laborious profession. Sometimes women are brought to Venice from Dalmatia, and, even better, from Friuli, women who are accustomed to indefatigable diligence, who do not complain, who sleep little, knead the bread, and pass from the oven to the well a hundred times to fill pails of water, with which to whiten the napkins, the linens, and any other soiled cloth. In past centuries, when the Republic possessed vast realms and provinces in the Levant, such tasks were intended for slaves, and every government envoy brought back more than one on his return, caring for them jealously as adoptive daughters."[18] In a more glorious age of Venetian empire, someone like Franceschini might have hoped to obtain his menial servants as well as his "adoptive daughters" from Venice's sphere of imperial and commercial domination in the eastern Mediterranean. In the eighteenth century, with the Venetian Empire reduced to the Adriatic region, the Massara was much more likely to be a Furlana, like Maria Lozaro.

Massara. Female laborer, working as a laundress, like Maria Lozaro. From Giovanni Grevembroch, *Gli abiti de veneziani.* By permission of the Biblioteca del Museo Correr, Venice.

The labor of the Massara could be oppressively hard, and Grevembroch specified a variety of medical problems. "These women, the laundresses especially, become sick with various illnesses contracted from the practice of standing always in humid conditions, from which wet hands and feet become emaciated; the women get old on the job and become dropsical and oppilated." The woman presented by Grevembroch actually looked rather healthy and was voluptuously laced into her bodice with full breasts almost revealed to the viewer.[19] The text enumerated the hardships of her life and clearly indicated that the Furlana, as a working woman, was exploited in Venice, but the image suggested, perhaps even encouraged, the further possibility of sexual exploitation.

In another image Grevembroch represented the "Nutrice," the wet nurse, again in the blue dress and red bodice of the Friulian costume. Here the breast was lifted above the unlaced bodice and offered to a tightly swaddled infant, while the nurse looked lovingly down with a gaze that might be mistaken for maternal. The text actually spoke disapprovingly

Nutrice. Maria Lozaro was the wet nurse for an infant child of Elena Artico. From Giovanni Grevembroch, *Gli abiti de veneziani.* By permission of the Biblioteca del Museo Correr, Venice.

of employing a wet nurse, for the wisdom of the Enlightenment held that women should nurse their own children. Patricians were further discouraged from making use of wet nurses because, according to Grevembroch, women of "the lowest condition" were made into virtual mothers to the infant charges, who then came to regard their nurses as parents. At the same time, wet nursing was hard on the nurse, who was often "tormented by hysterical passions," especially since she was expected to refrain from sexual relations with her own husband, based on the conventional medical wisdom that sex would ruin her milk.[20] Grevembroch thus gave another glimpse into the life of Maria Lozaro, who had nursed the child of Elena Artico while caring for her own daughter, the infant Paolina, as a sort of secondary responsibility.

Immediately following the figure of the Furlana, earnestly posed with spindle in hand, Grevembroch presented in a very different spirit the "Veneziana in Ballo," the dancing Venetian woman. Her swaying form, dangling earrings, and scarlet shoes, the red ribbons on her sleeves and the red rose in her hair, all created a contrast with the Furlana in the previous illustration, who was unmistakably a working woman. Yet the costume of the dancing Venetian was recognizably similar in style to that of the Furlana, a golden yellow dress with a blue bodice and a white lace-trimmed apron delicately raised between the fingers of the dancer. The crucial similarity was revealed in the text, which discussed the importance of dancing in the Venetian carnival season and explained the particular dance in the illustration. "No dance was better appreciated than that which was brought from Friuli and was called the Furlana, for which the women became so slender and agile that the men, however young and robust, were scarcely able to follow them." For "women of the people" [femmine popolari] holidays were the time for dancing the Furlana, since they did not have to work; they staged dances in their own neighborhoods, without even the formal accompaniment of musical instruments. The neighborhood of the Castello was particularly noted for dancing the Furlana. "Recently our ladies [nostre dame] have been enjoying this plebeian amusement," reported Grevembroch, by which he meant the ladies of the upper class; the artist himself enjoyed the patronage of the patrician Gradenigo family, and the reference to "our ladies" seemed to be addressed to the social circle of his patrons.[21]

A dual crossing of cultures was involved in dancing the Furlana: women of the elite who enjoyed the amusements of the popular classes, Venetians who adopted the dancing style of the Friulians. The woman in the illustration "Veneziana in Ballo" was not a Furlana but a Venetian woman imitating the rhythms, and even the costumes, of the Friulians. By a curious process of cultural appreciation and appropriation the poor Furlana, the wet nurse, the servant girl of the third rank, exploited in all the most unhealthful labors, became the model of gay and graceful agility in the carnival spirit of rococo entertainment.

The Venetian playwright Pietro Chiari, one of Goldoni's much less talented rivals, produced a comic musical drama for the carnival of 1771, *Le contadine furlane* (The Friulian Peasant Girls). The show was performed in the heart of Venice at San Moisè but idyllically set in the countryside of Friuli. On the stage the charming peasant Furlana could hope to marry a nobleman. The notion of a Furlana becoming a countess, from *contadina* to

Veneziana in Ballo. Venetian woman, probably dancing the Furlana. "No dance was better appreciated than that which was brought from Friuli, and was called the Furlana." From Giovanni Grevembroch, *Gli abiti de veneziani.* By permission of the Biblioteca del Museo Correr, Venice.

contessa, must have seemed very entertaining to the Venetian audience. They watched the Furlana Sandrina cheerfully sing to celebrate herself:

La Sandrina contadina	That Sandrina is a peasant
Non si crede in verità.	People don't truly believe.
Ho dell'aria da Damina	I have the air of a lady
Quando vado anche in Città.	Even when I go to town.[22]

It would be hard to conceive of a song more false to the spirit of the impoverished working conditions of the Furlana women, like Maria Lozaro, who went to town by immigrating to Venice. Yet it was perfectly true to the spirit of the Venetians who entertained themselves by dancing the Furlana. In a similar spirit, during the following decade, Marie Antoinette would construct her "village" at Versailles—*le petit hameau de la reine*—in the palace gardens, so that she could have the pleasure of playing milkmaid.

The Count, onstage in *Le contadine furlane*, addressed the two peasant girls as "you two little butterflies" (*voi due farfallette*) in a spirit of lighthearted flirtation.[23] However, when the Friulian peasants dressed up in noble fashion, they seemed a little ridiculous even to one another. Sandrina laughed when she imagined the peasant Menghino in a nobleman's powdered wig. He in turn derided her interest in French style and declared it an offense against Friulian honor:

Bell' onor del paese!	Beautiful honor of the country!
Una furlana in scuffia alla Francese!	A Furlana in a French cap![24]

She only had to hear the strumming of the guitar, however, to feel the beat in her dancing Friulian feet:

A suonar io sento appena,	As soon as I hear the playing
Brilla il Sangue in ogni vena.	My blood catches fire in every vein.[25]

The drama demanded that all the Friulian girls consummate the carnival entertainment by dancing the Furlana onstage.

Chiari's rococo musical entertainment reflected a distinctive aspect of Venetian perspective on Friulians in the eighteenth century. The impoverished and exploited immigrant Friulian community, as encountered in the streets of Venice, could be transformed into the dramatis personae of a gay carnival entertainment in the theater. Chiari's drama cast an aura of seductive pastoral appeal around the figure of the female Furlana, performing for the prurient spectators in the audience, while Grevembroch's costumed images endowed the Furlana with colorful and sensual appeal. The charm of the Friulians was celebrated in song and dance in eighteenth-century Venice. Gaetano Franceschini would understand perfectly how to take advantage of Maria Lozaro's poverty and desperation while admiring the little Furlana girl and luring her to his apartment upstairs from the coffeehouse.

Inside Franceschini's Apartment

The delivery service of the coffeehouse brought the investigation right to the threshold of Franceschini's apartment, where cups of coffee, one or two, were passed to the servants, who offered in return some bits of information about what the master was doing in the bedroom. Yet the tribunal needed to penetrate further into Franceschini's private life in order to establish his "character and custom," which meant compiling some sort of sexual history that might illuminate his night in bed with Paolina Lozaro. When Father Fiorese was asked who could testify about whether the girl was in bed with Franceschini, he unhesitatingly answered that only the servants could tell. Certainly, the housekeeper, Maria Bardini, was not stinting in her testimony on that issue, but she had not been working for Franceschini long enough to provide details on his past sexual history. For that information it was necessary to find a former servant who could testify from the internal perspective of the apartment about the women Franceschini entertained there. Finally, the most precise details about his sexual character and custom would come from locating and summoning those women themselves.

Giacomina Menochi had recently left the service of Franceschini and now lived in the parish of San Luca, not far from Sant'Angelo. She had worked for him in the apartment for eight months, preceding Maria Bardini as his housekeeper and receiving a colorful impression of his character. It was this former servant who had provided information about Franceschini's reputation to Cattarina Bartoli, who then reported to Elena Artico. Now Giacomina Menochi reported on Franceschini's character to the Bestemmia, describing him as *sensualissimo*. She mentioned that he made advances toward her, but when repulsed, "he promised me that he would never take such liberties again."[1] Having been both the target of his sexual advances and the witness of his sexual adventures, she could offer an especially comprehensive perspective on his sexual history. There were visits from prostitutes, including one who made a particular impression by losing her earrings in the bedroom and sending for them later. Most notable, however, was Franceschini's prior history of interest in young girls, and Giacomina Menochi addressed that issue directly.

> In the line of girls, sometimes he brought into the house young girls of tender age [*tenere ragazze*] who seemed to be miserable beggars. He brought them into his room, and afterward he sent them away. However, he wanted to keep them to sleep with them, justifying himself to my reproaches that I made in this matter by saying that the doctor had suggested to him that he take a girl to sleep with him so that she might communicate warmth to him. In order to achieve this, he had an acquaintance with a certain Furlana who went around the city selling ladles and spoons, and he commended himself to her, asking her to find him such a girl from somewhere, as I learned from him, not from the Furlana, whose name I do not know, who sometimes came to the apartment with her daughter of seven years, named Agnese. In these encounters she brought the girl into his room, but I don't know what happened. I know well that by means of this Furlana on the last Sunday of carnival there came an older man who said he had a girl and had the idea that he was to bring her on the last day of carnival. The man told me to expect the girl, that he was going to give her dinner, and that then he would come. He did not come however.[2]

The Bestemmia was interested in whether the Furlana who sold ladles and spoons was actually a professional procuress. "That Furlana who procured those girls," the tribunal inquired, "did she know the purposes of Franceschini?" Giacomina Menochi, after having implied the worst, now denied the implications: "In truth, I do not believe it, because he told her he wanted to train the girl for his service."[3]

Franceschini failed to obtain the service of a Furlana girl in the urban turbulence of the carnival season, and he was only somewhat more successful during Lent. Giacomina Menochi recalled two girls who were actually delivered to the apartment. The first girl, Meneghina, was brought by her mother, Maria Dalla Giana, another Friulian laundress. "On the third Sunday of the past Lent she brought her daughter, about eleven years old, and left her, supposing that she had placed her well. He kept the girl that day at his table, and after lunch he compelled me to go out of the apartment, having already told me that in the evening I was supposed to put her to sleep in his bed. I had already protested to him that I would not do such a thing." Giacomina Menochi claimed that she had even considered taking it upon herself to get the girl out of the apartment and take her home to her mother. However, as it happened, there was no opportunity for the servant to put into practice her good resolution on behalf of Meneghina: "When I returned, I did not find her there anymore, and he told me that he had sent her away and that he had not been able to overcome her resistance [*superare la di lei resistenza*]."[4] Meneghina Dalla Giana, when located by the Bestemmia, would turn out to be not eleven, but thirteen.

Soon after Meneghina Dalla Giana, yet another Furlana girl was brought to Franceschini; she too appeared to be about eleven and demonstrated "a similar steadfastness [*costanza*]." Giacomina Menochi described this new girl's refusal to have any sort of sex with the master: "In spite of all the alluring promises intended to make her believe in rings, watches, and purses of money, alternating entreaties with threats, as I heard myself standing in the next room, he did not succeed in overcoming her virtue [*onestà*], so that, becoming indignant [*sdegnatosi*] after having spent almost two hours trying to succeed, he chased her out the door and made her depart, although in these moments of her leaving the apartment I was at attention in order to see her, to know who she was."[5] In spite of that attention, the Bestemmia never discovered the name and identity of the girl.

This unidentified girl, like Meneghina Dalla Giana, was able to put up a formidable resistance on behalf of her own chastity—almost as if these Furlana girls were familiar with such situations. Similar resistance was also evident in Casanova's encounter with mother and daughter in 1747: "The fact is that the daughter, when I wanted to get to the matter, began to play at fencing with me, so that I always made the wrong move." Casanova, enraged, beat the girl up, whereas Franceschini, merely indignant, sent the girl away.

The tale of the Furlana girls, as told by Giacomina Menochi, was almost a comedy: the story of an elderly gentleman lusting after young girls and offering all possible blandishments but unable to prevail upon them to get into bed with him. The account of another servant also fit with this comical picture of Franceschini's adventures. Elisabetta Segati came to the apartment only in the mornings to perform menial services. She testified that she had encountered women in the apartment with him but had not seen as much of them as she would have liked: "Because on those days he had me leave even before I finished my daily chores, just so that I wouldn't see them, I suppose." She did mention with interest having met one woman "who said she was French" and had heard from the other servants about the supposedly medical quest for a young girl to rejuvenate the master by communicating bodily warmth. "All these things together cannot but establish that he is a man of relaxed morals, and, as I hear from everyone, very scandalous, for doing such things in his own apartment, and also because of his advanced age."[6] The sexual activities of an aging gentleman were scandalous to "everyone" in the neighborhood but also evidently a subject of general human interest and even entertainment. In his "advanced age," Franceschini could be perceived perhaps in the character of foolish old Pantalone, one of the traditional figures from Venetian *commedia dell'arte*.

Giacomina Menochi certainly conveyed the impression that Franceschini, in her view at least, was not a rapist. If a girl persisted in saying no, he eventually got the message. In fact, Giacomina Menochi knew this from her own experience. "I must say though, in truth, that he did not practice open violence, since when he tried to get me to comply with his desires, as soon as I rejected him with steadfastness, he never again made even an attempt, and in that encounter he employed all his arts, and even some small violence, but not the most forceful, for I was alone, and perhaps he could have succeeded."[7] She, too, seemed to regard such advances as an inevitable and familiar occurrence in the life of a female servant.

Writing about masters and servants in Renaissance Venice, Dennis Romano has counted between nine thousand and thirteen thousand servants in the city in the sixteenth and seventeenth centuries, and roughly twice as many women as men. Unmarried female servants, who generally went to work in order to earn their dowries, often found themselves in situations of potential sexual exploitation by male masters. Joanne Ferraro further notes that such women rarely enjoyed the protection of Venetian law because of the system's class and gender biases.[8] In the theatrical season of 1750–51 at the Teatro Sant'Angelo, when Goldoni introduced *La bottega del caffè*, he also had a great success with *Pamela*, based on Samuel Richardson's English novel of 1740, about the tribulations of a virtuous female servant facing the relentless sexual advances of her master. Goldoni's Pamela resisted her master with a servant's sense of self-respect: "Signore, I am a poor servant; you are my master. You are a Cavaliere; I was born an unhappy woman. But two things are equal between us, and those are reason and honor." She articulated her outrage in a language of enlightened personal dignity, almost revolutionary in its democratic implications of equality between masters and servants. Goldoni celebrated her steadfastness. "Every moment that I remain in this house," she soliloquized, "is compromising and injurious to my virtue [onestà]. My master has lifted the restraint from his passion. He persecutes me, and it suits me to flee. Oh God! Is it possible that he cannot gaze upon me without contemplating my ruin?"[9] Pamela's experience reflected the common experience of any female servant who faced the menace of sexual exploitation. Like Giacomina Menochi in Franceschini's service, Pamela was determined to resist her master's pressures and refused to comply with his desires.

In 1786 the Venetian Lorenzo Da Ponte wrote the libretto for Mozart's *Le nozze di Figaro*, based on the French comedy by Beaumarchais, the comedy of a master's sexual predation upon his female servants. In the first scene Susanna, the servant girl, sings to Figaro, her intended husband, about what happens when the servants are summoned by the bell, *din din, don don*:

Così se il mattino	So in the morning
Il caro Contino:	The dear Count:
Din din, e ti manda	Din din, and sends you
Tre miglia lontan;	Three miles away;
Don don, e a mia porta	Don don, and to my door
Il diavol lo porta. . . .	The devil brings him. . . .

Both Mozart and Da Ponte, like Beaumarchais, showed themselves well aware that a servant girl was very vulnerable to her master's advances. Franceschini seemed to take for granted that a servant girl was a sexual target, so much so that it might have been difficult to determine, in his case, whether sex was a condition of employment or whether employment was a mere pretext for sex.

The servant Giacomina Menochi remembered a girl named Meneghina being brought to Franceschini's apartment by her mother, a laundress. The Bestemmia located the mother, Maria Dalla Giana (born Maria Zambon), in the parish of San Geremia near Santa Lucia, where Venice's railroad station would be established in the nineteenth century. She told the tribunal that she had two daughters, a seven-year-old and a thirteen-year-old. The older girl, Meneghina, had been brought to Franceschini's apartment during the previous Lent and would be remembered by Giacomina Menochi as seeming to be about eleven. The mother began her testimony with reference to a certain Friulian vendor whose reputation was becoming ever more suspect before the Bestemmia.[10] Most witnesses remembered catching sight of the woman who sold ladles and spoons, and many found her to be somehow sexually suspect, but Maria Dalla Giana actually knew her personally.

> A woman who usually stays in Venice during the winter, lending and selling ladles and spoons, and who was sleeping in my house, said to me that there was a gentleman who was looking for a girl to raise, that he was a good gentleman, and that if I wanted to turn Meneghina over to him, I would make her fortune. I believed it was a stroke of Providence, and I accepted the offer. One Sunday morning during the past Lent, and together with the girl and also with the Furlana, I went to an apartment in Sant'Angelo, and we found that the gentleman was in bed. He got up, and then I consigned my daughter to him, and he assured me that she would be well treated. He gave me a coin worth thirty *soldi*, and I left. When it was evening, at midnight, I saw my daughter come home, and, surprised by that, I asked what happened, and she told me that she did not like staying there, that she had dined at table with the master, and he promised to take her for some amusement, and she did not like that sort of thing. She also said that when she wanted to go away and was going down the stairs, the gentleman told her that I should go see him the next morning, but I did not go anywhere. I never knew the gentleman's name.[11]

Maria Dalla Giana, a Friulian laundress like Maria Lozaro, also initially believed that Franceschini's favor was a stroke of Providence. Did Maria Dalla Giana decide not to go see Franceschini the next morning so that he would not be able to ask her to return the thirty *soldi*?

When pressed by the tribunal to reveal the true motive for the girl's midnight return, Maria Dalla Giana hesitantly added some further details of what she had learned from her daughter: "She did not tell me anything else, and I made no inquiry, because she is a girl who speaks little, and it takes an effort to make her speak. Now it comes to me that she also told me that he wanted to put his hands on her breasts, and it was for that reason that she fled. And in truth she is a girl who rejects with all steadfastness [*costanza*] the least hint of liberties in such matters, and in this case I reproached the Furlana who had me bring him the girl, and she replied that she did not know that he had that sort of character."[12] This situation was perhaps not shockingly new for thirteen-year-old Meneghina, since her mother felt that the girl already had an established record of rejecting liberties and preserving her virtue. Maria Dalla Giana came out ahead, with a coin worth thirty *soldi*, twice as much as the coin that Franceschini would later give to Maria Lozaro to get her out of his apartment.

There remained one crucial question to be asked: "Where is this Furlana who usually sells ladles and spoons?" In fact, Maria Dalla Giana knew exactly where she was and replied, "In her hometown [*paese*]."[13] Like the woodcutter's friend she had returned to Friuli. Like many other Friulians in Venice she moved back and forth, seasonally, between province and metropolis. The tribunal was sitting in September, but the Furlana was considered most likely to be in Venice during the winter months, which also happened to be the carnival months. She was needed perhaps in her Friulian hometown during the farming months of the summer and then came to Venice in the winter to sell whatever could be sold. It would not necessarily be an easy thing for the Bestemmia to summon her now to testify. By the time winter came, any of the Friulians who had already testified would have been in a position to send word that she should lie low, that her own role in these affairs had aroused the interest of the law.

Meneghina, or more formally, Domenica, was summoned herself to testify before the Bestemmia. At thirteen she lived with her mother and had a job in a workshop for weaving woolen blankets. She remembered that during Lent the Furlana who sold ladles and spoons was sleeping at her house and arranged for her to go into service with a gentleman in Sant'Angelo. Meneghina explained to the Bestemmia why she was uncomfortable in his house. "Because he wanted to put his hands on my breasts, and I didn't want it, and he said to me that if I didn't do what he wanted, then I would have to go away, and he told me to go, and I told him I was going, and I took my cloak, and I went away, and he accompanied me as far as the Rialto, because I did not know how to go, and he told me to tell my mother to go see him, but she didn't go."[14]

San Geremia was on the other side of town from Sant'Angelo, and the Rialto would not even have been halfway home for Meneghina. She remembered the inducements that Franceschini had offered to try to persuade her to stay. "He said he would give me a clean dress, and that he would take me for a walk, and to the comedy," she recalled. The promise of a theatrical excursion was perhaps particularly Venetian, an invitation to the poor girl to participate in the city's celebrated dramatic culture. She could not know that just around the corner, at the Teatro Sant'Angelo, in the previous generation, Goldoni's Pamela had acted out precisely her own circumstances, a servant girl in the house of a lecherous master. A Furlana by descent, Meneghina was born in Venice and testified in the Venetian dialect that Goldoni sometimes employed in his dramas of the people. "As soon as he did to me what I told you he did, I fled, and he told me that it did no harm, and I replied that I didn't want to and that I would rather die of hunger, and he became angry and said to me to go away, and I did."[15] In the context of Meneghina's simple Venetian testimony, the notion of preferring to die of hunger might have struck the tribunal as an unexpected rhetorical flourish. Still, it is possible that the daughter of the laundress had a more than rhetorical acquaintance with hunger.

Vicenzo Comin, a priest in the parish of San Geremia, was summoned to testify to the character of Meneghina and her mother. He knew the mother not just as a parishioner but also as the laundress who sometimes worked for him. The priest had seen her "exaltation because she had been given a coin worth thirty *soldi*" and had noted her conviction that Franceschini's offer to her daughter was a "stroke of Providence." He claimed to have warned the laundress against the "imprudence" of sending her daughter into a situation about which so little was known. He told the Bestemmia that the girl had come home, and he knew the reason, but he had not questioned her closely, "dealing with a girl of good custom, as I can assert in all truth, and fearing to insinuate to her any evil."[16] In general, his pastoral intervention in the lives of mother and daughter seems to have been minimal, but his character reference offered evidence to the tribunal that the mother and daughter were not professionally experienced in dealing with predatory gentlemen.

More worldly was the woman "who said she was French." The boy who worked in the coffeehouse spoke of a Frenchwoman in the neighborhood "who seems to be bad" and who asked, when he brought her coffee, whether Franceschini was prosperous. Summoned to testify, she gave her name as Petronilla, a native of France now living in Corte Barbarigo in the neighborhood of Sant'Angelo. She was a neighbor, and she knew Franceschini "very well," because he sometimes came to her shop where she sold perfume, pomade, and sealing wax. A Frenchwoman selling perfume in a shop might seem distinctly superior in caste to a Friulian woman who went through the streets selling ladles and spoons—yet perhaps there was some resemblance in their business, after all. When asked by Franceschini whether she knew any foreigners who might come to work for him in service, Petronilla promptly proposed a young German protégée. In fact,

Petronilla claimed to have another prospective employer for the German woman, the patrician Contarini family—a circumstance suggesting a rather distinguished circle of clients.[17]

Asked if she had ever been to Franceschini's apartment, the Frenchwoman Petronilla replied that "he sent for me to provide him with sealing wax and for nothing else." She introduced him to her German candidate, and the meeting was such a success that Franceschini went home with the young woman: "for *vin* and *viands*, as far as I know," commented the Frenchwoman archly, with her suggestive French vocabulary. The next morning the German woman followed Franceschini to his house, but that very evening he happened to be arrested.[18] Later, Francesca Ravasin would remember this foreigner, with a trunk and a hatbox, who provoked laughter in the neighborhood as she "could not even spend one night with him because of his arrest." Both the Frenchwoman and her German protégée had made appearances in Franceschini's apartment. His sexual history could be traced through the shadowy demimonde of Venice, where ambiguously semiprofessional sexual circumstances involved French and German, Venetian and Friulian, mothers and daughters, trunks and hatboxes, ladles and spoons, and usually coffee.

The world of fully professional sexual relations was represented before the tribunal by Malgarita Bianchi, who lived in Calle de' Zendali, the street of the silk shawls, and was the mistress of a "public place." She was born in Friuli and had been living in Venice for eight years, apparently enjoying some success as a woman of business. Asked whether she knew Gaetano Franceschini, she replied, "Very well [*benissimo*]," and explained the circumstances.[19]

He came several times to my women, although he was old and not very able [*poco capace*], according to what the women themselves told me, and as I myself was aware. Finally one day he said to my women that he wanted to drink coffee with me. They told me, and I said yes, and it happened the next day. He came to the house, around eight o'clock, three months ago, and I wanted to send for the coffee, but he said he didn't want it, and that I should go to his house, that he would go ahead, and I should follow. So I did that, and at that encounter I took my earrings from my ears and put them under the bed cushion, and after I had been there half an hour, he gave me a silver ducat and had me leave. Arriving home, I became aware of having forgotten the earrings, and I sent a servant of mine to recover them. That's how I know him.[20]

Her directness was absolutely professional, and she testified with the poise of one who practiced a lawful profession in solidly established premises. She would be no more embarrassed to tell the tribunal about receiving a silver ducat for her services than to send for the earrings that she forgot in Franceschini's bed. Guido Ruggiero has surveyed the many levels of prostitution in Renaissance Venice, from brilliant courtesans to impoverished part-timers, and he has noted that the Venetian state, while tolerating prostitution, also sought to monitor, limit, and control the profession. Indeed, the Bestemmia was implicated in the monitoring of prostitution, which occupied an important place among the causes of "scandals." In the sixteenth century such institutions as the Convertite (for reformed prostitutes), the Soccorso (for unchaste women), and the Zitelle (for dowerless girls, starting at the age of nine) offered alternatives to lives of prostitution. It was feared that sexual venality would otherwise be a likely outcome of economic penury.[21]

The French traveler Charles de Brosses, visiting Venice in 1739, wrote about the prostitutes as constituting one of the sights of the city: "They compose a truly respectable corps by their good behavior. It is not necessary to believe still, as is said, that the number of them is so great that one steps upon them; that does not happen except during carnival, when one finds as many women lying down as standing up, under the arcades of the Procuratie; otherwise, their number is no more than double that of Paris; but they are also heavily employed. Every night regularly, at midnight or at twelve-thirty, and after, they are all occupied. So much the worse for people who come later. And unlike those of Paris they are all of gentle spirit and charming politeness."[22] It was also possible to make the acquaintance of these charming prostitutes around the coffeehouses of San Marco. When Franceschini made his sexual overture to Malgarita Bianchi, he sent word "that he wanted to drink coffee with me."

Grevembroch, in his volumes of Venetian costumes, included five distinct images to survey the profession, from the soberly dressed concubine and courtesan, to the more colorfully attired prostitute [*meretrice*], the scarlet-skirted whore [*puttana*], and the woman of the bordello, standing tall on bright blue clogs. Gaetano Franceschini brought some of the local color of Venetian prostitution right into his apartment. His servants, like Giacomina Menochi, and his neighbors, like Francesca Ravasin, were profoundly attentive to the presence of "this prostitute quality of women who frequently went to his place." Franceschini seemed eager to explore the variety of sexually available women and, having already tried the women of the bordello, he was willing to pay a silver ducat for half an hour with the mistress. That he was limited in his sexual capacity only seemed to make him more avid for female alternatives to stimulate his equivocal libido. The tribunal asked Malgarita Bianchi whether she ever went home with him again: "Never again, because it is known to me that he is a man who goes around to all the places, changing women, for I have seen him going to another place near mine, and, then, these are things that are known among us women."[23] The Bestemmia decided that these were things that also needed to be known to the tribunal.

Franceschini seems to have made himself particularly well known among the Friulian women of Venice, and perhaps he was stimulated by some sense of their immigrant vulnerability. A solid professional, like Malgarita Bianchi, with a house of her own, ran a more regular business than the Furlana who sold ladles and spoons in the streets, occasionally procuring little girls for domestic service. Franceschini was not too fastidious to make use of the neighborhood brothel in Sant'Angelo, but he also explored the more remote neighborhood of Santa Maria Maggiore and cultivated more irregular connections for obtaining girls, like the Friulian man who waited outside the coffeehouse on the last Sunday of carnival. On the third Sunday in Lent Franceschini brought Meneghina Dalla Giana into his apartment, tried to overcome her resistance, and then sent her away again. Eventually, Franceschini's restless pursuit of sex in Venice brought him to Maria Lozaro and her daughter, Paolina, and that encounter would bring the secret investigation of the Bestemmia into the private space of Franceschini's apartment.

The Dalmatian Widow

Rise of gossip

Sixteenth of Booksellers
Private life

The gossip of the coffeehouse on Calle della Cortesia helped make the private affairs of Franceschini's apartment into matters of public interest, and ultimately helped the Bestemmia build a comprehensive case against him. The testimony before the tribunal revealed just how much it was possible for eighteenth-century Venetians to know about their neighbors in a densely inhabited city. The population of about 140,000 in the eighteenth century was more than double today's population of 60,000, though less than the Renaissance peak of 200,000 inhabitants—always within the same strictly limited urban space of islands in the lagoon. The privacy of private life was inevitably compromised by the density of urban population, and the judicial investigation of Gaetano Franceschini became, at the same time, an exploration of the boundaries between public life and private life in Venice.

The internal dynamics of the building on Calle della Cortesia were certainly not conducive to privacy. While Francesca Ravasin positioned herself on the internal balcony of the top floor for the best view of who came and went, Franceschini was bringing women in and out of his apartment on the floor below and addressing hopeless warnings against gossip to his own servants. On the floor below him, however, just above the coffeehouse, there resided another inhabitant of the building, perhaps even more attentive than Francesca Ravasin, and with more reason to harbor hostility toward Franceschini. This was the patrician widow Antonia Bon.

The trial included testimony from laundresses, servants, prostitutes, and priests, but Antonia Bon belonged to the patrician class, the very same class as the judges themselves who served on the tribunal and in every other political and judicial institution of the Venetian Republic. The building above the coffeehouse on Calle della Cortesia could even be seen as a sort of social microcosm with different levels on different floors: the *caffettiere* Ravasin residing on the fourth floor, the prosperous gentleman Franceschini on the third, and the patrician widow Bon on the second, with servants of the lower classes employed in each apartment. Antonia Bon and Gaetano Franceschini were actually closest to one another in standing, both belonging to the social elite, though her patrician status was arguably more grand. They were also both provincials by origin, neither a native Venetian, for Franceschini came from Vicenza, and Bon was born across the Adriatic in Dalmatia and was presumably elevated to patrician status by her Venetian marriage.

Dalmatia, the narrow province along the eastern coast of the Adriatic, was even more remote than Friuli, and the predominantly Slavic population even more alien. Venice had first staked out an imperial presence in Dalmatia around the year 1000 and had governed the province continuously from the early fifteenth century, regarding the Dalmatian coast as crucial to maritime control over the Adriatic Sea. Adriatic domination had once been the foundation for Venetian power in the eastern Mediterranean, but the Venetian imperial domain had long been receding, with the loss of Cyprus to the Turks in the sixteenth century, and the loss of Crete in the seventeenth century. By the eighteenth century, Venice still ruled its Italian possessions to the west of the metropolis—cities like Padua, Vicenza, and Verona—and its provinces around the Adriatic—like Friuli to the north of the sea and Dalmatia along the eastern coast.

In the eighteenth century the Venetian administration of Dalmatia was based in the coastal cities, such as Zara and Spalato (Zadar and Split today, in Croatia), whose inhabitants often spoke Italian and whose culture was generally Venetian. The Republic, however, saw itself engaged in a great civilizing mission in Dalmatia, bringing the benefits of Venetian civilization to the supposedly barbarous Slavic population, the Morlacchi, of the inland mountains.[1] The Bon family was active in Venice's military administration of Dalmatia, and the records of the patriciate, taken from the Libro d'Oro indicate that Gerolamo Bon held office in Spalato in Dalmatia in the eighteenth century, and his son Antonio Giorgio Bon was born there in 1717.[2] This son was probably the deceased husband of Antonia Bon, since she was recorded as the widow of Antonio Bon. He would have met and married her in Dalmatia, where she was born as Antonia Barbetta. Her husband, had he lived, would have been almost seventy in 1785, and if she were some years younger, as was usually the case, she would have been roughly Franceschini's contemporary in age. By 1785 she had been living in Venice for eighteen years and was well established in the city. The account of Antonia Bon was unlike any other testimony in the case against Franceschini; it showed him in some sort of relation to a woman of his own age and equal, if not superior, status. "I know him very well [*benissimo*]," she replied to the first question of the tribunal, and she proceeded to tell the story of their unfortunate acquaintance.[3]

> I will recount with all sincerity how I made his acquaintance and also how it dissolved. Around last November, one day after dinner, I was leaning on the balcony with my servant, passing the time abstractedly, and I saw passing by, and passing again several times, Franceschini, whom I did not know at all then. I did not think about this until a little later there was a knocking at the door that leads into my apartment. My woman went to answer, and hearing some sort of dialogue when I was passing through my room, I opened the curtain and saw Franceschini. I asked him what he wanted, and he replied by excusing himself for having made a mistake in supposing that he knew me. There was some reciprocal talk that I do not remember, but I recall that the conversation arrived at his asking me about an apartment for his use. The floor above me was actually for rent, and as he had indicated to me that he was of the Franceschini family, known for its business and for the virtue [*onestà*] of their relatives, who included two priests of great esteem in the Somaschi Order, and as his manners seemed polite to me, I offered to take an interest to help him get the apartment. When this arrangement succeeded, he renewed his visits and showed himself partial to me to the extent of wanting to court me [*di volermi corteggiare*], explaining also that he did not want me to have anything to do with anyone else, and especially with gentlemen. The proposition was repulsive to me to such an extent that from then on I did not want to receive him any longer in my home, and though he had then succeeded in coming to live on the floor above me, not only did I not deal with him, but I also avoided the occasion of having to greet him for the sake of civility.[4]

The testimony of Antonia Bon suggested that Franceschini was quite capable of making a respectable first impression, especially by invoking the

fine reputation of his family from Vicenza, including members of a religious order, the Somaschi, known for their particular dedication to the
charitable care of orphans. Franceschini himself would later deny before
the tribunal that he had ever been in keen pursuit of the widow Bon and
would testify that she had been rather more interested in him than the
other way around. Indeed, her testimony about looking out abstractedly
from the balcony, hearing his voice from within her room, drawing open
the curtain to meet him, and intervening to get him the apartment all
suggested that she was not indifferent to his acquaintance. As for him, his
indiscriminate record of omnifarious romances, from the children of immigrants to the mistresses of whorehouses, might perhaps have extended
to the widows of patricians. Yet, once he was established in the apartment,
his conduct quickly canceled the favorable first impression that he made
on Antonia Bon, so that she, like Francesca Ravasin, was soon pointedly
avoiding the exchange of civilities with Franceschini on the common staircase. Whether he felt the snubs may perhaps be doubted, since he obviously had no lack of sexual pursuits and preoccupations to distract him.

Antonia Bon must have hated Gaetano Franceschini, and all the more
in proportion to her original romantic interest in him. Da Ponte and
Mozart vividly envisioned the outrage of a noblewoman spurned when
they created the character of Donna Elvira in *Don Giovanni* in 1787. At
her first appearance onstage, she was hunting for her hated seducer and
singing her outrage:

Ah, se ritrovo l'empio,	Ah, if I find the impious one,
E a me non torna ancor,	And he does not return to me,
Vo' farne orrendo scempio,	I'll commit a horrible murder,
Gli vo' cavar il cor.	And cut out his heart.[5]

Donna Elvira, like Antonia Bon, felt both betrayed and humiliated, and
though still in love perhaps, she longed for revenge against the libertine.

Mi tradi il scellerato! È questo il premio
Che quel barbaro rende all'amor mio?
Ah, vendicar vogl'io. . . .

The wicked man betrayed me! Is this the reward
that that barbarian gives in return for my love?
Ah, I want to take revenge. . . .[6]

Donna Elvira readily joined the other conspirators in the campaign of vendetta against the man who had scorned her romantic interest in him. Revenge, however, came too slowly.

. . . Ah no, non puote	. . . Ah no, it cannot
Tardar l'ira del cielo!	be delayed, the anger of heaven!
La giustizia tardar!	Nor justice be delayed![7]

When Gaetano Franceschini was arrested, his first thought was that Antonia Bon was driving a judicial campaign of vendetta against him. He knew that she had reason to hate him and might want to avenge herself. He knew that, as a member of the patrician class, she was better placed than anyone else in the building to put in a discreet word against him with the patrician officials of Venetian justice. Yet the records of the Bestemmia suggest that Antonia Bon, for all her resentment, was not the motivating force in the prosecution. Maria Bardini, the humble housekeeper, played a far more decisive role, and Father Fiorese made the secret denunciation, while Elena Artico gave encouragement to Maria Lozaro. Without directly intervening herself, except to testify, Antonia Bon enjoyed the satisfaction of witnessing the downfall of the man who had treated her so casually.

Just as Donna Elvira was further humiliated by having Leporello sing to her about Don Giovanni's catalogue of conquests, so Antonia Bon was forced to go on living in the same building with Franceschini and therefore had to witness his ongoing sexual adventures. She may have avoided greeting Franceschini but could not help being aware of his visitors and his personal reputation, so different from the family reputation for honest business and religious virtue. "I will say that he had a universal bad reputation [*mala fama*] with regard to women and was regarded as a dissolute man [*uomo dissoluto*] in this regard," she testified. This was based in part on conversations she had with Franceschini's servants, who reported that "bad women" came to the house for him.[8] In 1787 Mozart and Da Ponte would present *Don Giovanni* with the alternative title *Il dissoluto punito* (The Dissolute Man Punished).

Antonia Bon could see for herself the disreputable women who walked down the street and stopped to flirt with Franceschini.

What I saw was that many times he stayed at the street door, playing the gallant with the tawdry women who passed by, and when it happened that there were some of bad conduct, he engaged them also in conversation. However, I never saw him bring any into his apartment. Except once, after dinner two or three months ago, there came knocking at the door of my apartment a prostitute, and she was looking for a pair of earrings, saying that her mistress had forgotten them under the bed cushion, and it then emerged that that prostitute had been at Franceschini's, and as this was made known, it encouraged the scandalous laughter of the neighborhood.[9]

At carnival, when the mysterious man was waiting outside the coffee-house to deliver an adoptive daughter to Franceschini, but then failed to bring the girl in the end, it might have been Antonia Bon who scared him away. She said nothing about this herself in her testimony, but the servant Giacomina Menochi, who was so well informed about so many other things, pointed a finger in that direction: "Living on the floor below is a certain Antonia Bon, and I don't know whether from her or from her servants, as I gathered, the man was warned not to bring the girl."[10] If true, the story would suggest that Antonia Bon took more than merely a spectator's interest in observing the course of Franceschini's sexual adventures. She may have intervened directly to thwart his lust.

More recently, Antonia Bon had heard the story of Paolina Lozaro: "I have heard it said publicly [*pubblicamente*] in these last days that he had taken a little girl into his apartment, and that he took her also to bed, but I did not see her." She did, however, have one final face-to-face encounter with Franceschini's female company after his arrest. It seems he had left a key to his apartment above the street door to the building, and someone found the key and—"motivated by curiosity to hear something"—brought it to Antonia Bon, his downstairs neighbor. She herself was not immune to curiosity and therefore decided to deliver the key to Franceschini's servants, opportunely taking a good look around the apartment, which, to her regret, she had originally obtained for him.[11]

"I found in that apartment a rather young German girl together with his usual housekeeper, and the housekeeper told me that he had taken the girl for his chambermaid the previous morning. Whether that was in fact the object, I do not know. I do know, however, that she was dressed inappropriately [*sbricamente*], with a colorful cap on her head, and she did not carry herself like a chambermaid."[12] Life with Franceschini in the building was clearly an education in sexual worldliness for his neighbors, who watched him flirting gallantly with every woman who passed by the entrance to the coffeehouse. This was a building in which a patrician's widow could come face-to-face with a prostitute looking for lost earrings, or with a chambermaid who did not look like a chambermaid.

The zone of privacy marked by the door to each apartment in the building was susceptible to various violations, as when Franceschini knocked at Antonia Bon's door to pretend to know her from somewhere, as when Antonia Bon rushed to Franceschini's door as soon as he was arrested with the pretext of having to deliver his key. It is noteworthy that Antonia Bon, despite some pretense at patrician aloofness, was fully involved in the networks of gossip and public discussion that circulated around the building and the coffeehouse. She knew of Franceschini's dissolute reputation, listened to complaints from his servants, and was fully aware of "scandalous laughter" in the neighborhood concerning his adventures.

The tribunal wanted to know whom they should further consult to confirm the testimony of Antonia Bon. She recommended the baker's man Bastian Todesco, who would have seen Franceschini talking to women in the street, and who "made remarks to me several times, and said some words indicating that he was scandalized by such behavior." It was notable in itself that Gaetano Franceschini provided common material for conversation between a baker's assistant and a patrician's widow. She further mentioned to the tribunal that testimony could be taken from her own servants, though they were unfortunately unavailable at the moment: "a certain Lucietta who served me as chambermaid and a certain Iseppo who was my servant, these could easily know something, but Lucietta left the other day for Udine where she is going into service, and Iseppo fled from Venice fifteen days ago on account of his criminal behavior."[13] He would thus have fled on the last day of August, the day that Franceschini met up with Maria Lozaro in the church of Sant'Angelo and took her daughter home with him. Probably this was a coincidence of criminal enterprises, but Iseppo's illicit or illegal conduct may well have been related to the shady operations that occurred in the vicinity of the coffeehouse.

The departure of Lucietta to go into service in Udine was also notable, for Udine was the principal city of Friuli, and she would hardly have made such a move, from the metropolis to the province, if she herself were not a Furlana with a longing to return to her hometown. Probably her departure, a few days after Franceschini's arrest, was another coincidence, but this was certainly a moment when a Furlana in the neighborhood of Sant'Angelo would have had reason to reflect upon her vulnerability as an immigrant and a servant in Venice.

The case of Gaetano Franceschini and Paolina Lozaro brought to light the hidden desperation of the urban underworld, just as it illuminated the secret sexual exploitation of children by supposedly respectable members of society. The judicial investigation of the Bestemmia ranged across the entire spectrum of Venetian society, from the patrician widow Antonia Bon to the Friulian laundress Maria Lozaro. The investigation also ultimately revealed the permeability of public and private life in eighteenth-century Venice, illustrating the different ways in which judicial procedure and neighborhood scandal penetrated to the mysteries of what happened behind the closed door of a private apartment, upstairs from a public coffeehouse.

PART THREE

The Libertine

I began to live truly independently of everything that could place limits on my inclinations. As long as I respected the laws it seemed to me that I could despise prejudices. I thought I could live perfectly free in a country subject to an aristocratic government.

—Casanova, *Histoire de ma vie*

The Interrogation of Franceschini

He was brought forth from the prisons on Saturday, September 10, to appear before the tribunal: a rather tall man, of ordinary build, with gray eyebrows that betrayed his age of sixty years, but wearing a fashionably curled eighteenth-century wig. He wore a long, pale gray jacket of fine material, with silver buttons, over a white vest and black silk breeches to the knee. White silk stockings and shoes with silver buckles completed the picture of an elegantly dressed elderly gentleman, in shades of black, white, silver, and gray. He identified himself before the tribunal: "My name is Gaetano Franceschini, the son of Giovanni; I am a native of Vicenza, living in this city for about two years, and for several months I have had an apartment in Calle della Cortesia in Sant'Angelo, and I live on my income." He had been arrested at six o'clock on Thursday evening by the policemen [*sbirri*] who were waiting for him at the door of his apartment. Now Franceschini had already spent two nights in prison and still managed to attire himself in a manner that emphasized social respectability and significant income. Yet he claimed not to know the reason for his arrest: "This is the thing that surprises me, since when I examine myself, I find no reason for which I would deserve to be subject to the censure of this most excellent magistrature of the Bestemmia."[1] One of the features of secret justice was that the accused criminal, upon his arrest, was not even informed of the charges against him.

Though the tribunal had collected a lot of testimony about Franceschini during the previous week, he was supposed to know nothing about the proceedings, to have no idea that they were contemplating his arrest and prosecution. In fact, his housekeeper, Maria Bardini, wondered whether he had managed to obtain some inkling of the case, when she saw the gondola hovering mysteriously in the canal near the house as if readied for a quick getaway. If that was indeed what Franceschini was planning, his stratagem was foiled by the tribunal's order of arrest.

The arrest was carried out by a certain captain of the police, Pietro Bonaretti, who included the expense of a boat in his bill to the Bestemmia. It was not a difficult arrest for Bonaretti, who had already spent years making arrests for the Bestemmia and had faced some rough customers. Fifteen years earlier he had been sent to break up a suspected ring of homosexual prostitution and walked in on a Turkish gentleman with two teenage boys: "The Turk, upon seeing me, presented himself with a dagger in hand." Just the previous year in 1784 Bonaretti came to arrest a violent young blasphemer, who brandished a short sword before jumping out the window. Franceschini seems to have made no such athletic efforts at resistance. Furthermore, Franceschini was taken in the privacy of his own home, whereas a few weeks later Bonaretti would have to make a more awkward arrest in a public place, that is, the Sultana coffeehouse. In that case, the prisoner was a priest, and Bonaretti had to confiscate his collection of pornography.[2]

Franceschini's arrest took place on Thursday, September 8, and now on Saturday, for the first time, he confronted the tribunal of the Bestemmia face-to-face. He would have had some forty-eight hours in prison to contemplate his situation, to try to guess what charges were being made against him, and, even more challenging, to guess what evidence had been gathered by the tribunal. Still, an innocent man would claim not to know why he had been arrested, and Franceschini was determined to play the part of an innocent man.

His silk breeches and silk stockings might have reminded the tribunal that Franceschini belonged to one of the great silk manufacturing families of the Venetian Republic, a family of wealth and prominence in nearby Vicenza. To arrest and interrogate such a personage was a larger undertaking than the tribunal's more usual disciplining of impoverished Venetians for their improper modes of conduct. Franceschini's costume and composure were surely intended to remind the law that he had some claim upon their consideration. He said that he had spent his time in prison examining his conscience but that he could imagine no reason for his arrest. One might guess at Franceschini's physical and spiritual experience of prison in 1785 by considering Casanova's memoirs, which describe his own experience of Venetian arrest and imprisonment from thirty years earlier.

Casanova was arrested in Venice in 1755 by order of the Inquisitors of State, under suspicion of magical practice and religious disbelief. A captain of the police conducted him by gondola through the network of canals, into the Grand Canal, and to the Doge's Palace. By the famous Bridge of Sighs Casanova was brought from the palace into the adjoining prison building, and deposited in the notorious *piombi* (the "leads"), which were the uppermost cells of the attic, just beneath the lead-covered roof. Casanova, who vividly described in his memoirs his own experience of imprisonment, was installed in a cell with six-inch-thick iron bars, very limited light, and a low ceiling that constrained him to keep his head down. His greatest fear in the *piombi* was the rats, "as big as rabbits"—and seemingly unintimidated by his presence. There were no furnishings except a bucket in which to relieve himself and a plank bench upon which Casanova placed his silk-trimmed cloak and his hat with a white feather plume.[3] As a prison inmate he must have presented an even more elegant appearance than Franceschini.

Like Franceschini, Casanova reflected in prison upon what could have been the reason for his arrest. "The examination of what I could have done to deserve such cruel treatment could not last for more than a moment, since I could find no motive for my arrest. In my character as a great libertine, a bold speaker, and a man who only thought to enjoy life, I could not find myself guilty but saw myself nevertheless treated as guilty. I spare the reader all that which rage, indignation, and despair made me say and think against the horrible despotism that oppressed me." Did Franceschini's private self-examination of his conscience in his own cell also produce a defiant self-justification of his life as a libertine, as a man who only pursued his own enjoyments? Did he, too, curse the government of Venice, seeing himself as the innocent victim of an oppressive despotism? Casanova was frankly revolutionary in his outrage: "I burned with the desire for a vengeance that I did not conceal from myself. It seemed to me that I was at the head of the people, exterminating the government and massacring the aristocrats. Everything was to be pulverized. I was not content to give orders to the executioners for the slaughter of my oppressors, but it was I myself who had to carry out the massacre."[4] Such was the level of fury of someone suddenly arrested by order of the government and subjected to the mysteries of secret justice.

Casanova, terrorized by the rats, assaulted by the fleas, and suffering from bowel disorders and painful hemorrhoids, was kept awake by the striking of the hours by the clock in the Piazza San Marco. Franceschini must have wakefully listened to that same clock as he reflected upon his situation. "Fantasy made reason the victim of chimerical hope or terrifying despair," wrote Casanova of his nights in prison, but he collected his thoughts. "For the first time in my life, at the age of thirty, I called upon the assistance of philosophy."[5] Casanova, behind bars, would eventually be able to think philosophically enough to plan and carry out a daring escape.

Franceschini was locked up not in the *piombi* but in the *camerotti*, cells at street level with windows that even permitted some communication with people on the outside.[6] His experience of prison, therefore, was probably less oppressive than Casanova's, to the bowels and to the spirit. Still, Franceschini petitioned for mercy from the tribunal—for a different prison, or even just for a different cell—to moderate the misery of being "condemned to have to mingle with known criminals in the opprobrium of convicted impiety, amid the horror and the abyss that is reserved only for established guilt." He begged to be relieved of "such grievous, humiliating, and degrading" imprisonment, not only for his own sake but for the sake of his family in Vicenza, "an honest, innocent, and honorable family that is not involved in the concerns of the court but finds itself degraded by my own situation." He pleaded, even exaggerated, his old age—"almost septuagenarian"—and his poor health, endorsed by a doctor's note that cited a "convulsive asthmatic condition." He appealed for "compassion" on all these counts of misfortune, and the tribunal eventually agreed to some easing of his situation within the prison, moving him to a different cell.[7]

Though perhaps he exaggerated his age and ill health, Franceschini was not overstating the importance of his honorable family. Antonia Bon confirmed the family reputation in her testimony, mentioning the virtue and piety of the Franceschini family in Vicenza, as well as their business. The fortune and reputation of the family were made in the manufacture of silk, an article of historical importance in Venetian trade and industry, dating from the Middle Ages when silk formed part of the eastern commerce at Constantinople, followed by the domestication of silk weaving in the Venetian Republic itself. When Casanova visited Vicenza in the 1750s, he was responding to a proposition for making money by purchasing six thousand florins' worth of silk from the factories of the city. This deal might very well have involved the Franceschini family, since they produced so much of Vicenza's silk. Predictably, the particular scheme that Casanova was pursuing turned out to be shady and fraudulent. He took away a somewhat sour impression of Vicenza, where he stayed in a hotel and went to bed alone.[8]

In 1765, when Francesco Griselini published the first issue of his pioneering journal, *Giornale d'Italia*, a landmark of the Enlightenment in Venice, he focused on the economic life of the Republic and wrote with great enthusiasm about the manufacture and commerce of silk in Vicenza. He particularly mentioned the Franceschini family, whose enterprise "had no equal inside or outside Italy, both for its vast size and systematic method." In 1770 an official report from Vicenza to the Venetian government praised Giovanni Franceschini, the head of the family, as "that ingenious Franceschini who is always adding new things to his renowned factory."[9] In fact, it was in the year 1770 that Giovanni Franceschini built a grand new family palace in Vicenza, designed by the celebrated neoclassical architect Ottavio Bertotti-Scamozzi, a worthy successor to the most famous figure of Vicenza's Renaissance, Andrea Palladio. The eighteenth-century Franceschini family home was constructed alongside the silk works in an extensive economic complex, with weavers living in the houses around the palace courtyard. The enterprise undertook important technical innovations in the use of hydraulic energy to power the machinery, and the Franceschini family operated seven hundred looms, more than a quarter of the total in Vicenza. Their silks were sent all over Europe, and the factory was also known for its production of the *zendale*, the sort of silk shawl that Maria Bardini was wearing at her first meeting with Father Fiorese.[10] Giovanni Franceschini stood at the center of a continental economic empire in silk and was a very prominent figure among the important businessmen of the Venetian Republic. Befitting his wealth and standing, he was the father of ten children. One of them was Gaetano, who identified himself to the tribunal as the son of Giovanni, a name that the judges would certainly have recognized.

Giovanni Franceschini died in 1774, and his last will and testament, preserved in the archives of Vicenza, revealed his provisions for five children in religious orders, including his only daughter, who became a nun. His worldly property was then divided among five other sons—Giacomo, Bartolo, Gerolamo, Antonio, and Gaetano—with the neoclassical palace and the silk manufacturing complex concentrated in the hands of Giacomo, presumably the eldest son. The testament invoked the celestial intercession of the Virgin Mary, promised three hundred ducats for the poor, and insisted that his sons follow precisely his testamentary provisions—"and whichever sons by whatever means disturb and molest the peace of the others will lose all benefit from my inheritance."[11] Antonio became the most active of the brothers in operating the family business, and Gaetano, a decade after his father's death, was living in Venice, bringing disgrace on the family name. His income from Vicenza was enough to rent an apartment and pursue the leisured life of a libertine in Venice.

Like Casanova, Franceschini may well have been aware of his vices, without ever reflecting that they could offend against the state. Franceschini, too, was a libertine, a man who freely pursued his own romantic and sexual satisfactions without worrying over the moral or religious implications. The eighteenth century was the great age of libertinage, witnessing its most spectacular exemplars in life and in literature, from Casanova to Don Giovanni, for the age of Enlightenment helped liberate the libertine from the scruples of piety. Franceschini, like Casanova, must have considered his own libertine enjoyment to be his private business and no affair of the Venetian Republic. Yet, alone in his cell for two nights, Franceschini would have had to ponder a response to his eventual interrogation by the tribunal. If he, like Casanova, raged inwardly against Venetian despotism, there was no hint in his courteous address to the "most excellent magistrature." Though he claimed to have no idea why he had been arrested, he had come up with a theory about who might have maneuvered against him, and now he strategically tried to undercut the charges, without knowing yet exactly what they were.

> When I was going to prison, I asked the policemen if they had any knowledge of the motive for my arrest, and one of them asked me if there was a noble lady who lived beneath my apartment, so I started to suspect that it was a sentiment of vendetta that had brought some calumny against me. The motive for which she could have conceived such bad will could have come from what I am about to recount. One day last November, as I was passing by Calle della Cortesia, I observed that on the balcony there was a refined woman with her chambermaid, and there was also a parrot. The immodesty [*sbriccheria*, in Venetian] of her dress, and the smile that she repeatedly turned on me as she gazed, encouraged me to go up the staircase, since the door was already open, out of curiosity to know who she was. I knocked at the door that led into her apartment, and the servant met me, and I asked who her mistress was, saying that I thought I knew her. The servant replied that it was the noble lady Antonia Bon, though I later learned that she was not even of civil birth.[12]

This was the same story that she had told about their first encounter, but obviously, it seemed very different from his perspective. She might almost have been a courtesan rather than a patrician as she gazed smilingly upon him from her balcony, as if inviting him to come up and see her sometime, and Franceschini was not the man to hesitate over an invitation of that sort. In his testimony he naturally attempted to discredit her, since he supposed that it was she who had calumniated and accused him. He not only suggested that she dressed like a courtesan but went so far as to challenge her patrician status. It was marriage into the Bon family that had made her a "noble lady," and the provincial obscurity of her birth in Dalmatia would have placed her outside the general categories of Venetian society.

According to his testimony it was Antonia Bon, after that first encounter, who had romantic designs upon him, and who therefore tried to set him up in the apartment above hers.

> She thought about it and took every means to procure it for me. I meanwhile went to see her from time to time and went out with her, and she had formed the intention of making me her escort [*servente*], and I would have agreed to that, except that I recognized in her a character too contrary to my own, which is quiet, and so I decided to abandon her, knowing her friendship to be extremely expensive and inconvenient for me. The affair of the rental was not yet concluded, however, and I then obtained that apartment, which suited me, so from then on I fulfilled the duties of civility by greeting her upon meeting, and nothing more. This matter, which was indifferent to me, was not so to her, and she showed her displeasure, and so I began to suspect that she wanted revenge.[13]

The prospect of becoming the widow's *cavaliere servente*, something ambiguously between an acknowledged lover and a public escort, must have seemed inconvenient indeed to Franceschini in a life that was dedicated to the frantic pursuit of prostitutes and servant girls, according to his not particularly "quiet" character. That he should have obtained the apartment through her good offices, and then given her nothing in exchange but polite greetings on the staircase, must have seemed like ingratitude to her, and he himself called it a kind of abandonment. When he reflected in prison about his acquaintances and asked himself who might have held a grudge, Antonia Bon would not only have come to mind as a woman scorned, and therefore perhaps vindictive, but her patrician status, even by marriage, might have seemed likely to give her the means and connections to carry out a judicial vendetta.

It is impossible to determine from the transcript of the interrogation whether Franceschini was truly surprised, or merely pretending to be surprised, at the next question: whether he knew a certain Paolina, the daughter of Maria Lozaro. The transcript does not report whether there followed a long pause, whether his face presented an expression of astonishment or embarrassment or sudden understanding, whether he took some time to think before formulating his response to the names of mother and daughter. He spoke, however, as if he had experienced a revelation, as if everything—the whole reason for his arrest and imprisonment—was suddenly clear to him: "Now I understand. There has been formed a most atrocious calumny against me. Listen."[14]

Franceschini then launched into a long, rambling tale of the domestic misadventures of his housekeeper, Maria Bardini. She was honest, he thought, but she was hopelessly incompetent and extremely confused and absent-minded. Once she even ruined a tablecloth by cutting it in half. Finally, her master had to ask her why she was so distracted, to which she replied that she was thinking about her two children, who were being cared for in the country while she was working in service in the city. So Franceschini, "moved by sentiments of humanity [*sentimenti d'umanità*] and to see if she would awaken from her confusion," decided to permit one of the children to come and live with her in his apartment, but the plan was derailed by objections from the patrician Erizzo family who had employed her late husband as a servant. In the meantime, the housekeeper was becoming more and more incompetent, falling asleep on the job, and creating a risk of fire in the building. She herself recognized the problem, and it was she who came to Franceschini with a request: "to take another steady woman or a big girl [*ragazzona*] to train, which would minimally increase my expenses, and I would have better service, and she would have company since she was not accustomed to remain alone."[15] The point of his meandering narrative was becoming increasingly clear as he affirmed that it was entirely the idea of his housekeeper to bring a girl into the apartment.

The master was therefore only thinking of his housekeeper when, soon after, he happened to be taking a walk around the town : "I saw a Furlana girl who was doing washing in the canal, and the project of my servant came into my mind, so I asked the girl if she wanted to go into service, and had her call her mother so I could make the same inquiry of her." The mother was all too agreeable, as she herself had already admitted to the tribunal, and Franceschini claimed that he was the one who hesitated on account of the girl's tender age. Again, however, it was the housekeeper who supposedly insisted on proceeding: "In fact, I recounted the matter to my housekeeper, who told me that it did not matter that the child was little, since she would feel greater pleasure with a child the same age as her own, and indeed she would be able to train the child all the better and more easily."[16] Franceschini's narrative was intended to demonstrate that any seemingly compromising circumstances concerning the presence of the child in his apartment occurred without the least initiative coming from him.

Now Franceschini told the tribunal what happened, from his perspective, after the arrival of Paolina Lozaro in his apartment.

> In the presence of the mother I consigned the girl to my housekeeper, and I recommended to her that she attend to the girl, and have her say her prayers morning and evening, and encourage the girl, who was crying at the separation from her mother. Then I went out, and upon my return I found the girl asleep with her hair combed differently. I woke her up and told her that if she wanted to sleep, she should throw herself upon some bed. I also said to the servant that little by little she should try to dress the girl better, because she was a poor girl wearing some blouse and a pair of old stockings that I would not use anymore. Meanwhile, I went to the table, and to provide myself with some distraction and to have someone to converse with, I had the girl come to the table with me. To give some idea of my character, which is eager for distractions: I have several times had come to visit me at the dinner hour one or another of these poor women with children, and it was pleasing to me to share a portion of my meal and to see them eat with that voracious appetite, passing with them a half hour in conversation, and then I sent them away, giving some coins in charity.
>
> That day when the meal was ended, the girl got up from the table, and I said to the woman to put her to bed to sleep. She put the girl on my bed, dressed as she was, and I, after finishing the meal, found her already asleep, and I also went to rest on the bed without undressing. I woke up while she was still sleeping. I groomed myself and went out of the house, having already told the housekeeper that morning that for the night she should manage to keep the girl with her until the next day when I would have a bigger bed made, as I had ordered my manservant. Then that evening when I came home, I found that she had put the girl in my bed. So as not to wake her, I also went to bed and fell asleep, though my first impulse was to awaken the girl and the woman, so that the woman could take the girl in bed with her, but I reflected that they were both asleep and that it was the same as if she were sleeping with her father, so I, too, as I said, went to bed.
>
> I woke up the following morning at my usual hour, opened the door, and the housekeeper came to open the shutters, and I asked her the reason

why she had put the girl in my bed when I had told her to keep the girl
with her, and she justified herself by saying that she had seen the girl in
my bed after lunch, and since her own was so narrow, she had thought it
better to put the girl in mine, being certain that it would not disturb me.
I replied to her that after lunch for half an hour, and dressed, was different
from the whole night, and undressed, and I was accustomed to sleeping
alone. I got up while the girl was still sleeping. I got dressed and went
out of the house after she had awakened, and she talked with me while I
groomed myself. When I returned home at lunchtime, the servant woman
said to me that a tall, thin woman had come, someone unknown to her,
accompanied by a priest and another man, and they had taken the girl
away. And I knew nothing else about it. This is certain: that that girl left
my house just as she was when she came. [*Questo è certo che quella ragazza
è partita tal quale è venuta in mia casa.*]"[17]

By this point Franceschini seems to have grasped very clearly what sort of
case was being prepared against him, so he decided to stake his innocence
on the unequivocal assertion that the girl remained a virgin after spending
the night in bed with him. That was what it meant to declare that she left
his house just as she was when she came. Whatever else might or might
not have occurred in bed would be difficult to determine with judicial cer-
tainty, so he would insist on having slept beside her, "as if she were sleeping
with her father." Everything else, in his telling, was a comedy of innocent
circumstances: a housekeeper so incompetent that she needed a child to
assist her, a charitable old gentlemen who liked to chatter with children
over his dinner, and a misunderstanding about where the new servant girl
was supposed to sleep. Franceschini made himself into Pantalone, the stock
figure of the ridiculous old gentleman from the Italian dramatic tradition of
commedia dell'arte, a figure all too often made into a fool by his scheming
servants. Franceschini's self-justification before the tribunal appeared as a
parody of libertine machinations, the old gentleman doing all he could to
preserve the decency of the poor child who nevertheless kept turning up, in
spite of all precautions to the contrary, in his own bed.

Franceschini's self-deprecating account of his domestic misadventures
was very different in spirit from the libertine braggadocio of Casanova in
his memoirs, titillating himself and his readers with the boldness of his
stratagems for obtaining satisfaction. Remembering Paris in the early 1750s,
Casanova wrote about "la petite Morfi," whom he also called "Hélène," a
thirteen-year-old girl who offered him her bed at the price of a coin. She
was pretty, but poor and dirty, and the bed was just a straw mattress on

some boards, so Casanova, still in his twenties, began to explore exactly what his coin might buy.

> "Do you call that a bed?"
> "That is my bed."
> "I do not want it, and you will not have the coin."
> "Are you thinking about getting undressed to sleep there?"
> "Without doubt."
> "What an idea! We have no sheets."
> "Do you then sleep dressed?"
> "Not at all."
> "Well then! Go to sleep yourself, and you will have the coin. I want to watch you."
> "All right. But you won't do anything to me."
> "Not the slightest thing."[18]

For Casanova the circumstance of the humble little bed and the negotiations over dress and undress were recounted with relish, as he proceeded in the pursuit of his own pleasure, making her bed and body into the materials of his own libertine adventure.

If Franceschini's incitements and calculations were similar to those of Casanova, they had to be completely revised as comic inadvertency in the self-exculpating narrative before the tribunal. Casanova, as it turned out, hesitated to purchase the virginity of poor little Hélène but had her portrait painted, with her undressed. The picture, he claimed, was then brought to Versailles, where King Louis XV, a royal libertine, took an interest in the model and installed her in the Parc-aux-Cerfs to become his mistress for three years, earning her a dowry of four hundred thousand francs.[19] It was the ultimate "stroke of Providence," beyond anything that Maria Lozaro might have imagined for her daughter in Venice. Furthermore, Louis XV, as an absolute monarch, was above the law and would never need to justify his libertinage before any tribunal as Franceschini did. It is also true that Hélène was thirteen, and Paolina only eight.

Asked whether there had been any intimacies with Paolina Lozaro, Franceschini replied, "None, except for some kisses to comfort her when she was crying, as one does with children [*come suol farsi colli ragazzi*]."[20] He now knew for certain the reason for his arrest, had presented his own narrative of the crucial events, and admitted to kisses but not to anything more. In particular he insisted on the medically verifiable fact that her virginity was intact: "That girl left my house just as she was when she came." At the same time, his appearance spoke on his behalf, for even after two nights in prison, he presented himself to the Bestemmia as a gentleman from an honorable family in the silk trade, dressed in black silk breeches and white silk stockings, with silver buttons on his jacket and silver buckles on his shoes. He had described his own character as "eager for distractions," and his interest in the child Paolina Lozaro as one of those innocent distractions. Even that interest was, he implied, only an incidental outcome of his need to find assistance for an incompetent housekeeper. As for kissing the child, he knew that kissing in itself was not a crime. He was merely comforting the little girl, "as one does with children." Indisputably, Paolina Lozaro was a child.

Casanova's Girls

When Franceschini first presented himself to the Bestemmia as a fond, paternal employer, he must have supposed that no one but himself and the child could know what really occurred behind the bedroom door. He may have been surprised to discover from the questions that followed how sweepingly the tribunal had investigated the pockets and corners of his private life. In particular, the interrogation sought to establish a pattern of conduct in Franceschini's relations with young girls. The trial of Franceschini stood at the threshold of modernity precisely because he recognized a norm of conduct for adult relations with little girls—"as one does with children"—which implied, by contrast, some recognition of abnormal, immoral, and even criminal conduct with children. The tribunal had to confront the modern notion of abnormality to discern a perverted pattern of relations between adults and children as represented in the case of Franceschini.

> TRIBUNAL. Do you know a certain Domenica, the daughter of Maria Dalla Giana, an inhabitant of the neighborhood of San Geremia?
> FRANCESCHINI. I do not recall anything; I don't remember.
> TRIBUNAL. Besides the already mentioned Paolina, did you take other young girls into your service?
> FRANCESCHINI. Never. This was an accident.
> TRIBUNAL. During the last days of carnival, were you offered a girl as a servant?
> FRANCESCHINI. No such offer was ever made to me.

TRIBUNAL. Do you know a certain Furlana, named Maria, who usually goes
    through the city selling ladles and spoons?
FRANCESCHINI. I do not know such a woman and do not have the least idea
    about her.
TRIBUNAL. Do you know a certain girl named Agnese, the daughter of a
    Furlana who usually sells ladles and spoons?
FRANCESCHINI. This girl, yes, she is one of those girls who comes with her
    mother, whose name I do not know. Actually, there were two or three
    little girls together.
TRIBUNAL. Were there any intimacies with that girl?
FRANCESCHINI. Oh, if it was a girl of two or three years, she was one of
    those girls whom it pleased me just to watch while she was eating.[1]

This line of interrogation, delicately pursuing the recurrence of equivocal
interludes with children in Franceschini's recent Venetian experience, was
striking in its underlying intention to delineate a particular kind of sexual
character, unnamed though not unknown in the world of the eighteenth
century. Indeed, it has been argued—in the introduction to Foucault's *History of Sexuality*, for instance—that the very notion of a sexual identity, a
character defined by a man or woman's sexual nature, became a fundamental aspect of modern life only in the nineteenth century, along with the
modern concepts of sexual normality, and correspondingly, sexual perversion. It would be a hundred years after the trial of Gaetano Franceschini, in
1886, that Richard von Krafft-Ebing, professor of psychiatry and neurology
at the University of Vienna, would write in his *Psychopathia Sexualis*, his
grand taxonomy of sexual psychopathology, about "a psycho-sexual perversion, which may at present be named erotic paedophilia (love of children)."[2]
Krafft-Ebing thus established and defined this category of classification. No
such taxonomy existed in the time of Gaetano Franceschini, but the details
of the case were such as to make of his interrogation a sort of tentative exploratory foray into the sexual psychopathology of the future.

The eighteenth century recognized the concept of libertinism, but the
case of Gaetano Franceschini called for an investigation of the margins of
libertinism, its extreme and unusual manifestations. This was perhaps what
witnesses meant, when for lack of a better word, they characterized his reputation as that of a "pig" (*porco*). Such an epithet crudely marked the gap
between the eighteenth-century role of the libertine and the modern category of the pervert. Franceschini himself seemed to recognize that questions
about children, however superficially innocuous, needed to be answered
with the utmost care. His denials, evasions, and notable lapses of memory

("I do not recall anything; I don't remember") suggested that he was alert to
the advent of modern cultural anxiety concerning sex and children.

In 1785, the year that Franceschini stood trial before the Bestemmia, his
contemporary Casanova, also sixty, was no longer living in Venice. He had
to leave town in 1783 after publishing a libelous satire against his various enemies. In 1785 Casanova settled in the Bohemian castle of Dux (Duchcov),
as the guest and librarian of Count Joseph Karl von Waldstein. There Casanova began to write the memoirs that would make his the most famous
name of eighteenth-century libertinism, and Casanova, unlike Franceschini,
was determined to remember everything.

"I began to live truly independently of everything that could place limits
on my inclinations," wrote Casanova, recalling his younger years in Venice.
"As long as I respected the laws, it seemed to me that I could despise prejudices [*mépriser les préjugés*]. I thought I could live perfectly free [*parfaitement
libre*] in a country subject to an aristocratic government."[3] This libertine
declaration of independence, true to the spirit of the Enlightenment in its
rejection of tradition and prejudice, in its celebration of freedom, offered
a philosophical vindication of himself, "a man who only thought to enjoy
life." The memoirs became almost a parody of Montesquieu and the *Spirit
of the Laws*, when Casanova cited Venice's aristocratic government, with its
privileges and liberties, as the political form apparently most conducive to

Casanova, age sixty-three. From Pompeo Molmenti, *La storia di Venezia nella vita privata*.

the pursuit of sexual satisfaction. "I believed that everything was permitted to me," Casanova recalled, though he would have to learn the political lesson that "true liberty does not exist and cannot exist anywhere," not even in Venice.[4] Franceschini would learn the same lesson. True liberty, however, remained the libertine ideal, a political and romantic fantasy, even if it could not exist in mundane reality.

The cultural icon of eighteenth-century libertinism, the dramatization of that fantasy, was Don Giovanni, as musically conceived by Mozart with the libretto of the Venetian libertine Lorenzo Da Ponte. Their collaboration dated from precisely the period of Franceschini's trial: they introduced the *Marriage of Figaro* in Vienna in 1786 and *Don Giovanni* in Prague in 1787. Casanova was in Bohemia in 1787, writing his memoirs, and it is possible that Da Ponte consulted with his fellow Venetian in preparation for the premiere of *Don Giovanni*.

At the conclusion of the first act the virtuous conspirators against the libertine Don Giovanni put on masks so he could not recognize them when they entered his palace. Thus, Mozart and Da Ponte created an evocatively Venetian moment onstage, the arrival of masked revelers at the scene of a carnival celebration. The invitation to enter the palace and join the fes-

Lorenzo Da Ponte, Mozart's Venetian librettist.
From Pompeo Molmenti, *La storia di Venezia nella vita privata.*

tivities, issued by the servant Leporello and seconded by the master Don Giovanni, seemed to suggest the staging of an orgy and culminated in the exclamation "Viva la libertà!" (Long live liberty!). It could have been Casanova's own ideological affirmation of libertinism:

LEPORELLO.	Venite pur avanti	Come along
	Vezzose mascherette!	Pretty ladies in masks!
DON GIOVANNI.	È aperto a tutti quanti:	It's open to everyone:
	Viva la libertà!	Long live liberty![5]

The masked conspirators then sang the same phrase in response—"Viva la libertà!"—as if it were the secret password of libertinism, admitting them to its rites and celebrations, its sacrifices and offerings.

Casanova's sexual adventures, considered in their variety, offer some clues to the norms and standards of libertinism. In particular, the age range of Casanova's romantic conquests testifies to the libertine's perspective on young girls and illuminates the intimations of criminal abnormality in Franceschini's case. The man who believed that everything was permitted to him was inevitably the advocate of liberty in its most extreme manifestations. Casanova's memoirs may test the question of how young was too young for the taste of an eighteenth-century Venetian libertine. Like Franceschini's testimony before the Bestemmia, Casanova's memoirs underline the difficulty of distinguishing between libertinism and perversion at the end of the eighteenth century.

Variety was a fundamental principle of libertinism for Casanova, as it was for Don Giovanni, whose multifarious conquests were recorded by his servant Leporello in a catalogue and celebrated in the famous catalogue aria with lyrics by Da Ponte:

V'han fra queste contadine,	Among them are peasant girls,
Cameriere, cittadine,	Chambermaids, citizens,
V'han contesse, baronesse,	Countesses, baronesses,
Marchesane, principesse,	Marchionesses, princesses,
E v'han donne d'ogni grado,	And women of every level,
D'ogni forma, d'ogni età.	Of every form, of every age.[6]

Franceschini, though he seemed to favor servants and prostitutes, flirted with at least one noble lady and later regretted it. Casanova, also wide ranging in his preferences, often specified the ages, as well as the forms and levels, of his individual conquests.

In 1741 Casanova himself was only sixteen and had been tonsured in preparation for a career in the priesthood. He was fascinated by the very expensive Venetian courtesan Juliette, age eighteen, and also by the niece of his ecclesiastical patron the Abbé Grimani, a girl named Angela, close to Casanova's own age; neither girl, however, was bestowing any sexual favors on him. Then one day, during a visit to a country estate, he encountered another, and younger, object of interest. She brought him his morning coffee when he was still in bed: "I am Lucie, the daughter of the concierge. I have neither brothers nor sisters, and I am fourteen years old. I am very glad you do not have a valet, for I will serve you myself, and I am sure that you will be content." He was content indeed, drinking his coffee and admiring her beauty as she sat on the end of his bed. Her parents appeared just then and commented to Casanova on the girl's excellent qualities with one qualification:

> "She fears God, is as healthy as a fish, and has only one fault."
> "What is that?"
> "She is too young."
> "Charming fault."[7]

She was fourteen, though Casanova thought she looked seventeen. He found her simple and innocent and charming, so he began to experiment with her innocence.

> The next morning, as soon as I awaken, I ring, and there is Lucie who reappears before me just as she was the day before, astonishing in her reasonings and her manners. Everything within her was shining beneath the charming surface of her candor and innocence. I could not imagine how, being good and virtuous and not at all stupid, she did not know that she could not expose herself thus to my eyes without fear of inflaming me. It must be, I said to myself, that in attaching no importance to certain bantering, she might not be too scrupulous. With this thought in mind, I decide to show her that I appreciate her. I do not feel guilty vis-à-vis her parents, since I suppose that they are as careless as she is. And neither do I fear to be the first to alarm her beautiful innocence and to introduce into her soul the somber light of mischief. Finally, not wanting to be the dupe of sentiment, nor to act against sentiment, I wish to clarify matters. I casually extend a libertine hand toward her, and by a movement that seems involuntary, she draws back, blushes, and her gaiety disappears. She turns around, as if looking for something, but not knowing what, until she feels relieved of her disquiet. That happened within a minute.[8]

At fourteen, Lucie was almost twice the age of Franceschini's prey, but, for Casanova, the childlike quality of Lucie was precisely her allure, and the exploratory foray of his libertine hand tested not only her innocence but his own sense of guilt and responsibility. Though he claimed to feel none, blaming her and her parents for their carelessness, nevertheless the monitoring of his own conscience was an inseparable part of the titillation that her innocence excited.

> Everything made me recognize that she was an angel incarnate who could not fail to become the victim of the first libertine who made an attempt upon her. I felt quite sure that it would not be I. The thought alone made me tremble. My self-esteem guaranteed the honor of Lucie to her virtuous parents who abandoned her thus to me, based on the good opinion that they had of my manners. It seemed to me that I would become the most unhappy of men if I betrayed their confidence in me. So I took the part of suffering, and, confident of preserving victory, I decided to struggle. I was content that her presence should be the only recompense of my desires. I had not yet learned the axiom: as long as the combat lasts, the victory is always uncertain.[9]

Casanova, for the moment, promised himself that he would respect her innocence, even if it meant struggling against himself. Her angelic innocence, however, was precisely the erotic stimulus to his libertine fantasy.

The articulation of the innocence of childhood—in a secular rather than religious sense—was an important ideological project of the Enlightenment in the eighteenth century, destined to become an overwhelming cult in the Victorian society of the nineteenth century. Rousseau gave the concept its most famous and original formulation in *Emile* in 1762. "Love childhood [*Aimez l'enfance*]," he commanded his readers. "Encourage its games, its pleasures, its lovable instinct. Which of you has not sometimes longed for the age when laughter was always upon the lips, when the soul was always at peace. Why would you wish to take from these innocents the joy of such a short time that is slipping away from them, of such a precious good that they cannot abuse?"[10] Rousseau meant to perorate against a dreary system of formal education that robbed children of their childhood, but his message also emphasized that childhood's innocence could be brutalized and abused. Rousseau himself was not immune to the erotic appeal of children's innocence, and there was perhaps an ambivalent libertinism implicit in his injunction to "love childhood," his plea not to deprive children of their innocence.

Casanova loved childhood in the form of Lucie and was aroused to the point of frenzy at the contemplation of her innocence.

> The company of this angel caused me to suffer the pains of hell. In my continual temptation to cover her physiognomy with kisses, when, laughing, she put her face two inches from mine while telling me she wished she were my sister, I guarded myself well against taking her hands between mine. If I had given her one sole kiss, the whole edifice would have been blown up into the air, for I felt myself becoming a thing of straw. When she left, I was always astonished at having won the victory, but insatiable for laurels I longed to see her return the next day for the renewal of the sweet and dangerous combat. . . . After ten to twelve days, I found I either had to stop, or else become wicked. I chose to stop because nothing made me feel sure of obtaining the reward of my wickedness [scélératesse] through the consent of the object.[11]

Maria Lozaro described Franceschini as that wicked man [quel scellerato uomo], and Casanova put the same epithet to his own account, but it only served to enhance the excitement of the impasse. He claimed to have resolved to give up his morning sessions with Lucie, and, stimulated as always by the morning coffee that she brought him, he tried to explain the moral dimensions of the situation to her. She, however, was too innocent to appreciate them and remonstrated: "You would banish me from your presence, because your love makes you afraid. What would you do if you hated me? Am I guilty because I have caused you to fall in love? If that is a crime, I assure you that I had no intention of committing it, and you cannot in good conscience punish me for it." Thus, the issue of innocence, guilt, and crime was peculiarly twisted so that it was she, the child, who pleaded her case before him, the libertine, urging him to countenance his own love for her. "My dear abbé," she exclaimed, reminding him of his junior ecclesiastical status, "if love is a torment for you, I am sorry about that, but would it be possible for you to have been born and not to love?"[12]

Casanova recognized in her naive speech "the eloquence of nature," and, he, born to love if anyone ever was, surrendered to her romantic reasoning and took Lucie in his arms. Somewhat in the spirit of Rousseau, Casanova came to recognize her innocence as bestowing a natural immunity from the prejudices of morality, the same prejudices that he would learn to discard as a libertine. In short, her perfect innocence was paradoxically akin to complete depravity, and it was the child who led him into the kingdom of guiltless libertinism. That she was "too young" was, in his view, a "charming fault," and he was thoroughly charmed. They spent the next eleven nights together, making love, while he fought the fight to preserve her virginity: "That which made us insatiable was an abstinence that she did all she could to make me renounce."[13] Right up until his return to Venice, he waged war against himself, and it was clearly that struggle that gave the adventure its special erotic character, the excitement of making love to a child.

Lucie, at fourteen, though she may have been a virgin, was not exactly a child, and Casanova himself, at sixteen, was little older than she. One cannot help concluding that Casanova, the writer, deliberately emphasized the childlike nature of Lucie because he enjoyed remembering the adventure as his seduction of a child, or rather, as he related it, his seduction by a child. "In recalling the pleasures that I have had, I renew them for myself," reflected Casanova, about the writing of his memoirs.[14] Writing in the 1780s about the erotic encounters of the 1740s, he relived the pleasures once again, but this time as a man of sixty. In other words, the childlike innocence of Lucie can only have been highlighted in the memoirs of a man who was no longer a teenager when he wrote but a gentleman of Franceschini's age. In the fantasy induced by writing, the aging Casanova displaced his teenage self in bed with Lucie, and under those literary circumstances the discrepancy in their ages was indeed dramatic.

In 1744 Casanova had reached the more mature age of nineteen, and that year he encountered at an inn in Ancona a touring theatrical family, which included a beautiful boy castrato of seventeen, Bellino, an opera singer; a younger brother, Petronio, who danced female roles; as well as two younger sisters: Cecilia, a twelve-year-old who studied music, and Marina, an eleven-year-old who studied dance. Casanova fell in love with Bellino (who later turned out to be a girl just pretending to be a castrato), but the other siblings also encroached upon the libertine's erotic consciousness. Petronio, for instance, brought Casanova's morning coffee, and, in gratitude for a tip, bestowed a kiss on the lips. Casanova, though not particularly interested in Petronio, was free from prejudice, and his general preference for women did not prevent him from contemplating the seduction of the supposedly male Bellino: "I had Bellino sit upon my bed with the idea of treating him as a girl, but his two sisters ran in, and so interrupted my project." So, almost accidentally, Casanova was compelled to take note of the younger sisters, Cecilia and Marina: "The two little girls were true living rosebuds, and very worthy of being preferred to Bellino, if I had not gotten into my head the idea that Bellino was a girl like them. Despite their extreme youth one saw the signs of their precocious puberty on their white bosoms."[15] For these children Casanova had a vocabulary of description that evocatively expressed their barely pubescent appeal. He had hoped to interrogate Cecilia—"mon petit ange" (my little angel)—about Bellino's genitals, to establish whether the latter was male or female, but the girl, with her mother's encouragement, offered herself in the place of her ambiguous sibling. She was "charming" in bed: "When I woke up, after giving her an amorous salutation, I made her a present of three doubloons that she would love better than oaths of eternal fidelity—absurd oaths that a man is in no condition to make to even the most beautiful of women. Cecilia went to take her treasure to her mother, who, crying with joy, confirmed her faith in Divine Providence."[16] Indeed, eternal fidelity would have been a peculiar promise to make to a twelve-year-old girl whose alleged virginity had just been purchased by a payment to her piously avaricious mother.

The very next day Casanova was already being tempted into inconstancy by the predictably providential candidate, Cecilia's eleven-year-old sister, Marina:

> "Cecilia has passed the night with you. You will depart tomorrow with Bellino. I am the only unfortunate one."
> "Do you want some money?"
> "No, I love you."
> "You are too much a child. [*Tu es trop enfant.*]"
> "Age means nothing. I am better formed than my sister."
> "And is it also possible that you have had a lover?"
> "As for that, no."
> "Very well. We will see tonight."
> "Then I am going to tell mama to prepare sheets for tomorrow so that the servant of the inn should not guess the truth."[17]

Casanova's merely perfunctory objection—"You are too much a child"—was immediately put aside out of deference to her perseverance. Yet he also meticulously recorded her childlike exclamations and summed up their agreement by remarking that "these farces supremely amused me."[18] He did not specify whether the amusing farce was the phenomenon of an eleven-year-old girl performing the part of a whore, or an eleven-year-old whore performing the part of a virgin in her concern for the sheets. Casanova, writing about her in his memoirs, cast her in the role of a child, not troubling to evade the implications of her youth. "She unfolded for me all the amorous ideas of her soul. She spoke to me in detail of all that she knew how to do. She displayed all her doctrines, and she detailed all the occasions that she had had to make herself a grand mistress in the mysteries of love."[19] Thus, in a farcical spirit, he recorded the childishness of her chatter, ridiculing her pretenses to adult sexual sophistication, even as he prepared to have sex with her himself, in this case with no scruple about her virginity, which he rather doubted anyway.

Casanova delighted Marina by telling her that he found her sexually superior to her sister, but he paid the same price of three doubloons. Marina carried the money off to her mother, "who was insatiable to contract ever greater obligations with Divine Providence." Casanova took cheerfully for granted that roadside society included venal mothers who would eagerly offer virginal daughters, at least as young as eleven and twelve, for his satisfaction. Franceschini had similar expectations in Venice in the 1780s, and Casanova, writing his memoirs at that time, not only assumed that readers would find the tale of Cecilia and Marina amusing but also summed up the episode as the philosophical antidote to human unhappiness. "Those who say that life is only a collection of misfortunes mean that life itself is a misfortune," wrote Casanova. "These people have written thus without good health, without a purse full of gold, and without the contentment of the soul that comes from holding in their arms the like of Cecilia and Marina, and being confident of having others of that sort in the future."[20] Sex with children was thus elevated to a principle of enlightened optimism in Casanova's libertine philosophy.

In Voltaire's *Candide*, published in 1759 with the subtitle *Optimism*, the argument against Providence, against the idea that "all is for the best" in "the best of all possible worlds," was invested with the brilliant satirical energy of the Enlightenment. Casanova rebutted Voltaire's pessimism and argued for a sort of libertine Providence. "If pleasure exists, and if one can only enjoy it in life, then life is happiness," concluded Casanova, who, even when he was unhappy, could enjoy the prospect of future happiness. "It pleases me infinitely when I am in a dark room, and I see the light through a window looking toward an immense horizon."[21] His dark room was, inevitably, a bedroom, and, like Don Giovanni, like Franceschini, he looked out upon a social horizon of multifarious female forms, of all kinds and all ages, and it pleased him to imagine them all, by turns, in the room with him, the human proof that life is happiness.

In the case of thirteen-year-old Hélène in Paris in the early 1750s, Casanova stopped short of intercourse, not for concerns of conscience but only because they could not agree on a price for her virginity. When he was in St. Petersburg in 1765, Casanova, now forty, had no trouble settling on the price of a thirteen-year-old Russian peasant girl, advertised as a virgin, and purchased not as a prostitute for a single night but as a slave who would belong to him for the duration of his stay in Russia. He negotiated a price of a hundred rubles with her father, employing a Russian officer to translate and explain the terms of the agreement.

"And if I were disposed to give a hundred rubles?"
"Then you would have her at your service, and you would be the master with the right to go to bed with her."
"And if she did not want it?"
"Oh! That never happens. You would be the master with the right to beat her."
"Suppose then that she may be content. I ask you if, after having enjoyed her and having found her to my taste, could I continue to keep her?"
"You become her master, I tell you, and you can even have her arrested if she escapes, as long as she does not pay back the hundred rubles that you paid for her."[22]

For Casanova such an agreement seemed exciting and also exotic, premised upon the brutal conditions of Russian society in which peasant serfs could be treated almost as slaves. Casanova, with his freedom from prejudice, was intrigued by the prospect of sexual slavery, but, in spite of the implied exoticism, there must have been aspects of the situation that were perfectly familiar to him from his native Venetian circumstances. He was quite accustomed to negotiating the price of a girl's virginity, and he regarded a servant girl, "at his service," as someone generally available to his sexual appetites. Furthermore, even in Venice, on the Giudecca in 1747, he beat a girl on the buttocks with a broomstick when she did not cooperate with his sexual expectations. The Russian circumstances seemed to offer a straightforward codification of the sexual conditions that, at home in Venice, were sometimes fraught with legal complications, as Franceschini also discovered.

Casanova named the Russian girl Zaire, after the heroine of Voltaire's Oriental harem drama, and taught her his own language so that they could communicate: "The pleasure I had in hearing her speak to me in Venetian was inconceivable."[23] Thus, he domesticated the romance, for so it seemed to him, though the circumstances seem less romantic from a modern perspective. Casanova remained always conscious of the difference in age between himself and his slave, taking particular pleasure in the curiosity of others. Away from St. Petersburg, on a trip to Moscow, he made a mystery of their relation: "Pretty as a little angel, wherever I took her she was the delight of the company, and people did not care to enter into the question of whether she was my daughter, my mistress, or my servant."[24] Lucie at fourteen, Zaire at thirteen, Cecilia at twelve were all his little angels; it was one of the endearments by which he marked their childlike charm.

In the case of Zaire her appeal was emphatically prepubescent: "Her breasts had still not finished budding. She was in her thirteenth year. She had nowhere the definitive mark of puberty."[25] Thus, the sexagenarian memoirist in the castle in Bohemia relived the pleasure of possessing a slave girl, and though he had become older, she remained in his memory eternally thirteen—or perhaps only twelve, "in her thirteenth year"—and it was in that youthful condition that he offered her up to the erotic fantasies of his readers. When Casanova left Russia, he returned Zaire to her father, but with the understanding that she was to be sold again, this time to an Italian architect in St. Petersburg, a gentleman of seventy.

In St. Petersburg in 1789, John Paul Jones, formerly the naval hero of the American Revolution and now in the service of Catherine the Great, was charged with raping a ten-year-old girl named Katerina. He himself claimed that the charge of rape was concocted by the girl and her mother, that the girl seemed older than ten, that she was a prostitute whom he paid for her sexual services, that he never had intercourse with her, but that, stopping short of intercourse, she visited him regularly "to do all that a man would want of her." Jones was thus not embarrassed to admit to sexual play with a young girl who might have looked older than her actual age, and though the scandal did not lead to legal prosecution (either against him or against the girl), he ended up leaving Catherine's court and service.[26]

In the 1750s Casanova achieved the peak of his romantic complications in Venice, the simultaneous intricacies of relations with the women he discreetly denominated as C.C. and M.M. C.C. was only fourteen years old when she encountered Casanova; M.M. was older but possessed the special attraction of being a nun. Casanova made use of a servant named Laura as his messenger to the convent on Murano and, despite his busy involvement with C.C. and M.M., found time and energy for sex with Laura's fifteen-year-old daughter, Tonina. "With this girl I passed twenty-two days, which today, when I recall them, I consider as among the happiest of my life."[27] Casanova, blissful though he may have been in the arms of the adolescent Tonina, inevitably became aware that she had a sister, Barberina, one year younger still. The girl captivated his attention when she climbed a fig tree to pick some figs, and he, down below, looked up between her legs. He called up to her in the tree.

> "Ah! my charming Barberina. If you knew what I see."
> "What you must have often seen with my sister."
> "It is true. But I find you prettier."

Barberina, instead of answering, rearranged her limbs up in the tree:

> Pretending that she was unable to reach the figs, she put a foot upon a higher branch and offered me a tableau more seductive than anything that the most consummate experience could have imagined. She saw me in ecstasy, she did not rush herself, and I knew she was pleased. Helping her to descend, I asked her if the fig that I was touching had been plucked, and she let me clarify that point by remaining within my arms with a smile.

Her promise of a rendezvous at which she would refuse him nothing was particularly thrilling, since "this is the language that makes a man happy when it comes from a novice mouth."[28] Her youth and inexperience as a fourteen-year-old girl, even relative to her fifteen-year-old sister, were important aspects of her charm for Casanova.

The unembarrassed account of sex with Barberina further emphasized her inexperience, as she eagerly disposed of her virginity with Casanova. He seemed to feel that he was doing her a favor, or, indeed, that he was indulging the importunate whim of a child.

> The celebration was new for Barberina. Her transports, her green ideas that she communicated to me with the greatest naiveté, and her compliance flavored by the charms of inexperience would not have surprised me, if I were not feeling something fresh myself. It seemed to me that I was enjoying a fruit whose sweetness I had never so fully tasted in the past. Barberina was ashamed to let me know that I had hurt her, and this same sentiment of dissimulation excited her to do everything to convince me that the pleasure she felt was greater than it actually was. She was not yet a big girl; the roses of her budding breasts were not yet in bloom. Perfect puberty was present only in her young spirit.[29]

In other words, she was a prepubescent child, embarking upon sexual relations as a novice, and it was precisely her naive newness to the game, her "greenness," that made the unripe fruit seem especially fresh to the jaded palate of Casanova. Yet Casanova clearly did not consider himself sexually abnormal in his appreciation of her prepubescence, and he unashamedly told the story in his memoirs.

Casanova's contemporary, the Venetian dramatist Carlo Gozzi, had a sexual relationship with a thirteen-year-old girl when he was a young man in the 1740s. Gozzi (the brother of Gasparo Gozzi, who wrote about the virtues of coffee and coffeehouses) would become Goldoni's literary archrival and the celebrated author of such theatrical fables as *The Love of Three Oranges*, *King Stag*, and *Turandot*. He began his career, however, in the Venetian military administration of the province of Dalmatia and was stationed at Zadar, where he rented a room from a shopkeeper and his wife. "The couple were not blessed with children, but the man had adopted a poor girl [*giovinetta*], in order to perform an act of Christian charity. This child, who had scarcely reached her thirteenth year, dined and supped with us, as the adopted daughter of the house, and with behavior of supreme innocence [*di somma innocenza*]."[30] In short, her position was very similar to the one proposed for Paolina Lozaro, an adoptive daughter in the home of Gaetano Franceschini in Venice.

Gozzi, who was in his early twenties, enjoyed the company of the girl, and they were soon kissing one another playfully. "I began to perceive that her kisses, which were accompanied by labored breathing, were not as innocent as I supposed. Respecting hospitality, I offered her a gentle but serious correction, in such a manner as not to cause her harm, but warning her that such kisses between man and woman were forbidden by our confessors. She laughed and told me in a lowered voice to be quiet and not to cause a commotion. She begged me to leave my bedroom door ajar that night, because when everyone had gone to bed and was asleep, she would come and visit me." The first thing she had to tell him when she came to his room that night concerned her adoptive father: "He is a real swine. He took me into his house, with a show of charity, as his adopted daughter; but in secret the brute has always had his way with me, and still does now, though his good wife suspects nothing."[31] This was precisely the situation that Franceschini sought to establish in Venice forty years later, without even the hindrance of a wife on the premises. Gozzi did not seem particularly outraged by what he learned about his landlord but received the news of the girl's abuse simply as a reason to discard his own scruples and hesitations.

Gozzi was sixty years old in 1780, when he wrote his memoirs and remembered the Dalmatian episodes of his youth. Looking back across the years, he insisted that it was he who had been seduced and corrupted by the child. "My powers of reasoning evaporated before this sprite of thirteen years, more naked than dressed, beautiful as a celestial spirit. Under the compulsion of a bold, impetuous passion, she sucked up my soul between her parted lips and breathed her own soul into my mouth in return."[32] The seemingly celestial innocence of childhood revealed itself as a sort of demonic depravity. Gozzi's attitude of moral condemnation was all the more emphatic because he himself, in the intervening decades, had become a conservative moralist in eighteenth-century Venetian intellectual life, an enemy of the Enlightenment, and no advocate for the liberty of the libertines. If he had sex with a child when he was a young man, it was morally convenient to remember it later as her fault. When Gozzi then learned that the girl had other lovers besides himself, and besides her adoptive father, he pronounced himself "horrified" (*raccapricciato*) at the conduct of this "thirteen-year-old Messalina." Yet he described her amorous exploits with a dramatic sense for the comedy of the circumstances, and he left Zadar "cheerful" three days after the discovery of her promiscuity.[33] Gozzi's memoirs, alongside Casanova's, suggest that the moralism of the one and the libertinism of the other were not so far apart in their unreserved and undisturbed perspectives on sexual relations with young girls.

Da Ponte, whose libertinism as a young priest also earned him the attention of the Bestemmia, did not actually specify the precise age range of Don Giovanni's many lovers, but Leporello clearly indicated that they were "of every form, of every age." Furthermore, the operatic libertine distinctly preferred youth to age:

Delle vecchie fa conquista	He makes conquests of the old ones
Pel piacer di porle in lista:	For the pleasure of putting them on the list:
Ma passion predominante	But his predominant passion
È la giovin principiante.	Is the young beginner.[34]

How young is the young beginner? Da Ponte did not specify, but Don Giovanni, if his libertinism bore some resemblance to that of the Venetian Casanova, might have included in his catalogue virgin beginners of fifteen, fourteen, thirteen, twelve, and even eleven.

In the catalogue aria Leporello also discusses the physical size and shape of the women whom Don Giovanni seduces:

Vuol d'inverno la grassotta,	In winter he likes a fat one,
Vuol d'estate la magrotta;	In summer he likes a thin one;
È la grande maestosa,	The big one is majestic,
La piccina è ognor vezzosa.	The little one is always charming.[35]

How little is the little one? This was a question that Mozart himself addressed musically in the archly playful setting of the words *la piccina*. Anyone who knows the aria knows that at that point Leporello launches himself into a hypnotically driven repetition, marked by playful staccato, dotted rhythm, and an almost complete collapse of articulation: "La piccina, la piccina, lapiccinalapiccinalapiccinalapiccinalapiccina." Leporello, Don Giovanni's Boswell, his fellow *basso*, his biggest fan, his faithful servant, his alter ego, sings a sort of riff on the diminutive expression *la piccina*, with a musical effect that is at once ironic, comic, knowing, dirty-minded, and infinitely suggestive. It is as if the little girl, the young beginner, were getting littler and younger with each repetition of the diminutive. *La piccina* is Don Giovanni's child victim, as young as you would dare to imagine her.

Franceschini also had a long and varied list of sexual partners, which took the form of a written catalogue only when the tribunal began to gather information about his private life. When he was interrogated about his sex life, he replied in a spirit of relatively frank and unembarrassed acknowledgment. He was a libertine, he pursued his own enjoyment, and he made no apologies for that. Like Don Giovanni, he liked women in all sizes, and the figure of the *grassotta* (the fat one), from Leporello's catalogue aria, made her plump appearance also in Franceschini's courtroom testimony.

> TRIBUNAL. Have you received bad women [*di mal fare*] in your apartment?
> FRANCESCHINI. Sometimes.
> TRIBUNAL. Do you know the mistress of one of those public places situated in Calle de' Zendali?
> FRANCESCHINI. Rather, a big fat woman, and she has also been at my place.
> TRIBUNAL. Did she come there frequently?
> FRANCESCHINI. As far as I recall, she was there only once.
> TRIBUNAL. Did any of those women ever forget anything in your apartment?
> FRANCESCHINI. That was precisely the already mentioned mistress of that place, who forgot her earrings in my apartment.
> TRIBUNAL. Have you brought such women to your apartment at night?
> FRANCESCHINI. Once or twice, I think.
> TRIBUNAL. Did you during the past Lent intend to have in your apartment any girl as a servant?
> FRANCESCHINI. That I do not know, or I do not remember.[36]

While Franceschini was perfectly happy to acknowledge libertine sexual relations with *la grassotta*, his testimony became more reticent and evasive as soon as the tribunal asked about *la piccina*. Suddenly, when it came to little girls, he could not remember anything from as recently as Lent, though Casanova and Gozzi had no trouble remembering some little girls they had known decades earlier. Franceschini was evidently well aware that relations with girls could be legally awkward for him, so questions about children, however superficially innocuous, needed to be answered with the utmost care.

"What I have done does not, I believe, merit that punishment that I am enduring," Franceschini affirmed before the tribunal, after spending two nights in prison. He appealed to his lifelong record: "my reputation as an honest man who has never committed any action in the entire course of my life that was contrary to equity, to probity, and to honor."[37] He was sixty after all, and if there was not already a criminal record of encounters with the law, it was certainly not because he lived chastely. Rather, the episodes of his private life were perhaps merely conventional according to the recognizable patterns of eighteenth-century libertinism. Yet Franceschini recognized a code of acceptable conduct—"as one does with children"—and by implication a sense of what was unacceptable. He admitted taking pleasure in watching children eat at his table but knew that if a little girl was sleeping in his bed, that circumstance might require some explanation before a court of law. The memoirs of Casanova suggest that a libertine like Franceschini would have felt privately uninhibited about pursuing his pleasure with prepubescent girls as young as eleven, like little Marina. Casanova considered her "too much a child" for a mere moment, until he decided that that was part of her appeal. Paolina Lozaro was younger still, even more a child, but not perhaps "too much" for Franceschini's libertine interest.

Casanova never completed the history of his life. He put down his pen in 1797, the year before his death. He had finished twelve volumes, the longest erotic memoir ever written, but he had told the story only up until 1774, when he was about to reach his fiftieth year. We do not possess the complete catalogue of Casanova's continuing sexual career into his fifties and beyond, the sexual adventures of Casanova at sixty, when his contemporary Gaetano Franceschini was searching for very young girls along the canals of Venice. The last pages of Casanova's memoirs, however, offer some clues to the direction of his libido at the threshold of older age. By 1774 he had been an exile from his native Venice for eighteen years, ever since he had escaped from the *piombi* in 1756. "At the age of forty-nine it seemed to me that I should hope for nothing more from fortune, the exclusive friend of youth and the declared enemy of mature age," wrote Casanova, who wanted to go home. "It seemed to me that in Venice I could live happily without having need of the favors of the blind goddess."[38] He thought he might obtain a general pardon if he put himself at the service of the Council of Ten and the Inquisitors of State. In 1773 and 1774 he lingered along the borders of the Venetian Republic, in the Habsburg port of Trieste, and in Habsburg Gorizia, adjoining Venetian Friuli. He was feeling old and was all the more intrigued by the young.

At Trieste in 1774 he was delighted to encounter a former lover, the actress Irene, now the mother of a nine-year-old daughter. Casanova soon received a visit from Irene: "A few days later she came, with her daughter, who pleased me and who did not reject my caresses. One fine day, Irene met with Baron Pittoni, who loved little girls as much as I did [*aimant autant que moi les petites filles*]. He took a liking to Irene's girl and asked the mother to do him the same honor sometime that she had done me. I encouraged her to receive the offer, and the baron fell in love. This was lucky for Irene." It was lucky for Irene, because she was involved in illicit gambling, and Pietro Antonio Pittoni was a police official in Trieste, who was able to protect her once he had become "her friend."[39] He was her friend, however, in Casanova's understanding, because she was so obliging about permitting some sort of amorous relation between the baron and her nine-year-old daughter. Casanova claimed only to have indulged in "caresses," and if Pittoni was permitted merely "the same honor," then the relation would have been a matter of molestation by libertine hands, like the case of Franceschini. Of course, it is possible that to obtain police protection, Irene would have had to offer the baron some larger interest in her daughter. Casanova's memoirs do not specify the full sexual extent of the "offer" that he encouraged Irene to accept from Pittoni. Whatever its terms, he thought Irene was lucky to have made the bargain, and, in fact, perhaps Casanova himself was lucky, inasmuch as a man who enjoyed lecherously caressing children was fortunate to have a friend in the police force who happened to pursue the same gratifications.

Casanova, as he noted, was forty-nine in 1774, Pittoni was forty-four, and neither gentleman seemed to feel that there was anything particularly reprehensible or abnormal about extending their libertine hands to a nine-year-old girl. This clearly establishes the social and cultural context for Franceschini's molestation of an eight-year-old girl in 1785. While nervous about the legal implications, and therefore evasive in replying to questions about children, Franceschini would have considered Paolina Lozaro a merely minor item in his libertine catalogue of sexual encounters: *la piccina*.

The actress Irene had been performing on the stage in Trieste in 1774 during carnival, and carnival season was the context for gentlemen caressing *les petites filles*. Every carnival, however, must come to an end. Lent inevitably arrives, and the very last sentence of Casanova's epic romantic autobiography notes the conclusion of carnival with Irene's departure from Trieste. "At the beginning of Lent she left with the whole troop, and three years later I saw her at Padua where I established with her daughter a much more tender acquaintance."[40] At that point Casanova concluded his memoir, and we have no detailed record of his sexual exploits after 1774, but his libido was obviously very much alive. When he remembered caressing the nine-year-old girl in Trieste, he was already anticipating, in memory, some fuller consummation of the relationship three years in the future when the girl would have been twelve and Casanova fifty-two. Casanova received permission to return to Venice in 1774, and he remained for a decade until 1783, the same year that Franceschini moved to Venice from Vicenza. Briefly the two aging libertines inhabited the same city, perhaps haunted some of the same equivocal Venetian locales, and maybe crossed paths as they pursued women of every form and every age.

THIRTEEN

The Scandal of Franceschini

On November 11, 1785, two months after his interrogation on September 10, Franceschini was once again brought forth from prison, this time to hear read to him, to his face, the indictment that had finally been formulated against him by the Venetian state. In fact, all the witnesses had been summoned and deposed in September, so the month of October that Franceschini spent in prison while waiting for his case to proceed reflected either the law's routine delay or, perhaps, the problematic nature of his particular crime. "When I examine myself, I find no reason for which I would deserve to be subject to the censure of this most excellent magistrature," declared Franceschini on September 10. "That girl left my house just as she was when she came."[1] Thus, he challenged the tribunal to formulate precisely what it was that he had done to incur the intervention of Venetian justice, and, after passing two months behind bars, he finally received the reply to his challenge.

Casanova in the 1750s found that money could ameliorate the conditions of his imprisonment in the *piombi*, and his friends obtained for him food and wine, clothes, and books. Franceschini in the 1780s was certainly wealthy enough to purchase similar favors, as he waited for the Bestemmia to present its case. Now at last, with the reading of the indictment—called the *opposizionale* in Venetian justice—he would know exactly what evidence had been gathered against him and what charges he faced.[2] It was not unusual for the accused to remain ignorant of the particular charges up until this moment in the judicial proceedings. Yet, in this case, the indictment as finally read to Franceschini expressed a powerful sense of moral outrage, without being particularly precise about infringements of the law.

> It is not on account of calumny coming from evil vendetta, as you affected to suppose, that you find yourself subject to the authoritative censures of this most grave magistrature, but on account of your own depraved customs, not satisfied to vent yourself by impudently frequenting the public brothels but causing more scandal and making it more public [*maggiormente palese*] when you came to live in Calle della Cortesia in Sant'Angelo, where trampling without reserve upon the most definite duties of virtue and religion, you made yourself a mirror of turpitude [*specchio di turpitudine*] by showing your sensual dissoluteness in common sight, by prostituting without shame your own house, receiving by day and entertaining also for whole nights libertine women, causing the greatest scandal [*sommo scandalo*] and universal commotion. Not limiting your dissoluteness to this, but pushing it still further, you went so far as to procure innocent girls of tender age [*più oltre spingendo ti dasti perfino a procurarti tenere innocenti fanciulle*], treacherously disguising your guilty intentions with alluring promises, in order to obtain the girls, seeking then with chimerical pretexts to obscure the circumstances of your turpitudinous purpose, and to achieve it, you attempted by seductive means to deceive the feeble mentality of the girls in order to bend them to your satisfactions [*compiacenze*], and thus by your lewd acts and dishonest licentiousness in perpetrated malice, taking from them that innocence that was supposed to form the most sturdy rampart of their virtue [*quella innocenza che formar doveva il più valido presidio alla loro onestà*].[3]

From the very first grand rhetorical formulations of the indictment it was evident that Franceschini's single night in bed with Paolina Lozaro was the crucial concern of the tribunal. The accusation was formulated with a distinctly modern conceptual vocabulary, in phrases that would not sound out of place in a modern court case concerning the sexual violation of children by adults: the deceptive allurement by the adult aggressor, the helpless innocence of the child victim. What was also clear from the opening of the indictment of 1785 was that the outrage inspired by Franceschini's conduct would not be easy to articulate in terms of precise criminal offenses according to the legal conventions of the eighteenth century. To entertain prostitutes in your house was not necessarily a crime, and neither was it clearly a culpable matter either to make deceptive promises to children or even to compromise their innocence and virtue. From the first, the Bestemmia focused on an arena of its own undeniable jurisdiction, the provocation of public scandal. Gaetano Cozzi has noted that in the eighteenth century, Venetian indictments often included "among the accusations" that of constituting a "scandal or bad example to people."[4] In Franceschini's case this charge became not just a secondary addition to the indictment but the most prominent aspect of the entire prosecution. Franceschini was charged with causing scandal at a historical moment when robbing young girls of their innocence was more clearly a scandal than a crime.

The indictment against Franceschini was structured to establish first his "sensual dissoluteness in common sight," that is, the fact that his sexual conduct was "causing the greatest scandal"; and second, that such dissoluteness did not suffice for him, "but pushing it still further," he pursued innocent young girls. The first part of the indictment thus focused on the conventional aspects of libertine conduct, such as his relations with prostitutes, and demonstrated straightforwardly that his bad character led to a bad reputation, thus causing scandal. The second part addressed the more unusual and disturbing aspects of his sexual behavior, his relations with young girls, on the historical frontier between the recognizable libertinism of the eighteenth century and the emerging modern conception of psychopathological perversion. The case for the prosecution argued that while Franceschini's general libertine conduct caused conventional scandal, his unconventional preferences and pursuits made the scandal that much greater and all the more culpable. The indictment thus resembled Leporello's catalogue aria, with an enumeration of all Franceschini's female conquests, as known to the tribunal, followed by a lengthy and historically unprecedented exploration of his relations with young girls, that is, the explication of *la piccina*, a category that Mozart and Da Ponte preferred to leave to the imagination of their operatic audience.

Don Giovanni's catalogue famously counted his conquests by country: 640 from Italy, 100 from France, 91 from Turkey, and 1,003 from Spain: *mille e tre*. Casanova, of course, was a traveling libertine, who made conquests across the continent of Europe, from Russia to England, from Turkey to Spain. Franceschini's indictment, with much smaller numbers, also gave a notion of national variety, with a French tradeswoman who sold perfumes and pomades, and a German chambermaid whose appearance "did not correspond to that of a chambermaid." Franceschini's women, like Don

Giovanni's, ranged in size from *la grassotta* to *la piccina*, and the women summoned to testify represented a full spectrum of Venetian society from the world of lowly laundresses to the elevated sphere of the patrician nobility.

The indictment particularly censured Franceschini for his insolence toward the patrician class in the person of Antonia Bon: "All that you said tending to denigrate the character of that lady who, also on account of the patrician subject whose wife she was, was owed more respect from you, and all that you said and confessed with regard to the way that you made her acquaintance is enough by which to recognize the proclivity of your spirit toward sensuality."[5] Though the tribunal denied that the case against Franceschini was the product of a vendetta, the patrician court rallied around the patrician's widow and, in some sense, proposed to avenge the offense against her honor through the system of Venetian justice. Franceschini's testimony about Antonia Bon had been offensively disrespectful.

The drama of *Don Giovanni* is chiefly driven by the libertine's fatally wrong move in offending the noblewomen Donna Anna and Donna Elvira, the former by murdering her father, the latter by betraying her love. They devote themselves to seeking revenge against Don Giovanni, coming as masked conspirators to visit his castle and expose his supposed crimes. At the same time that the conspirators literally unmask themselves, they also figuratively unmask him, publicly denouncing him as a murderer as well as a libertine. Mozart and Da Ponte composed the operatic indictment:

Trema, trema, o scellerato!	Tremble, tremble, oh wicked man!
Saprà tosto il mondo intero	Soon the whole world will know
Il misfatto orrendo e nero,	Your black and horrendous misdeed,
La tua fiera crudeltà.	Your proud cruelty.[6]

One of the ironies of the opera is that the conspirators are threatening to expose Don Giovanni for wickedness that the audience has known about from the very beginning: wickedness, in fact, that Mozart and Da Ponte have rendered not altogether unlikable. In the judicial case of Gaetano Franceschini the tribunal had to uncover the secrets of his private life and then, paradoxically, prove that these were not really secrets at all, but publicly known, and therefore culpable scandals.

It was not enough to establish that the accused had a character marked by libertine sensuality. "That it was such, and that accordingly you established depraved customs, is proved by the reputation that circulated concerning you [*la fama che di te correva*]." Character explained reputation, but reputation was also evidence of character. The tribunal had culled from the testimony seven statements of Franceschini's bad reputation, though secret justice meant that the indictment did not attribute the statements by name. It was "commonly" said that he was a sensual man, an extremely sensual man (*sensualissimo*), a dissolute man, an old pig, that he enjoyed a "universal reputation" for being "brutally" inclined toward women, that he was treated with "coldness and austerity" by virtuous women, and that he was rejected for membership in a casino on account of his character.[7] Thus, the public scandal of Franceschini's reputation was first secretly investigated through the testimony of individual witnesses and then formulated to his face as a phenomenon of anonymous universality.

The honorable renown of his family in Vicenza only made the scandal of Franceschini's conduct all the more condemnable. Because the family name was known to the public, the disgrace of Gaetano Franceschini was a matter of general interest and public concern. His sexual misdoings, once known to anyone, could no longer be concealed by the veil of privacy: "These offenses, most serious in themselves, become all the more conspicuous and aggravated inasmuch as you have almost reached old age and have come from a virtuous family, whose honor is recognized in utility to commerce, decorum to your country, luster to religion, for which account it attracts all the more attentive universal observation, and so there was a greater and more precise obligation on your part to be an edifying exemplar, and instead all the greater and more effective is the scandal that you have caused."[8] His five siblings in their various religious orders only served to dramatize the scandal of his own impious conduct. The fame of his deceased father as a titan of the silk industry in Vicenza simply guaranteed that the disgrace of a surviving son would receive scandalous notice. Even the old age of Gaetano Franceschini added to the conspicuousness of the scandal by making his sexual adventures seem inappropriate and ridiculous, in the comic spirit of Pantalone.

"You have already confessed yourself in your deposition that you sometimes received in your house bad women," read the indictment. "You confessed that you knew the mistress of one of the public brothels in Calle de' Zendali, saying that she had also been to your apartment only once, as far as you recalled, and that she forgot her earrings." Franceschini's casual relations with prostitutes, at the brothels and in his own apartment, were cited as evidence of a scandalous reputation. The indictment further cited an unnamed witness "to whom it was known that you went around through all the places of prostitution, changing women."[9] In this case, the witness in question was actually the mistress of one of the brothels, so her knowledge of his visits could hardly have been considered evidence that his depravity was scandalously known to the neighborhood at large. Yet, by citing her anonymously, the indictment conveyed the crucial message that Franceschini's conduct was "known" to others and was therefore the occasion for scandal.

Further evidence of Franceschini's scandalous conduct could be found in the streets of the neighborhood: "the witness recounting having seen you several times stopping at the street door playing the gallant with tawdry women who were passing by, holding conversation even with bad women."[10] Franceschini was not told, but would not have been surprised to learn, that the source for this information was none other than the noble lady Antonia Bon, whom he regarded as his nemesis. This was conduct of a public character, transpiring on the street, where anyone could have seen and been scandalized by the encounters with disreputable women. Pursuing a circuitous and sometimes circular correspondence between episodes of conduct and epithets of reputation, the indictment made the case against Franceschini as an object of public scandal.

The tribunal cited one witness who had testified to standing just outside the closed door of Franceschini's bedroom, at the threshold between private sex and public scandal: "He came into your apartment, heard it said that you had a whore with you in bed, and conjectured ever afterward about encounters in your apartment, whenever you made some notable alteration from the routine, that you then had in your room a woman of that quality, and he conjectured all the more inasmuch as the concept was universal of you as a pig with regard to women, as people were saying."[11] The unnamed witness could only have been the man from the coffeehouse, Zuane Lorenzini, conjecturing on the basis of the number of coffees ordered, but his testimony was inserted into the indictment as if it reflected universal opinion and, therefore, general scandal.

"Judging from the full extent of all these vile actions of yours, so well proven by evidence, and rendered so notorious, you can see that these are not limited to the crime of simple fornication committed with circumspection, for which the judgment is reserved to Divine Justice." Thus, the indictment reminded Franceschini that he stood before the tribunal of state not simply for the sake of sex. Rather, he had committed "a crime engaging the peculiar authority of this magistrature to suppress and avenge it," inasmuch as his conduct, as a whole, constituted "a triumph of turpitude that necessarily caused scandal."[12] Sex itself was not the criminal action in this case, but rather, corresponding to the "peculiar authority" of the Bestemmia, the issue was notoriety and scandal.

Franceschini represented the "triumph of turpitude" (*trionfo di turpitudine*), a phrase that almost seemed to recognize the compelling power of the libertine ideal. In composing the full catalogue of his vile actions, and measuring the extent of his libertine reputation, the tribunal articulated his triumph even as it orchestrated his downfall. The more people who considered him to be a pig, the greater was the scandal, the more culpable his conduct before the court, and the more triumphant his libertine turpitude.

The first part of the indictment thus denounced Franceschini generally as a libertine whose conduct had caused serious scandal. The second part addressed his more distinctive and more disturbing sexual interest in children: "Though grave are the offenses set forth against you up to this point, and particularly for the scandal that you have caused, you will recognize as all the more grave those that derive from procuring innocent girls of tender age for the venting of your indecency. You too know the seriousness of this offense, and therefore you have sought to conceal it in your testimony, in part absolutely by denying the facts, and in part by an incredible forgetfulness holding back from confessing them."[13] Franceschini's relations with young girls were thus stipulated as particularly serious offenses, more serious than his relations with adult women, and, indeed, it was on account of one particular young girl that the case was brought against him in the first place.

The libertine had unhesitatingly admitted to receiving visits from prostitutes, but he was, as the indictment noted, much more reticent, and even purposefully "forgetful," about his relations with children. He would admit only to an odd but not indecent pleasure in watching little children eat at his table, and he conceded that he might have kissed Paolina Lozaro to comfort her, "as one does with children." His sexual offenses with children were difficult to prove from the evidence of testimony, and the investigation involved the tribunal even more intricately in the paradox of prosecuting scandal. As Franceschini refused to incriminate himself, the Bestemmia had to ferret out his secret history with young girls, while also arguing that it was no secret at all but a public scandal, and therefore a punishable crime. The indictment clearly revealed the problematic disjunction of public disapproval and disgust at Franceschini's conduct with children and, at the same time, the absence of any modern conceptual framework in medicine or law for formulating and prosecuting a pedophile who perpetrated the sexual abuse of children.

The indictment was, however, ambitiously modern inasmuch as the presentation of the case was not exclusively concerned with Paolina Lozaro. Rather, the law sought to establish a pattern of procuring young girls, which would impute a particular sexual character to the accused, a specific form of libertinism. In this sense, the indictment looked forward more than a century to the age of Krafft-Ebing, who would have identified Franceschini's case as a clinical instance of the "psycho-sexual perversion" of "erotic paedophilia." No such vocabulary was available to the Bestemmia in 1785, as it sought to make the case for an aggravated criminal offense based on the age of the girls in Franceschini's catalogue.

The list began with the youngest, Agnese, the seven-year-old daughter of the Furlana who sold ladles and spoons, a child who had barely been mentioned in the case, except by a single witness, Franceschini's former servant. When Franceschini himself was asked about Agnese, he had thought she might have been "one of those girls whom it pleased me just to watch while she was eating." The indictment now questioned the plausibility of such innocent entertainment of young girls: "What in fact was the object for which you received such girls and various others of greater and lesser age—who were frequently seen to visit you with these sorts of Furlana women, as several witnesses testify—is not evident to the court, although valid may be the presumption of a vile intention."[14] The tribunal persistently tried to determine Franceschini's "object" or "intention" in seeking to befriend, entertain, and employ young girls.

The next child in the catalogue of the indictment was never seen by any of the witnesses. This was the girl who was supposedly promised for delivery by the man who was waiting to speak to Franceschini during the last week of carnival. The man was tall, thin, middle-aged, apparently Friulian, and he waited around the house for about two hours, but the girl, possibly his daughter, was never brought, and therefore never seen, either because the man was warned away by the neighbors, or because he had an unsatisfactory exchange with Franceschini himself. Although the testimony gave the tribunal a glimpse into an underworld of itinerant Friulians who came and went in the streets of Venice, and could recommend or even deliver young girls for unspecified forms of service, such shadowy and elusive characters did not leave behind a solid base of evidence for judiciary proceedings.

It was after carnival, during Lent, that the Furlana who sold ladles and spoons happened to mention to Maria Dalla Giana that a place could be found in service for her thirteen-year-old daughter, Meneghina. Franceschini may have intended to sleep with her in his room, but since she did not stay the night, there was little for the tribunal to investigate, except her reasons for not wanting to remain. Her mother testified that he wanted to put his hands on her breasts. Meneghina herself said that he had offered to take her to a comedy but that she would rather "die of hunger" than let him touch her. He accompanied her to the Rialto, leaving her to find her way home to the Cannaregio district from there, and leaving the Bestemmia with no positive evidence concerning his vile intention.

Still less legally useful was the very vague information about another Furlana girl, said to be eleven years old, whose name no witness knew; she, too, was provided for Franceschini by the Furlana who sold ladles and spoons and spent about two hours in his service. According to the indictment, "Alternating threats and allurements, you did not succeed in overcoming her virtue so that, becoming indignant, after having spent almost two hours trying to succeed, you chased her out the door."[15] This anonymous Furlana girl proved equally useless to Franceschini for his sexual satisfaction and, later, to the Bestemmia for its judicial prosecution. The incident, however, was purposefully included in the indictment in order to prove a pattern of sexual interest in children.

Casanova and Gozzi were both rather casual about sex with thirteen-year-old girls, and it is interesting that the indictment against Franceschini counted the thirteen-year-old Meneghina among the "innocent girls of tender age" whom he had attempted to corrupt. Similarly, Francesca Ravasin's servant—"a girl of about thirteen years"—was mentioned in this section of the indictment: "You asked her to abandon that family and pass into your own service, and because she responded negatively, you proceeded to ask her if she had at least another girl, as you expressed it, her equal."[16] The tribunal understood that he was looking for other girls "equal" in age, that he was pursuing a particular cohort and category of juveniles, ostensibly for domestic service but also, by implication, with "vile intention." The indictment insisted on the difference between such pursuit of young girls and the merely routine libertinism of paying prostitutes or playing the gallant with random women who came along Calle della Cortesia. The court was even careful to try to quote Franceschini, supposedly in his own words, to show that he was specifically seeking a girl of a certain age.

"Your denials serve only as further proof that you understood the grave guiltiness of these matters, and so tried to conceal them, flattering yourself that they were not known, or not proved before the law," declared the indictment. "Since you then understood that the matter of the young girl Paolina Lozaro could not be successfully concealed, you must recognize that the basis of the present trial comes from that matter, and from the bad reputation of your wicked inclinations [*della mala fama delle prave tue inclinazioni*]."[17] The encounter with Paolina Lozaro was the key that made sense out of the series of approaches to young girls, from seven-year-old Agnese to thirteen-year-old Meneghina, and the case thus rested on a remarkably modern and perhaps unprecedentedly detailed investigation not just of a libertine's misdeeds but of the particularly wicked "inclinations" by which he deviated from the libertine norm.

Combining and integrating the assortment of testimonies, the tribunal was able to narrate the entire story of Franceschini's encounter with Paolina Lozaro, telling it to him in the indictment, from the moment that he first set eyes upon the child by the side of the canal on the embankment of Santa Maria Maggiore, to the rendezvous with mother and child at the church of Sant'Angelo, to the delivery of the child to the apartment in Calle della Cortesia. Franceschini now learned, probably for the first time, how Maria Lozaro had told her side of the story to the tribunal. Her account of leaving the girl in his apartment was read to him as part of the indictment: "She asked your name and surname, which she still did not know, and you refused to tell her, saying that it was of no importance to her; and after having stayed there for a little while, she was going to leave, with the intention of returning the following day according to the agreement, but you told her that she was not to come until the following Sunday, with the pretext that the girl had to become accustomed, and when the mother had left, she made inquiries and learned not only your name and surname but also, at the same time, your perverse character [*il perverso tuo carattere*], which put her in extreme consternation."[18] The indictment thus argued that Franceschini had sought to conceal his identity, and along with it his reputation, thus suggesting that his true motives were such as needed to be kept from the mother. The formulation of his "perverse character" could not, in 1785, have carried the sexually clinical connotations that belong to its modern meaning, but even if *perverso* implied only general depravity, the word nevertheless carried its Latin sense of something turned the wrong way, something crooked, distorted, and awry in Franceschini's wicked inclinations.

For the first time Franceschini now learned that his servants had been listening outside the door of his bedroom during the night that he spent in bed with Paolina Lozaro, that they had heard the child crying. He also learned what the girl herself had to say about the night in his bed: "she had been awake the whole night because you had been tickling her and pinching her."[19] Concluding its indictment, the Bestemmia had to try to move from tickling and pinching to criminal charges that clearly articulated the nature of Franceschini's alleged guilt.

> On account of the innocence of the girl [*per l'innocenza della ragazza*], and the necessary reserve in opportune inquiries, the vile treatment that you employed with her did not emerge more precisely, but nevertheless it is abundantly proved, and the innocence that you attempted to attribute to yourself in your testimony has been shown to be a lie. This is the end of your indictment by which you will be able to recognize clearly, to your consternation, how well founded are the proofs that qualify you as a man of depraved custom, confirming that you have without reservation constituted yourself as a mirror of turpitude. In remedy therefore to the extreme scandal that you have thus caused, and as your suitable punishment, you may expect from the authority of this most grave magistrature that heavy penalty that would be sufficient, through the example made of you, to restrain others from committing similar crimes, and to summon you once more to recognize and observe the laws of God and the state, and of virtuous society.[20]

With the innocence of the child at the center of the concluding argument, both as the crucial indication of his depraved character and as the obstacle to articulating precisely the details of that depravity in practice, the tribunal sought to delineate in Franceschini a criminal subject whose conduct lay beyond the bounds of decent society, and even outside the norms of conventional libertinism. The scandal was declared to be extreme and superlative (*sommo scandalo*), and his conduct was condemned as accordingly extreme. Yet Franceschini himself, after hearing the indictment, could take stock of just how much the investigation had discovered about his private life and just how little clarity and precision had been achieved in the legal articulation of the charges against him. He had consulted with his lawyer and replied in a simple sentence: "I reserve for the time of my defense the demonstration of my innocence."[21]

FOURTEEN

Child Pornography
and the Marquis de Sade

While Gaetano Franceschini was in prison in Venice facing the indictment of the Bestemmia in 1785, another libertine, the most notorious sexual criminal of the eighteenth century, the marquis de Sade, was a prisoner in the Bastille in Paris, just finishing his first large-scale work of pornographic literature, *The 120 Days of Sodom*. Sade in prison was permitted the comfort of his own furniture, his own clothing, his own books, and, above all, the basic necessities of pen and paper. On October 22, 1785, three weeks before the indictment for scandalous sexual turpitude was read to Franceschini in Venice, Sade began to write out his final copy of the *120 Days of Sodom*, a fictional celebration of sexual turpitude.[1]

In most respects the novel went far beyond Franceschini's sordid episode of molestation and explored the outrageous extremes of Sade's vicious imagination. The protagonists were four libertine gentlemen who assembled a harem for the purpose of enjoying an ongoing orgy in which they demonstrated their complete freedom from every possible "prejudice" in the sexual degradation and torture of their victims. Among the cast the libertines included a carefully balanced set of eight young girls and eight young boys, recruited by a team of professional procurers, who were commissioned to abduct the children from convent schools and noble homes. The targeted age range was from twelve to fifteen—"everything that was above or below was pitilessly rejected"—and the lower limit suggested that Sade, as he penned his pornographic fantasies in the Bastille, was not principally focused on prepubescent children.[2] In this chronological respect Franceschini's night with Paolina Lozaro could be considered more turpitudinous than even the pornographic imagination of the marquis de Sade, at least at that early stage of his literary development.

Yet, just as a study of Casanova's sexual encounters, assorted by age, reveals the parameters of contemporary libertinism in relation to young girls, similar attention to Sade's pornography, as it developed in the 1780s and 1790s, offers some insight into the significance of young girls for the most extreme libertine fantasies of the late eighteenth century. Though the *120 Days of Sodom* remained unpublished until the 1930s, the succeeding pornographic fictions *Justine* and the *History of Juliette* were published in the 1790s, which implied the possible existence of some limited public that consumed and appreciated Sade's personal libertine fantasies. Franceschini himself, or his French counterparts and contemporaries, might have read and responded to the scenarios of Sade's novels. While the *120 Days of Sodom* stipulated an age range of twelve to fifteen years, Sade's later fiction would include younger child victims, and his literary fantasies about sex with children may have been published with the presumption of an interested reading public.

In the *120 Days of Sodom* there were gathered more than a hundred girls, each of them subject to a process of libertine inspection and selection: "She was made to undress, and in that condition she passed and passed again, five or six times in succession, from one to another of our libertines. They turned her around, and around again; they handled her and smelled her. They spread and examined her virginity." Thus, the libertines selected for pubescent perfection, fully conscious that innocence was one of the principal stimulants to orgiastic excess, as in the case of Hébé: "She was twelve, and the daughter of a cavalry captain, a nobleman living in Orleans. The young girl had been enticed and carried off from the convent where she was being educated; two nuns had been won over with money. It was impossible to envision anything more seductive and more charming."[3] She was destined to be anally raped by the four libertines on New Year's Day. Just as innocence stimulated depravity in Sade's calculus of erotics, so fragility provoked violence. Childhood was thus inevitably implicated in his sadistic fiction.

Some participants in the orgy played the merely narrative role of story-tellers, a quartet of debauched older women telling tales to excite the four presiding gentlemen. These tales included reminiscences of rape and abuse in earlier childhood, as in the case of Madame Champville, who lost her virginity at the age of five to a man who preferred sex with girls between the ages of three and seven. Likewise, Madame Martaine was introduced to sex at the age of four, and her brother was sold by their mother at the age of seven to another gentleman who preferred boys.[4] Here Sade's fictional fantasy domain almost corresponded to the authentic urban sphere of commercial sex where Franceschini looked for little girls in the 1780s. Yet the orgies whose narration constitutes the substance of the *120 Days of Sodom* did not involve victims under the age of twelve. The most notorious instance of orgiastic criminality in Sade's own biography, at the Chateau La Coste in Provence in the 1770s, was known as the "young girls" scandal, because it involved five girls around the age of fifteen. Parents protested against their children's abduction, and a criminal case took shape; some of the girls could not be sent home, because their bodies were covered with the bruises of sexual abuse. Sade seemed to relish the public sensation in Provence: "I pass for the werewolf of these parts. Poor little chicks [*les pauvres petites poulettes*] with their words of terror!"[5] In 1775 he took refuge from the law by traveling to Italy.

In the age range of his victims, both in his biographical orgies of the 1770s and in his pornographic fictions of the 1780s, the marquis de Sade, like Don Giovanni, like Casanova, favored women of every form and every age, with a preference for the young, though not usually as young as eight. The hallmark of Sade's sexuality, of course, was the infliction of pain, the humiliation, flagellation, and torture that constituted what came to be known as sadism. In considering the case of Sade, the ambiguous boundary between eighteenth-century libertinism and modern perversion becomes all the more evident, since it was the eighteenth-century libertine himself, declaring himself free from every moral prejudice and sexual restriction, who bequeathed his name to the most notorious of the modern perversions.

Both Krafft-Ebing in the *Psychopathia Sexualis* and Freud in *Three Essays on the Theory of Sexuality* described sadism as a perversion not very remote from normal sexuality. "As regards active algolagnia, sadism, the roots are easy to detect in the normal," wrote Freud. "The sexuality of most male human beings contains an element of aggressiveness—a desire to subjugate." Krafft-Ebing considered sadism to "vary in monstrousness according to the power exercised by the perverse instinct" but found the instinct to be present in the normal male pursuit of sexual conquest. "It affords man great pleasure to win a woman, to conquer her," wrote Krafft-Ebing. "This aggressive character, however, under pathological condition may likewise be excessively developed, and express itself in an impulse to subdue absolutely the object of desire, even to destroy or kill it."[6] Well aware that such an instinct could be directed against children, Krafft-Ebing cited the Roman emperors Tiberius and Nero as well as sexual criminals of the nineteenth century. For Sade himself, both the erotic infliction of pain and the sexual victimization of children were aspects of radical libertinism. He did not see his life or his literary work as matters of sexual psychopathology but rather as the fullest expression of contemporary libertinism, achieved by refusing to accept traditional prejudices and restrictions concerning sex.

On trial in Aix-en-Provence in 1778 Sade was condemned for "immoderate libertinage" and punished with a fine.[7] Though the court was leniently inclined to leave him free, Sade ended up being imprisoned nevertheless by the royal order of *lettre de cachet*, at the instigation of his mother-in-law. First at Vincennes, then at the Bastille, he was deprived for years of the very liberty that was so essential to the life of a libertine; that liberty now became the central subject of his pornographic writing, his literary libertinism. Transferred from the Bastille in July 1789, ten days before the storming of the fortress by the people of Paris, Sade was then installed in the insane asylum at Charenton. He was liberated in 1790 by order of the revolutionary government, which quashed the royal order of his arrest. The *120 Days of Sodom* had been written in the Bastille for his own satisfaction but never published; in 1791 Sade became a published author with the appearance of his novel *Justine, or The Misfortunes of Virtue*.

The novel began with the bankruptcy and death of rich Parisian parents, leaving their convent-educated daughters to make their own penniless way in the world. The girls were Justine, age twelve and very virtuous, and Juliette, age fifteen, and less inclined to virtue; their ages precisely bounded the range that Sade had considered ideal for the victims of orgies. The real misfortunes of Justine began from the moment that she was expelled from the convent for want of tuition, with no resources but her big blue eyes and her manifest youth: "an air of virginity" along with the attraction of "naive graces and delicate traits."[8] Thus, Sade made the charm of childhood into the literary bait of his pornographic fiction.

The very first priest to whom Justine appealed for assistance responded with a kiss that seemed "much too worldly for a man of the Church." The virtuous child rebuffed him: "I am soliciting advice on account of my youth and misfortunes, and you want me to buy it at a rather dear price."[9] Then she appealed to a rich Parisian tradesman, Monsieur Dubourg: "I am a poor orphan not yet fourteen years old, who already knows all the nuances of misfortune. I implore your commiseration." Monsieur Dubourg, in reply, informed her frankly that "the services of a child like you are of little use in a home." He therefore posed the pertinent question: "How can a little girl like you show gratitude for what is done on her behalf, if not by abandoning herself to all that is demanded of her body?" Monsieur Dubourg assured Justine that her virtue was a mere "chimera," though she, on her knees, declared that she would rather die a thousand times than surrender it.[10] She then discovered to her horror that he was only further aroused by her abject entreaties, that he was finding a special sadistic pleasure in her desperate helplessness. The more Justine sought to defend her virtue, the more furious were the assaults upon it; the innocence of the child only aggravated the lust of the libertine.

In the history of Gaetano Franceschini thirteen-year-old girls successfully defended their virtue, such as Meneghina, who said she would rather have died of hunger than let him touch her, or the anonymous eleven-year-old girl mentioned in the indictment: "you did not succeed in overcoming her virtue so that, becoming indignant, after having spent almost two hours trying to succeed, you chased her out the door." The fictional world of Sade, however, made it possible to construct scenarios far more remote from attention and intervention than an urban apartment upstairs from a coffeehouse. The isolated castles and underground vaults of the Gothic imagination served Sade as the sites for his orgies, and Justine, a little older now, found herself wandering deep into the forest in search of asylum in a Benedictine monastery. Justine had been informed that the monastery was inhabited by monks of exceptional piety, and that the superior, Dom Severino, was "the most saintly of men," an Italian, age fifty-five, and a relative of the pope. When she finally met Dom Severino, she was not disappointed in his solicitousness. He listened sympathetically to her sad story and was especially interested in ascertaining that she was an orphan, that there was no one to take an interest in her fate, and that she had told no one of her intention to visit the monastery. Having reassured himself on all these points, Dom Severino had no further hesitations about offering asylum to Justine. He took her by the hand and led her into the church—"come, my child"— at which she began to feel strangely troubled. "What! You are afraid to pass the night with four saintly hermits!" exclaimed Dom Severino. "Oh! You will see how we shall find the means to divert you, dear angel, and if we do not procure for you great pleasures, at least you will serve ours at their most extreme extent."[11] Justine was promptly introduced into the harem of the saintly hermits, which consisted of eight women, ranging in age from ten to forty. The orgies then commenced.

During his years of liberty in revolutionary France, Sade's chief risk of arrest was as a noble marquis rather than as a criminal libertine. Though he was somewhat sympathetic to the French Revolution, his chateau at La Coste, where he had held his orgies of the "young girls," was ransacked by a revolutionary crowd in 1792; Sade ended up in the prisons of the Terror in 1793 and narrowly missed going to the guillotine as an enemy of the Revolution. The sexual abuse of children occupied a place in revolutionary consciousness as a royal and aristocratic vice, for when the queen, Marie Antoinette, was put on trial for her life in 1793, one of the charges against her as a supposed monster of depravity was the sexual molestation of her own son, the dauphin, eight years old at the time of his mother's trial.[12] It was a pornographic fiction worthy of the Marquis de Sade. When Sade was released from prison after the fall of Robespierre in 1794, the marquis had to try to earn a living in postrevolutionary France, and his need encouraged him to publish in 1797 the *History of Juliette*.

Juliette was the older sister of Justine, and as naturally depraved as her sister was virtuous. While Justine was learning the principles of virtue in the convent, Juliette was being sexually initiated by the Mother Superior Madame Delbène. This initiation began early—"the day that I entered into my thirteenth year"—that is, on Juliette's twelfth birthday.[13] The precocious girl, however, quickly reached the advanced stage at which she herself aspired to the abuse of even younger children. Juliette chose the child Laurette as a particular victim: "Her childhood (she was barely ten), her pretty lively little face, the splendor of her birth, everything excited me, everything enflamed me. The Mother Superior, seeing little obstacle since this young orphan had no other protector than an old uncle who lived a hundred leagues from Paris, assured me that I could regard as already sacrificed the victim whom my perfidious desires were sacrificing in advance."[14] With the *History of Juliette* the marquis de Sade had at last achieved the repulsive distinction of the authentic child pornographer, eager to detail the sacrifice of innocent children for the particular arousal of a specialized pornographic public.

The first hundred pages of the novel built toward the convent orgy at which the ten-year-old Laurette was sexually assaulted by the twelve-year-old Juliette, who narrated the scene: "Destined to play the role of high priest, I am invested with an artificial member. According to the barbaric orders of the abbess it is bigger than is preferable. Here is the arrangement of this session, both lewd and cruel: Laurette is bound upon a stool, in such a way that her ass, supported by a very hard cushion, rests only upon this little seat; her legs, spread far apart, are also constrained by rings, on the floor, and her arms equally so, hanging on the other side. In this attitude the victim presents in the most beautiful position the narrow and delicate part of her body where the sword must penetrate."[15] Sade described to his readers the tableau of the ten-year-old victim in meticulous detail, preparing and positioning the child for the imminent satisfaction of their pornographic fantasies. In fact, the scenario involved two children, for Juliette was scarcely older than Laurette.

The actual consummation brought forth blood and screams, to the great satisfaction of the orgiasts, and the child was left unconscious. Juliette seemed to speak for the pornographic public as she held out the hope of even more extreme brutality in the second round.

> Our exhaustion and the necessity of bringing Laurette back to life if we want to extract other pleasures, everything obliges us to give some attention to her. Laurette is unbound: surrounded, tapped, tousled, slapped, and soon she gives some sign of life.
> "What is the matter with you?" Delbène cruelly asks. "Are you then so weak that such a light attack already sends you to the gates of hell?"
> "Alas, Madame, I can take no more," says this poor little unfortunate whose blood continues to flow abundantly. "I have suffered great pain, and I am dying."
> "Good!" says the Mother Superior coldly. "Others younger than you have endured these attacks without risk. Let us continue."
> And without taking other care except to stanch the bleeding, the victim is bound on her stomach, as she was before on her back, so now her asshole is well within my range.[16]

The ensuing scene led to some uncertainty about whether the child was actually dying or already dead, to which Madame Delbène responded without much concern: "This is just pretending! And what does it matter to me anyway, the existence of this whore? She is here only for our pleasures."[17] Such a merciless credo was particularly apt for a pornographer like Sade, since he could afford to kill off any number of little girls in the pages of his fiction, purely for the excitement of his readers. If, however, in his earlier works, like the *120 Days of Sodom* and *Justine*, he tended to celebrate the abuse of girls between twelve and fifteen, in the *History of Juliette* he seemed more ready to make the sexual sacrifice of a younger child into a pornographic center-piece of the novel.

When Juliette encountered the ultimate sexual barbarian Minski the Muscovite, he boasted of a harem of two hundred girls between the ages of five and twenty, girls whom he not only possessed as sexual slaves but also eventually cannibalized. Juliette, fascinated, demanded to see him rape a seven-year-old girl on the spot for her entertainment. He obliged, of course, while she commented to the reader, "Nothing could be prettier than the lit-tle creature whom the barbarian was about to sacrifice, and nothing amused me more than the incredible disproportion between the assailant and the victim." That disproportion was enough to kill the child, but death did not put an end to the orgy: "turning her over, dead though she may be, the libertine sodomizes her."[18] As Sade sought ever-intensifying pornographic ef-fects in his fiction, he made the sexual brutalization of children into a dem-onstration of the limitless depravity of the libertine. The rape and murder of a seven-year-old girl, or the bloody sexual sacrifice of ten-year-old Laurette, tapped and tousled to bring her back to life for a second assault, went far beyond the pinchings and ticklings of Gaetano Franceschini in bed with Paolina Lozaro. Yet Sade presumed that someone like Franceschini might have been interested to read about the sexual abuse of children at the psy-chopathological outer limits of libertinism. The persistence of child pornog-raphy from the French fiction of the eighteenth century to the World Wide Web of the twenty-first century suggests that Sade was basically correct in his supposition of an interested public.

The details of the orgies in Sade's fiction were endorsed from within the novels by an audaciously conceived set of lengthy philosophical arguments against the principles of religion and morality. Justine virtuously affirmed: "There are within me religious principles that, thank God, will never leave me; if Providence makes the course of my life painful, it is in order to compensate me in a better world." A more worldly interlocutor within the novel, however, rejected such notions as "absurd" and argued philosophi-cally with Justine by suggesting that Providence seemed to favor evil quite as much as good.[19] Like Voltaire's Candide, Justine clung to her faith in Providence, to a belief that all must be for the best, and like Candide she was repeatedly overwhelmed by the arbitrary cruelty with which Providence proved her wrong.

Such philosophical considerations were not entirely new in the pornography of the eighteenth century, and the marquis de Sade may have looked to the precedent of a novel entitled *Thérèse philosophe* by the marquis d'Argens, published in 1748. The heroine's sexual corruption was accompanied by philosophical instruction, by lectures on materialist philosophy and against the principles of Christianity. As historian Robert Darnton has demonstrated, *Thérèse philosophe* was one of the "forbidden bestsellers" of the ancien régime, and its philosophical concerns, celebrated even in the title, were by no means incidental to its success. Darnton suggests that in becoming "philosophical," the heroine represented the Enlightenment to a reading public that was stimulated both intellectually and erotically by her adventures.[20] Justine thus continued the same tradition of receiving philosophical instruction on the road to sexual degradation. Justine clung to her virtuous principles and refused to become philosophical about sex, but Sade entertained himself and his readers by subjecting her to long lectures on the providential virtues of sodomy, incest, and flagellation. He almost seemed to be parodying the Enlightenment's spirit of intellectual criticism.

Sade might perhaps be seen as a philosophe who followed the Enlightenment to its most extreme implications in the rejection of traditional prejudices, and in this sense the libertine was always a philosophe, even on the verge of perversion. Justine, for instance, was first flagellated by a sadistic monk, Dom Clément, and then lectured by him philosophically, as he expounded what was, in effect, Sade's apologia for sadism. The girl, battered and bleeding, still reproached the monk for "the depravity of his tastes," and he replied in a philosophical spirit. "Without doubt the most ridiculous thing in the world," said Dom Clément, "is to want to dispute about human tastes, to contradict them, to blame them or punish them if they are not conformant to the laws of the land that one inhabits, or to the social conventions. What! Men never understand that there is no type of tastes, however bizarre, however criminal even one may suppose them, that do not depend upon the type of organization that we have received from nature!"[21] Thus, the philosophical defense of extreme libertinism was also an apologia for perversion, for the bizarre and criminal sexual preferences that, according to Sade, were nevertheless innate and therefore natural.

"Can we become other than what we are?" the monk rhetorically demanded, in a rather modern appreciation of sexuality. Pursuing the implications of the epistemological reasoning of the Enlightenment, the writings of John Locke and David Hume, Dom Clément discussed sensory perceptions and the ways in which they were regulated by subjective imagination. "Now, if we admit that the enjoyment of the senses is always dependent upon the imagination, always regulated by the imagination, there will be no longer any reason to be astonished by the numerous variations that the imagination will suggest in these enjoyments, the infinite multitude of different tastes and passions that are born from the different flights of this imagination." The disquisition went on for pages as the monk argued that a libertine was not responsible for his nature and that he should therefore be indulged rather than punished by society and the law: "If then there exist beings in the world whose tastes shock all the accepted prejudices, not only should one not be astonished at these beings, not only should one not lecture them or punish them, but one must serve them, satisfy them, annihilate all the restraints that embarrass them, and one must give them, if you want to be just, all the means to satisfy themselves without risk."[22] Dom Clément proceeded by mock syllogism and elaborate sophistry from point to point, with Justine, his victim and pupil, providing the objections that compelled him to continue elaborating the argument. Ultimately, he envisioned the advent of the supreme libertine, the man who would think only of himself, who would pursue his own satisfactions without any compunction concerning others. Justine objected, "But the man of whom you speak is a monster," and the monk replied serenely, "The man of whom I speak is the man of nature."[23] The libertine's impulse toward the liberation from prejudice became, in Sade's philosophy, an enlightened imperative, and the philosophy of the Enlightenment was invoked to vindicate the libertine's complete spectrum of perverse preferences, for any sort of sexual crime, practised upon sexual victims of every form and every age.

Juliette also received philosophical instruction, but unlike Justine, she was eager to learn the lessons of libertinism and was readily persuaded by its reasoning. Madame Delbène considered such instruction to be an essential part of a convent education, along with orgiastic sexual initiation. She felt that young girls in particular were in need of such instruction inasmuch as children might have been already indoctrinated with Christian religious precepts: "I fear that the bizarre ideas about this fantastical God that have poisoned your childhood may return to trouble your imagination in the middle of the most divine flights. Oh Juliette! Forget it, despise it, the idea of this vain and ridiculous God." The innocence of childhood was thus perversely reinterpreted as a condition befouled by religious belief, and sexual corruption was therefore accompanied by intellectual enlightenment.

Indeed, the hostility to religion of Madame Delbène was not so far from Voltaire's slogan "Écrasez l'infâme!" (Crush the infamy!). She explicitly cited Spinoza and the eighteenth-century treatise on atheistic materialism, *Le système de la nature* by the Baron d'Holbach, and she promised Juliette that "we will study them; we will analyze them together."[24] Philosophical study was inseparable from a libertine education.

After the brutal rape of ten-year-old Laurette, the philosophical explications and justifications of Madame Delbène became all the more emphatic: "Yesterday I saw that you were surprised at my tranquillity in the middle of the horrors that we were committing, and you accused me of lacking pity for that poor Laurette, who was sacrificed to our debauchery. Oh Juliette, you may be certain that everything is arranged by nature." The Mother Superior represented herself as a sort of superwoman, beyond the constraints of conventional morality. "If I saw that the only possibility for me to be happy was in the excess of the most atrocious crimes, I would commit them all instantly, without shuddering, being certain, just as I have already told you, that the first law that nature shows me is to take my own pleasure, whatever the cost to others. If she has given to my organs a constitution such that it is only by the unhappiness of my neighbor that my voluptuousness can bloom, it is in order to achieve her own destructive ends."[25] Nature was invoked to vindicate the most extreme inclinations of the libertine.

Sade's philosophical strategy in the *History of Juliette* also involved affirming the anthropological variety of customs around the world in order to subvert the pretensions of conventional European morality. Jean-Jacques Rousseau affirmed the moral superiority of noble savages to civilized Europeans. The voyages of Captain Cook in the South Pacific, providing new knowledge about primitive peoples, confirmed the heterogeneity of humanity and encouraged a culturally relative view of manners and morals. Madame Delbène was sufficiently learned to lecture Juliette against marriage, observing that "in Lapland, in Tartary, in America, it is an honor for a man to prostitute his wife to a stranger," and that "Cook discovered a society on Tahiti where all the women gave themselves indifferently to all the men of the assembly."[26] Madame Delbène could cite twenty instances from Iceland to Japan to make her point, and if Sade was not particularly rigorous about anthropological accuracy, he was nevertheless generally plausible in emphasizing the variety of sexual customs.

A later philosophical mentor, the libertine Noirceuil, offered Juliette another anthropological tour of the world, including a discussion of bestiality:

the Greeks with goats, the Americans with monkeys, and the Egyptians with crocodiles. He also included in the global variety of sexual customs the rape of children: "The Caribs buy children even inside the womb of the mother. They mark the stomach with annatto dye, and these children, when they are born, they deflower at seven or eight years, and they commonly kill them after having used them."[27] By such examples Noirceuil claimed to have demonstrated the preposterousness of European laws against supposed sexual crimes, and he enjoined Juliette to consider herself completely liberated from all sexual scruples.

When the marquis de Sade was arrested again in 1801, at the age of sixty, it was not as a sexual criminal but as a pornographer. During the years when Napoleon transformed France and conquered Europe, Sade lived ingloriously in the insane asylum at Charenton, with a diagnosis of "libertine dementia." He petitioned Napoleon for mercy in 1809, pleading medical debility, "almost blind, and afflicted with gout and with rheumatisms of the chest and stomach." The emperor, however, was advised that Sade was a man of "monstrous thoughts and actions," that "he is an unnatural being, and no effort should be spared to keep him out of society." In the asylum Sade noticed a nurse's daughter, a girl of twelve, who began to figure in his fantasies; by the time she was fifteen and he was seventy, he was paying the mother in order to have sex with the girl, a last libertine relation that continued until his death in 1814.[28] This sordid episode was certainly a far cry from the stupendous pornographic fantasies of the novels. Rather, the celebrated libertine now found his satisfaction in the venal nexus of maternal procuresses and juvenile victims, so similar to the sexual underworld that Franceschini frequented in Venice in the 1780s.

Sade's relevance to Franceschini appears in the literary exploration of libertinism's extreme limits. The tribunal in Venice in 1785 could only with difficulty articulate the monstrousness of Franceschini's sexual relations for lack of a legal or medical concept of psychopathological perversion. Sade, who would give his name to the most pervasive of perversions, refused to recognize any restrictions in the expression of deviant sexual tastes and celebrated an unlimited libertinism that discarded all conventional prejudices. In his pornographic fiction the sexual abuse of young girls was represented as the prerogative of this libertinism, and the commercial publication of a novel like the *History of Juliette* in 1797 must have presumed the existence of a reading public that would respond to such fantasies. Sade's biographer Maurice Lever notes that the *History of Juliette* was for sale beneath the arcades of the Palais Royal and that mothers may have been prostituting their children in the same locale. Lever suggests that Sade earned enough money from his publications at this time to pay off his debts, but not enough to live on thereafter.[29]

In the early 1950s Simone de Beauvoir polemically posed the question "Faut-il brûler Sade?" (Must one burn Sade?) in *Les Temps modernes*, addressing the ethical and philosophical significance of his work, including its implications for existential freedom.[30] In 1955, the same year that Beauvoir's treatment of Sade was published as a book by Gallimard, Vladimir Nabokov published in English the novel *Lolita*, which immediately became the subject of literary controversy and moral condemnation. For *Lolita* featured the libertine hero Humbert Humbert, who, like the libertine heroes of Sade's fiction, undertook not only to violate conventional sexual morality but to vindicate himself before the judgment of the public, his readers, whom he addressed as "ladies and gentlemen of the jury."[31] In his confession Humbert Humbert revealed to them the innermost impulses of a man who, like Sade's heroes, could not help being the way he was, who could not help finding romance in the figures of little girls, and who consummated his romantic fantasies in a sexual relationship with Lolita.

In Venice in 1785 the tribunal could not recognize Franceschini's conduct as perversion and could barely prosecute it as crime without invoking the pretext of scandal. In America in 1955 the categories of perversion and sexual crime were so thoroughly ingrained and established as fundamental axioms of modern society and culture that Humbert Humbert, defending himself with special pleading and cunning sophistry, seemed to destabilize the values of American society. For Franceschini in 1785, facing the secret justice of the Venetian Republic, there would be no jury and no public to address, but having heard his indictment, he pleaded innocent and prepared to present his legal defense.

FIFTEEN

The Freedom of the Libertine

"I am a free man, living by myself without family relations."[1] This affirmation of freedom was central to Franceschini's defense: "Io sono uomo libero." When he said that he was free, he meant, precisely, legally, that there were no family bonds and obligations that he violated or offended by the conduct of his private life. The marquis de Sade was a married man in the 1770s, and the father of young children, at the time when he was presiding over orgies at La Coste, orgies in which his wife actually participated. It was thus a family matter for his mother-in-law to seek the royal *lettre de cachet* by which Sade was arrested, locked up, and prevented from bringing further dishonor to his family. Franceschini, on the other hand, had no wife and no children to be implicated in the scandal of his conduct, and he had separated himself from his respectable family in Vicenza to come and live alone in Venice. He was a free man and therefore answerable only to himself in the conduct of his private life.

Yet *freedom* was a word with many implications in the age of Enlightenment, in the decade after the American Revolution, in the decade before the French Revolution. "Man was born free, and he is everywhere in chains," wrote Rousseau in the *Social Contract*. Rousseau, of course, was not think-

ing particularly about old men accused of seeking sex with young girls, but
Franceschini in the chains of prison might also have had reason to reflect on
the philosophical, political, and social implications of freedom. It was only
a short etymological leap from the *uomo libero* to the *uomo libertino*, and
then, as Sade recognized, it took only another little philosophical twist for
the libertine free from prejudice to become the criminal free from scruple.
"Io sono uomo libero," declared Franceschini in 1785. Don Giovanni in
1787 sang out, "Viva la libertà!"[2]

As Franceschini presented his defense, however, a formal "allegation"
[*allegazione*] that he prepared with the assistance of a lawyer, he remained
in chains, and the rhetorical thrust of the introduction was a lament for the
loss of his freedom.

> Most Wise Lords, Most Grave Magistrature, if ever false and arbitrary zeal
> and the force of unfounded deductions have been able to sacrifice innocent
> victims upon the altars of justice, and if ever an obscuring of the truth of
> the facts by means of the most inconclusive and audacious suppositions has
> been able to cast the simulated appearances of guilt and culpability upon
> the most indifferent actions, the origin of this trial and the actual situation
> in which I present myself—I most unfortunate Gaetano Franceschini, in
> the dolorous Iliad that envelops me—offer you the most pitiable and fatal
> example. Sixty years of irreproachable conduct were not in fact sufficient to
> spare me this fatal destiny, and unfounded rumors sufficed, illegal defama-
> tion, arbitrary deductions, to destroy in one moment that which cost me the
> long course of a life formed in the principles of virtue, and lived according to
> the paths of reputation and honor.[3]

With astute legal counsel Franceschini stood prepared to demonstrate
that the evidence against him was completely insubstantial. He was determined to transform a case in which he had been cast as the monstrous
scourge of an innocent victim into its mirror opposite, with himself as the
innocent victim of monstrous injustice. For rhetorical purposes he donned
the heroic mantle of an honorable man condemned to suffer the vicissi-
tudes of Homeric misfortune. Above all, however, he represented himself
as a victim in the violation of his privacy and invoked the "always respectable silence of the domestic walls."[4] From the beginning, the case against
Franceschini was dependent upon discovering the secrets of his private life,
determining what took place inside his apartment and, even more privately,
inside his bedroom. Making the affirmation of his domestic privacy into the
central principle of his defense, Franceschini insisted on a sharp distinction

between the spheres of private sexuality and public culpability. Sade, in his pornographic fiction, argued philosophically for the right of the libertine to find satisfaction for his sexual tastes. Franceschini, in his legal defense, argued for the right to privacy that began at his bedroom door. Addressing the relation between public and private life, he articulated a modern conception of what it meant to be a free man in the late eighteenth century.

Franceschini recognized that the principal charge against him, the crime that brought him under the jurisdiction of the Bestemmia, was simply causing scandal. His defense therefore commenced by discussing legally, and even philosophically, the nature of scandal and the ways in which it was constituted at the intersection of private and public life. "Scandal is a deduction made by some concerning the operations of others," declared the defense. "In order to establish someone's accountable action as a scandal, however, the judgment of others is not sufficient." A man could not be convicted of scandal just because others said he behaved scandalously. Rather, it remained to be demonstrated that his conduct could plausibly be considered the "legitimate cause" of scandal.[5]

Though Beccaria's *Crimes and Punishments* did not address the subject of scandal, Franceschini's lawyer must have been familiar with the author's enlightened style of analysis, the rational application of sense to traditional categories of criminality, such as adultery, homosexuality, and infanticide. The peculiar illogicality of scandal was that it might exist without reference to any actual basis in fact. If Franceschini himself was the subject of the scandal, but not its cause, then he should not be held responsible for unfounded defamations of his character. It was not enough to show that the scandal existed, unless it could also be shown that the subject had actually committed the stipulated scandalous acts. If those acts were not criminal in themselves, then could the scandal alone be logically considered to be criminal? The Bestemmia seemed to assume the plausibility of a don't-ask-don't-tell scenario in which private misconduct was reserved for divine justice unless it became the subject of public scandal. Yet it was the tribunal's own investigative machinery that cracked open the protective casings of privacy. In mounting an accusation against Franceschini, the prosecution had to pursue a paradoxical procedure: the secret investigation of a public scandal. Therefore, the investigation could actually have been creating the very scandal that it sought to uncover, rendering notorious what had previously been private.

Scandal was inevitably a human construction and subject to the inflections of human fallibility and human malice. "In fact, the most indifferent actions, the most innocent operations, may acquire in the spirit of a slanderous man this most fatal interpretation," according to the defense. Goldoni had made the same point on the Venetian stage when he created the character Don Marzio, the scandal-mongering gossip of the coffee-house. The accusation against Franceschini was characterized by the defense as mere "defamation," as "chimerical, imaginary deduction," and there-fore unfounded in criminal fact.[6] Not only did the defense refuse to admit Franceschini's guilt but it questioned the general category of crime with which he was being charged. Scandal always existed in the minds of others and was therefore fundamentally susceptible to chimerical and imaginary insinuations.

"Now I understand," said Franceschini at his first appearance before the tribunal. "There has been formed a most atrocious calumny against me." Ten years before, in 1775, Beaumarchais first introduced the character Figaro to the European public in the drama *The Barber of Seville*. In one of the celebrated speeches of the play, the crafty music master Don Bazile recom-mended "calumny" as the infallible method for assaulting an enemy. "There is no malice, no horrors, no absurd tale that one cannot get accepted by the idle people of a great city," he confidently declared. The course of calumny was narrated as a kind of music lesson with marked dynamics: "First a slight noise, skimming the earth like a swallow before the storm, *pianissimo* mur-murs and spins and plants the poisoned arrow. Someone's mouth receives it and *piano*, *piano* it slips neatly into your ear. The damage is done. It germi-nates, creeps, tramps, and *rinforzando* from mouth to mouth it goes like the devil." So the calumny finally culminates in "a public *crescendo*, a univer-sal chorus of hate and proscription."[7] This enlightened appreciation of the power of calumny, and its capacity to create public scandal out of nothing but malice, was clearly fundamental for Franceschini's defense in 1785.

In the eighteenth century, public scandal was also regarded as a literary staple of the publishing business, and scandalous accounts were consumed by avid readers all over Europe, especially in France. Such accounts, as Rob-ert Darnton has demonstrated, were prominent among the "forbidden best-sellers" of the ancien régime and were often classified as "philosophical." Semifictional and sometimes semipornographic works, called *libelles* (libels), purported to reveal the secret scandalous truth about notable figures of the French royal court. *Anecdotes of Mme du Barry* was a best seller of 1775, as was the *Private Life of Louis XV* in 1781, full of scandalous revelations about the recently deceased king. Such works fed the hunger of the reading public for scandalous sex in combination with criticism of the monarchy and thus played a part in the evolution of political consciousness in the public sphere.[8]

By far the most potent French scandal of the ancien régime, however, erupted in 1785, the year of Franceschini's trial in Venice, and permitted the public of Europe to contemplate the cultural and legal implications of scandal in general. This was the Diamond Necklace Affair, which destroyed the reputation of Marie Antoinette and undermined the credibility and legitimacy of the French monarchy in the period immediately preceding the French Revolution. In this scandal a scheming adventuress, Madame de la Motte, manipulated an ambitious cardinal, Louis de Rohan, and arranged for him a nocturnal meeting in the gardens of Versailles with a prostitute who impersonated the queen. Cardinal Rohan than undertook to purchase, supposedly in the queen's name, an immensely valuable diamond necklace, which the queen never received. The cardinal was arrested on August 15 at Versailles, a few weeks before Franceschini's September arrest in Venice, and the case received tremendous publicity in the Paris news chronicles, all the more since the actual involvement of the queen, if any, remained fascinatingly uncertain.

The Diamond Necklace Affair focused hostile attention on the French court but also allowed for reflection on the nature of scandal itself, on its plausibility, dissemination, and sometimes pernicious consequences, the same issues that Franceschini raised with regard to the allegedly chimerical and imaginary aspects of the case against himself. One French chronicle reporting on the Diamond Necklace Affair on August 18, 1785, observed that "although the story is very improbable, it is so widely spread about, and sworn to by people so well placed and so trustworthy, that it is very difficult not to believe it." The scandal fed upon the public trial of Rohan before the Parlement of Paris, and Sarah Maza, who has analyzed the case in her book *Private Lives and Public Affairs*, concludes that "within the nascent oppositional public sphere of the eighteenth century, private and public experience were not sharply distinct categories, but were located along a continuum so that the one shaded off into the other."[9] Franceschini's case revealed an analogous confusion of public and private affairs under the different circumstances of secret justice in Venice. At exactly the same time that witnesses were being secretly summoned by the Bestemmia to testify about Franceschini, the customers in the coffeehouses of Venice would have been reading in the gazettes about the Diamond Necklace Affair in France. In Franceschini's case, the defense was sufficiently attuned to current concerns about the equivocal nature of scandal to challenge its fundamental construction as a category of criminal conduct.

Franceschini's defense focused on the circular reasoning of the indictment, which explained his character by the scandal, and the scandal by his character, while neither was a subject susceptible to proof by concrete facts.

> Everything is arbitrary; everything is deduction; there is not any real fact; there is not valid proof that can offer true and real results. Regarding the accusation in the general aspect that includes the odious character of sensuality attributed to me, there are only reckless deductions presented. Regarding the alleged scandal, malice is absolutely apparent, rather than an innocent and legitimate scandal. In order to establish a guilty depraved custom, the most occult directions have not been neglected, and it has been allowed that the testimony that was supposed to argue and prove the deductions may wander freely and capriciously, interpreting in its fashion, defining in its fashion, circumstantiating in its fashion the things that it enunciates.[10]

Franceschini's defense seemed almost to echo the speech of Don Bazile in *The Barber of Seville*, a study in the dynamics of calumny as it was translated into testimony: creeping and tramping from mouth to mouth and ear to ear, arbitrarily wandering and interpreting in its own arbitrary fashion, moving from the occult whispering of malice, *pianissimo*, to a public *crescendo* of condemnation. The alleged scandal was not "innocent and legitimate," because it was maliciously concocted, and the legal indictment was also illegitimate, because the testimony was capriciously construed.

"There was no one who introduced, who exposed, who represented me as an irreligious man, as a blasphemer," Franceschini noted. The name and commission of the tribunal implied that blasphemy and impiety would be inevitably commingled with the other vices and crimes, but the prosecution had concentrated entirely on Franceschini's sexual activity. Boldly, the defense challenged the assumption that a man's private sex life was necessarily an essential aspect of his public reputation: "A man can be infamous in the face of society, without being sensual, and can enjoy the prerogatives of an optimal reputation even in spite of sensuality."[11] Sensuality, after all, could exercise its effect in private, within the domestic walls, within the bedroom chamber, without becoming the cause of scandal.

"If people call me sensual, they are wrong," wrote Casanova, in the introduction to his memoirs, "for the force of my senses has never taken me from my duties when I had them."[12] Franceschini, like Casanova, affirmed that sex did not definitively compromise character and that sexual relations were not the crucial determinant of social reputations. The hypocrisy of society, then as now, permitted perfunctory piety and pervasive impropriety to coexist. According to Franceschini's defense, however, it was not actually hypocritical but perfectly proper for a man to enjoy an optimal reputation in spite of his sexual activity; character was not simply a matter of sex, and the public conception of character was rightly separate from what occurred within the "always respectable silence of the domestic walls." He was a free man, and he dared to regard his libertinism as a prerogative of his freedom.

Indeed, Franceschini offered himself as proof that a free man with a freely cultivated private life might possess an optimal reputation. "I have always been received in whatever civil, virtuous, noble society," he announced, and it was one of the few points of his entire defense for which he summoned witnesses to corroborate his account.[13] Anzolo Zorzi, living in the neighborhood of Santa Maria Formosa, testified concerning Franceschini, "I have known him for four or five years on account of circumstances that draw him into that society that I also customarily frequent." The Zorzi were one of the grand patrician families of Venice, and this scion of the clan testified to seeing Franceschini received "in every civil, virtuous, and noble circle," mentioning particularly casinos and theater boxes. Since Franceschini supposedly settled in Venice only two years earlier, he must have been visiting the city regularly for some years before that to enjoy its social diversions. Carlo Foncel, also of Santa Maria Formosa, had known Franceschini for two years from another venue: "the coffeehouse at the Ponte dell'Angelo, which I customarily frequent." This referred, very probably, to the same coffeehouse beneath Franceschini's apartment. Foncel also claimed to have seen Franceschini received "in the most virtuous and noble society." Foncel was apparently of non-noble but privileged "civil" birth, a citizen, his status comparable to that of Franceschini himself. Felice Sartori was a lawyer who had known Franceschini as a client for about two years, but once encountered him also in a casino. "Was he received in noble and virtuous society?" the tribunal asked. "I saw him well received in that casino," replied Sartori, "and I saw him with the most noble and virtuous persons."[14]

Paolo Valmarana belonged to one of the great noble families of Vicenza, the family for which Palladio built the Villa Valmarana in the sixteenth century, but like Franceschini, Valmarana had moved to Venice and was living in the neighborhood of Sant'Angelo. He testified that he had seen Franceschini "well received among virtuous and noble families." Francesco

Panizzon was another transplanted native of Vicenza, who had been living in Venice for ten years and was serving as a public official. "I have known him very well from my earliest years," he said of Franceschini, "since he, too, is from Vicenza." In Venice they continued to move in the same society: "I have certainly seen him at the coffeehouse at the Ponte dell'Angelo, where he dealt with the best gentlemen."[15] Thus, a sampling of respectable society, from Venice and Vicenza, patricians and citizens, testified to the point that Franceschini was well received in their own circles. The defense sought to establish that Franceschini, as a man of good reputation, could not be considered the cause of scandal but must be the victim of arbitrary and malicious defamation. Such testimony must also have made clear to the patrician judges of the Bestemmia that Franceschini belonged to circles not so far from their own, that he was someone they might have encountered at the casino, in the theater, even at the coffeehouse. Franceschini's character witnesses simply certified for the judges what must have been evident from the start, that he stood far closer to their own social world than did the poor laundress Maria Lozaro and her daughter.

Valmarana and Panizzon, as natives of Vicenza, were further questioned concerning Franceschini's status as a "free man," without family obligations. "Does Franceschini have any family relations?" Valmarana was asked. "His family lives in Vicenza," was the reply. "He has separated from his family and has been living by himself, not being married, as far as I know and is universally known." Panizzon replied similarly to the same question: "For many years he has been living separated from his entire family, which lives in Vicenza, and not being married, he has therefore no relations."[16] Well received in Venetian society, embedded in respectable social circumstances and connections, a man without family relations or obligations susceptible to indiscretion or violation, Franceschini, in the view of the defense, was incapable of causing scandal. He was a free man, and whatever conduct he pursued in private concerned only himself.

Franceschini, in his own defense, even invoked the name of God, as if to demonstrate that there was nothing incongruous, let alone blasphemous, in a libertine's expression of religious sentiment. "Good God! [*Dio buono*!] what a weak foundation supported the absolute ruin of the good name, the honor, the reputation, of a sixty-year-old man." In the spirit of Beccaria, Franceschini objected to a system of secret justice in which testimony was "covered with the odious darkness of the most false suppositions." He presented the "moving spectacle" of himself, an old man who was now, in December, entering into his fourth month of imprisonment. He called upon the tribunal to reflect on what he had lost, "the irretrievable, demonstrable sacrifice of honor."[17] Whereas the indictment argued that it was his character and reputation that created scandal and made him culpable, Franceschini replied that it was the case itself that defamed his character, destroyed his reputation, and sacrificed his honor. The honor of a libertine was not merely a cynical expression: Casanova in Poland in the 1760s fought a duel when he was called a "Venetian coward," and Don Giovanni audaciously confronted his own damnation when he invited the ghostly statue to dine with him as a point of honor.

The indictment against Franceschini had been divided into two parts, focused first on the scandalous consequences of his "sensual dissoluteness," and second on his proclivity for "pushing it still further" by pursuing young girls. Correspondingly, the defense replied on both counts, and after having addressed the general issues of sensuality and scandal, then proceeded to refute the particular charges that made the case so remarkable. "I have heard the reproach," wrote Franceschini, "that I was also in the habit of introducing into my apartment girls of tender age." Bringing girls into his apartment, however, was not in itself a criminal act: "The most indifferent actions were clothed in the most odious appearances of doubt and uncertainty. It has been attempted to attribute to these actions the agitation of a culpable intention." He therefore asserted a sharp distinction between neutral (and undeniable) facts, such as the presence of a girl in his apartment, and guilty sexual intentions which were more difficult to establish. "If the simple fact of girls coming into my apartment is not a crime, to construct it as such, one needs the proof of a guilty intention."[18] Just as scandal and character were shown to be dependent upon intangible factors, susceptible to manipulation, so Franceschini's ultimate intentions, in the argument of the defense, were represented as fundamentally unprovable.

There were two witnesses who claimed to have heard Franceschini assert that he wanted a girl to have in bed with him for the sake of her warmth. He was not told the identity of those witnesses, but he rightly recognized the importance of that remark for the attribution of a "guilty intention." He simply claimed that he was joking. "This expression," said Franceschini, "certainly cannot appear to an enlightened judge as a legal proof of an existing fact, or even as a reasonable index of a concealed intention. Woe indeed [*guai infatti*], if such expressions in the course of pleasant conversations, playfully communicated [*giocosamente annunziate*], could form the proof of a criminal question! Woe, if in order to decide about volition, and about intention, which has always been an object concealed from the mind of man, which law and reason have set apart from the judge since it is recognized as the impenetrable work of Divine Providence, removing this from the penetration of men and reserving to itself the judgment; woe, if one can be convinced by the trifle of a vain expression!"[19] Franceschini pleaded his own jocularity in pleasant conversation; perhaps the expression was tasteless, the joke unfunny, but, he asserted, it could not be convincingly construed as the evidence for criminal intention.

Franceschini's defense was further obliged to comment on the testimony of the girls themselves: Paolina Lozaro had spoken of pinching, and Meneghina Dalla Giana had mentioned an attempt to touch her breasts. Surely such testimony gave some clue to Franceschini's "guilty intention." Yet his defense simply rejected the testimony of the girls as "unreliable" [inattendibile] and suggested that such girls, offered employment as servants at a young age, often resented having to do their work and therefore ended up inventing excuses for not wanting to remain in service. Little girls would naturally have regretted "the sacrifice of a liberty enjoyed up until that moment" and would have had to make up some story to tell their parents about why they found serving Franceschini to be oppressive. The question of why Franceschini had brought Paolina Lozaro into his apartment was therefore easy to answer: he employed her as a servant. Yet the tribunal insisted on twisting his intentions: "Not for the motive of personal service but for a vile [turpe] sensuality it is alleged that I procured the girl's coming into my apartment. Vague disseminations constitute the basis of this deduction, which, penetrating into the hidden darkness of a concealed intention [internandosi nell'occulte tenebre di una nascosta intenzione], would claim to show clearly a different contested motive."[20] Franceschini rejected such speculative probing into his personal motives. He affirmed not only the domestic privacy of his apartment but also the personal privacy of his interior self.

In Franceschini's case, the elaborate defense of his domestic and personal privacy was specifically related to matters of sex. He was arguing that both his sexual activity, within his home, and his sexual thoughts, within himself, were off limits to the law and belonged to him alone. The argument of the defense suggested that not only was the tribunal wrongly encroaching upon his privacy as a free man but also that it was virtually impossible for the law to penetrate into his private life to obtain legally meaningful evidence. In these respects, Franceschini's defense reflected the most modern legal criticism of the Enlightenment, as summed up by Beccaria in his discussion of "crimes difficult to prove." The crimes that Beccaria especially cited were adultery and homosexuality, noting that in such matters "the tyrannical presumptions of the quasi-proofs and the semi-proofs are admitted," in the absence of more rigorous legal evidence—"as if a man could be semi-innocent or semi-guilty."[21] Beccaria deplored such sloppy justice, and it was just this sort of sloppiness that Franceschini's defense undertook to demonstrate in the case of his supposed scandals.

Beccaria, however, went further, in discussing adultery at least, and critically addressed the general issue of sex as a subject of criminal justice: "Adultery arises from the abuse of a constant and universal need in all mankind, a need antecedent to and, indeed, foundational of society itself, whereas other socially destructive crimes result from transitory emotions rather than natural need."[22] Thus, the eighteenth century already adumbrated the enlightened idea that sex crime was legally problematic, founded as it was on human libido. Beccaria did not explicitly state the same argument for homosexuality, but an astute reader might have been able to make the connection. Sade's Madame Delbène offered the radically and outrageously extreme extension of this argument when she confided in Juliette that "if I saw that the only possibility for me to be happy was in the excess of the most atrocious crimes, I would commit them all instantly." Like Beccaria, Sade respected the compelling nature of the sexual impulse and critically questioned the classification of certain sexual acts as crimes.

In the twentieth century, when Michel Foucault composed his history of sexuality, he attempted to describe the emergence of a modern notion of sexuality in the eighteenth and nineteenth centuries through a "discursive explosion" of writing about sex. Foucault argued that this was the historical epoch that witnessed "the setting apart of the 'unnatural' as a specific dimension in the field of sexuality," that general prohibitions concerning sex became fragmented as particular taboos: "to marry a close relative or practice sodomy, to seduce a nun or engage in sadism, to deceive one's wife or violate cadavers, became things that were essentially different." Though he did not name them, Foucault surely had in mind both Casanova and Sade, the legendary seducer of nuns and the notorious patron of sadism. Furthermore, though the enumeration of unnatural practices did not strictly follow Leporello's catalogue, Foucault clearly recognized the importance of Don Giovanni. "Here we have a likely reason, among others, for the prestige of

Don Juan, which three centuries have not erased. Underneath the great violator of the rules of marriage—stealer of wives, seducer of virgins, the shame of families, and an insult to husbands and fathers—another personage can be glimpsed: the individual driven, in spite of himself, by the somber madness of sex. Underneath the libertine, the pervert."[23] In the shadow of Don Giovanni, Gaetano Franceschini.

 With a philosophical defense focused on his personal interior privacy, defiantly affirming that no external testimony could ever discover his concealed intentions, Franceschini seemed to invoke—with calculating and exculpating purpose—the mystery of modern sexual identity. Foucault found an epochal distinction between the traditional concept of sex, understood as the commission of sexual acts, and a modern idea of sexuality, understood as a person's essential sense of self. The nineteenth century was, for Foucault, the great age of emerging sexual identities: "Homosexuality appeared as one of the forms of sexuality when it was transposed from the practice of sodomy onto a kind of interior androgyny, a hermaphrodism of the soul. The sodomite had been a temporary aberration; the homosexual was now a species. So, too, were all those minor perverts whom nineteenth-century psychiatrists entomologized by giving them strange baptismal names." Foucault mentioned, for instance Krafft-Ebing's "zoophiles" and "zooerasts," the minor perverts who found love and sexual satisfaction with animals, but there was a multitude of such eccentric identities constituting the modern sexual taxonomy of the nineteenth century. Foucault argued that such identities were psychiatrically assigned to individuals and thus "implanted in bodies, slipped in beneath modes of conduct, made into a principle of classification and intelligibility."[24] It was this fitting of a category of sexual identity to each characteristic mode of sexual conduct that produced the modern notion of sexuality. While Gaetano Franceschini in the eighteenth century may have considered himself a free man, engaging without prejudice in different forms of libertine sexual relations, Krafft-Ebing in the nineteenth century might have "entomologized" him in the category of "erotic paedophilia."

As he defended his "character" from "chimerical" imputations, as he shielded his innermost intentions from the presumption of the law that sought to interpret them as the evidence of a libidinous identity, Gaetano Franceschini stood at the historical crossroads where sex was already being overtaken by the ideological principle of sexuality. In the modern sexual universe, according to Foucault, "it is through sex—in fact, an imaginary point determined by the deployment of sexuality—that each individual has to pass in order to have access to his own intelligibility (seeing that it is both the hidden aspect and the generative principle of meaning), to the whole of his body (since it is a real and threatened part of it, while symbolically constituting the whole), to his identity."[25] Casanova, to be sure, discovered the intelligibility of his life in a discursive explosion of endless writing about his sexual adventures. When he summed himself up at the age of seventy-two, in 1797 (the year of Sade's *Juliette*), Casanova proudly recognized the perverse aspect of his libertine identity. "I have loved foods of strong flavor," recalled Casanova. "The macaroni pie made by a good Neapolitan cook, *olla podrida*, the sticky codfish of Newfoundland, aromatic game, and the cheeses whose perfection appears when the little living things that inhabit them become visible. As for women, I have always found that the one I loved smelled good, and the stronger her sweat the more she seemed sweet to me. What depraved taste! How shameful to recognize it and not to blush! Such criticism makes me laugh. Thanks to my crude tastes I am sufficiently shameless to believe myself to be happier than any other, principally because I am convinced that my tastes render me more susceptible to pleasure."[26] Casanova unabashedly celebrated his own tastes for the extravagant and the extreme; like Don Giovanni he had broad interests and sampled women of every form and every age, but he recognized that his more unusual tastes more particularly summed up the unique nature of his identity.

The libertine was a free man who enjoyed the freedom to explore and cultivate personal tastes and preferences, even individual perversions. Franceschini declared himself "a free man without family relations" and therefore a man who could not give offense to society or the state by his private sexual conduct. "There is nothing strange [*niente di estraneo*] even in the alleged sensuality," he noted in his defense.[27] For his libertine freedom encompassed the prerogative of sensuality, as something essential, neither strange nor extraneous, to the life of a free man. The Venetian expression *niente di estraneo* might be read as the slogan of a libertinism diversely indulged, including an interest in little girls that was only just beginning to seem notably strange and problematically criminal, though not yet taxonomically perverse, in relation to the libertine values of the Enlightenment.

PART FOUR

The Innocence of Childhood

Aimez l'enfance.

—Rousseau, *Emile*

SIXTEEN

Rousseau's Simple Project

In the 1740s Jean-Jacques Rousseau spent a year in Venice, working as secretary to the French ambassador. Rousseau was then a young man in his early thirties, not yet the famous philosophe whose works would revolutionize the culture of the Enlightenment in the 1750s and 1760s—works that included his pathbreaking proposal for an enlightened pedagogy adapted to the true nature of children, published under the title *Emile* in 1762. From the eighteenth century to our own times, *Emile* has served as a crucial point of reference for considering the enlightened reform of education and for understanding the mystique of the child in modern society, culture, and fantasy.

Rousseau celebrated the innocence of childhood in *Emile* and appealed for the liberation of the child from a life of bondage and oppression that traditionally began with tightly wrapped swaddling clothes in infancy. Rousseau believed that the tedium of traditional education destroyed the happy simplicity of childhood as surely as civilization ruined the Arcadian spirit of noble savages. "Aimez l'enfance" (Love childhood), Rousseau commanded. "Favor its games, its pleasures, its lovable instinct. Which of you has not sometimes longed for that age when laughter was always upon the lips, and when the soul was always at peace? Why do you wish to take from these little innocents the joy of a time so brief in passing, such a precious good that they cannot abuse? Why do you wish to fill with bitterness and sorrows these first rapidly passing years, that will never return, no more for them than for you?"[1] Rousseau's intense conviction of the innocence, the preciousness, the transience of childhood laid the ideological and sentimental foundations for the modern appreciation of children.

"Respectez l'enfance" (Respect childhood), enjoined Rousseau in *Emile*, for childhood was to be not only loved but also respected, especially for the child's relation to nature. "Let nature act for a long time, before you intervene to act in its place, for fear of opposing its operations." Rousseau was thinking about pedagogy, but his argument suggested a broader concern about adults tampering with children and interfering with the natural course of childhood.[2] The growing respect, even reverence, for childhood in the eighteenth century created the cultural context for the charges against Gaetano Franceschini and made his conduct seem particularly monstrous. Rousseau's philosophical reflections would even offer a rhetorical language for articulating the "unnatural" monstrosity of men like Franceschini. Yet Rousseau himself was not absolutely immune to Franceschini's libertine inclinations.

In his autobiographical *Confessions*, Rousseau recalled the "celebrated amusements" of Venice in the 1740s, including the allure of Venetian women. The first instance that he cited involved the Venetian confraternities—the *scuole* where poor girls were trained to sing in chorus and mobilized for musical performances in church. "There are motets during vespers, for a large chorus and orchestra, composed and directed by the greatest masters of Italy, performed from the grated galleries uniquely by girls under the age of twenty. I had no notion of anything so voluptuous, so touching as this music: the richness of the art, the exquisite taste of the singing, the beauty of the voices."[3] Rousseau would later become deeply engaged in debates about musical style in France, would write articles on musical subjects for the *Encyclopédie* of Diderot and d'Alembert, and would even have some success as a composer.

As a young man in Venice Rousseau was already captivated by music and faithfully attended these church concerts whose casts consisted entirely of young girls. The music alone, however, though "voluptuous" to the ear, did not fully satisfy Rousseau, for he longed to see the girls who were singing.

> What distressed me were those cursed gratings, which permitted only sounds to pass through and hid from me the angels of beauty worthy of making

those sounds. I spoke of nothing else. One day when I was speaking about it at the home of Monsieur Le Blond, he said to me, "If you are so curious to see these little girls, it is easy to satisfy you. I am one of the administrators of the house. I want to offer you something to eat there with them." I did not let him rest until he had kept his word. Entering the salon that contained these coveted beauties, I felt a trembling of love that I had never experienced before. Monsieur Le Blond presented me to one after another of these celebrated singers, whose voices and names alone were known to me. "Come Sophie. . . ." She was horrible. "Come Cattina. . . ." She was blind in one eye. "Come Bettina. . . ." Smallpox had disfigured her. Almost every one of them had some notable defect. My tormentor laughed at my cruel surprise.[4]

Rousseau's account of his anticipatory trembling was a frank confession of erotic arousal, and Le Blond, the French consul, obviously recognized it as such when he staged his comedy of romantic disappointment.

Rousseau, however, so desperately needed an amorous edge to his musical appreciation that he persuaded himself that he loved the singers in spite of their appearances and returned to the concerts with his vision of their angelic beauty somehow unblemished. "I continued to find their singing delightful, and their voices so well disguised their faces that as long as they were singing, I persisted, in spite of my eyes, in finding them beautiful."[5] With such a precariously maintained conviction of their beauty there was little chance that Rousseau would presume to seek any less platonic acquaintance with the young girls of the chorus after the singing of vespers.

Yet somehow the subject of the young singers was so imbued with erotic romance that it seemed entirely natural for Rousseau, in his autobiographical narrative, to move immediately to the subject of sexual relations, especially prostitution, another of the "celebrated amusements" of Venice. "But, concerning girls, in a city like Venice one does not abstain. Someone could ask me: Do you not have anything to confess on that account?" wrote Rousseau, posing the question to himself. In fact he had something quite remarkable to confess concerning girls in Venice, but the story had to be told from the beginning. It began with a fundamental problem for Rousseau: "I have always felt disgust for prostitutes, and in Venice I had nothing else available to me." Venice was famous for its sexual venality, and Rousseau was there just a few years after Charles de Brosses, who noted the enormous number of prostitutes in the Piazza San Marco and found them "of gentle spirit and charming politeness."[6] Rousseau, after one reluctant encounter with a Paduan prostitute, became anxious about venereal disease. Another courtesan, Giulietta (Zulietta in Venetian), stirred him greatly ("the young virgins of the cloisters are less fresh"), but when he contemplated the fact that she was prostituting herself, he found himself suddenly impotent. He then became further incapable of arousal when he perceived that one of her nipples was malformed. Suddenly, in spite of her beauty she appeared to him as "a species of monster."[7] So Rousseau in Venice was unable to find sexual satisfaction with prostitutes, for his own neurotic imagination was too volatile, transforming whores into virgins, and angels into monsters.

From this impasse of frustration Rousseau arrived at "a simple project" (*un simple projet*) to provide himself with the perfect sexual partner.[8] He had a friend in Venice named Carrio, the secretary of the Spanish embassy, who was also interested in the project—so the two men together formed a partnership for the pursuit of sexual satisfaction. Rousseau at vespers was entranced by the singing voices of girls under twenty, and his initial attraction to Giulietta was based on her virginal freshness. Authentic virginity was furthermore of particular importance to a man who dreaded venereal disease. With Carrio's help Rousseau would find what he really wanted: a young girl.

> Since we were inseparable, he proposed to me the arrangement, not rare in Venice, to have one girl for us both. I consented. It was a matter of finding a safe one. He searched so hard that he unearthed a little girl of eleven to twelve years, whose unworthy mother was seeking to sell her. We went together to see her. I was moved to pity at the sight of this child. She was blonde and gentle as a lamb; one would never have believed she was Italian. People live on very little in Venice. We gave some money to the mother, and provided for the keeping of the girl. She had a voice: to gain her a useful talent, we gave her a spinet and a music master. All that cost us scarcely two *zecchini* each per month, and we saved on other expenses. But since it was necessary to wait until she was mature, there was a lot of sowing before the harvesting. We were content, however, to go there to pass the evenings, to chat and play very innocently with this child. We amused ourselves more agreeably perhaps than if we had actually possessed her. It is so true that the thing that attaches us most to women is less debauchery than a certain agreeability in living around them. Imperceptibly my heart became attached to little Anzoletta, but it was a paternal attachment, in which the senses played so little part that accordingly, as it grew, there would have been less and less possibility for the senses to enter into it. And I felt that I would have had a horror of approaching that girl when she became nubile, as if it were an abominable incest. I saw the sentiments of good Carrio, unknown to himself, take the same turn. We provided ourselves unwittingly with plea-

sures no less sweet but quite different from those that we at first conceived, and I am certain that however beautiful that poor child might have become, we, far from ever being the corruptors of her innocence, would have been its protectors.[9]

This unexpected episode in the life story of the famous philosophe offered a sort of supreme confession of moral degradation, ultimately vindicated by the ascendancy of sentimental virtue. Jean-Jacques Rousseau himself, a man whose name would become a byword for virtue in future decades of the Enlightenment, purchased a little girl from her mother in Venice with the intention of keeping her as his sexual slave, while sharing her services with a friend, for the sake of convenience and economy. "I have shown myself such as I was," declared Rousseau, on the opening page of the *Confessions*, "despicable and vile when I was so."[10] In the tale of little Anzoletta, eleven or twelve, as gentle as a lamb, Rousseau did indeed appear at first to be despicable and vile, but the simple project itself was not so extraordinary in the context of eighteenth-century Venice. In Venice at about the same time, in the 1740s, Casanova bought a girl's virginity from her mother and then beat the girl when she wouldn't carry out the bargain by submitting to sex. In the 1760s, in Russia, Casanova purchased a thirteen-year-old sexual slave from her father and violated her immediately without any thought of delaying gratification for a time of greater maturity. Rousseau and Casanova accepted certain common axioms about venal sex in Venice in the 1740s, including the terms of negotiation involving mothers and daughters. The crucial difference is that Casanova would probably not have experienced Rousseau's sentimental qualms and inhibitions. With Casanova the story would have had a different ending, something more like the story of twelve-year-old Cecilia or eleven-year-old Marina.

Rousseau and Casanova were perhaps the two greatest autobiographers of the eighteenth century, both narrating in a frenzy of frankness their adventures and depravities, their sexual pursuits and romantic frustrations. Casanova was still writing his memoirs in the 1780s, while Rousseau's were already being published in that decade after the author's death in 1778. Casanova recounted his conquests for the satisfaction of reliving his youthful pleasures, and perhaps sharing those pleasures with sympathetically stimulated readers, while Rousseau preferred to abase himself, to make his readers into a moral tribunal, and he found a sort of erotic satisfaction in literary self-exposure. From the outset of the *Confessions* he signaled his strategy with the account of his early masochistic susceptibility to the pleasure of corporal punishment. As a boy Rousseau was studying Latin with the pastor Monsieur Lambercier and receiving discipline from the pastor's sister Mademoiselle Lambercier. "I had found in the pain, even in the shame, an admixture of sensuality that left me with more desire than fear of experiencing it again by the same hand," Rousseau recalled. "Who would believe that this punishment of a child, received at eight years by the hand of a maid of thirty, determined my tastes, my desires, my passions, my self, for the rest of my life?" Rousseau himself, like Sade, must be counted among the early explorers of perversion, conscious of the "precocious instinct" of the child, the power of the adult, and the sexual current that could be activated between them, even in the routine application of domestic discipline.[11]

Rousseau's story of little Anzoletta did not culminate in the violation of the child, but the narrative, in its erotic restraint, possessed a special prurience of its own. The philosophe purposefully sought to focus on the forbidden aspect of sex with a child, the interplay of innocence and incest that made the envisioned sexual relation seem somehow horrific to his vividly engaged imagination. Indeed, in the humiliating confession of his depraved intention he recapitulated the cultural course of eighteenth-century perspectives on childhood, the increasing appreciation of innocence that would eventually make sex with children seem distinctly more extreme, that is, perverse, than the ordinary indulgences of voracious libertinism.

Rousseau was actually writing his *Confessions* in the 1760s, looking back at his time in Venice in the 1740s, remembering his change of heart about the child, noting the evolution of his sentimental attachment to little Anzoletta. Franceschini, in Venice in the 1780s, already lived in a cultural climate of considerably more complex ambivalence about children. The tribunal, the witnesses, the defense, all reflected an assortment of mixed sentiments and emotions. From some perspectives, Franceschini's conduct appeared as merely routine libertinage, while from others he appeared as a monster who preyed upon innocent victims. He himself actually claimed to be susceptible to the innocent pleasures of communion with children, the same chatting that Rousseau fondly recalled with Anzoletta—for Franceschini testified to a special satisfaction in having children keep him company at dinner. Rousseau drew a sharp distinction between relishing the innocence of a child and making her the object of adult lust, but Franceschini perhaps, like Casanova with little Marina, did not emphatically separate the spheres of chatter at the table and fondling in the bed.

Franceschini, in a similarly casual fashion, probably did not distinguish absolutely between the dual purposes of training the child as a servant and exploiting her as a sexual object. He, together with his generation of early modern libertines, must have assumed that overlapping roles permitted the girl to serve him multifariously. That he spent the night with her in bed did not necessarily mean, to him, that he was not also having her raised and instructed as a chambermaid; the latter was not necessarily a false pretext for the former but a complementary aspect of domestic dependency. Rousseau, on the other hand, could not combine his purposes, could not simultaneously enjoy the "agreeable amusement" of the child's company while aiming at her ultimate sexual violation. In fact, it is notable that Rousseau, destined to become the most important eighteenth-century philosopher of modern pedagogy, seems to have conceived his custodial relation to the girl as a problem of education. Perhaps inspired by the example of the singing girls of the *scuole*, with their exquisite voices and disfigured faces, he bought a spinet for little Anzoletta and hired a music teacher.

Twenty years later, when Rousseau published *Emile*, he proposed a comprehensive course of education for the eponymous hero but also added an account of an ideal female education for Emile's intended companion, Sophie. Rousseau was so completely convinced that boys and girls were of fundamentally unlike natures, requiring quite distinctive educations, that his proposals for the instruction of Sophie have been interpreted as an ideological argument for the modern differentiation of the sexes according to separate spheres. "The little girl wants with all her heart to know how to adorn her doll," Rousseau pronounced. "Almost all little girls learn with repugnance to read and write, but, as for handling a needle, that is what they always gladly learn."[12] On maxims such as these Sophie was educated to captivate the romantic attentions of Emile. The book concludes with their rapturous marriage. Yet the education of Sophie for the role of the virtuous wife was perhaps perversely anticipated in the "simple project" of training Anzoletta in Venice, preparing her for the role of a sexual slave to two men who had purchased her services from her compliant mother. Gradually appreciating the innocence of her childhood, Rousseau surrendered his sexual intentions toward Anzoletta. In the end, he regarded her in the same sentimental and companionable spirit that he would later prescribe for the education of Sophie, the model little girl of the Enlightenment.

It is, of course, impossible to know how Anzoletta herself understood her situation when she came under the custodial care of the two gentlemen who provided her with music lessons and visited her to chatter and to play, even as they evaluated the development of their investment. "Imperceptibly my heart became attached to little Anzoletta," recalled Rousseau, sentimentally; but did she grow attached to him? How much did she understand about the "simple project," the experiment in sexual economy for which she was the model specimen? Had she any notion of the gentlemen's ultimate intentions toward her, any sense that they were eventually wavering in their purpose, any awareness of Rousseau's growing resolution to become the protector, rather than the corruptor, of her innocence? Rousseau, who wrote in the *Confessions* with such detail and intensity of his own childhood consciousness, left no clue to the sensibilities of little Anzoletta.

The history of childhood is difficult to write in part because the historical record only rarely offers evidence of children's own perspectives. Rather, the historical child appears as the object of the attentions, projections, emotions, ambitions, and fantasies of interested adults, recording their own impressions and experiences. Childhood in the eighteenth century thus remains

Little girl playing with her doll, eighteenth-century Venice. Detail from engraving by Giovanni Cattini after painting by Pietro Longhi, *The Letter*, painted in the 1740s. This little girl would have been the exact contemporary of Rousseau's Anzoletta in Venice. By permission of the Biblioteca del Museo Correr, Venice.

largely opaque to the historian, even as modern notions about children were increasingly articulated: their innocence, charm, vulnerability—all the childlike qualities that distinguished them from adults. Only rarely, however, does the voice of the individual child speak out across the centuries, letting us know what it was like to be a child at the beginning of the modern age, telling us directly about the experience of childhood, and, still more rarely, about the sexual intrusions of adults upon the lives of children.

SEVENTEEN

Paolina Lozaro in Her Own Words

On September 5, 1785, there appeared before the tribunal of the Bestemmia in Venice an eight-year-old girl "dressed like a Furlana [*vestita alla Furlana*]," according to the court transcript. If she resembled the image of the Furlana in Grevembroch's volume of Venetian costumes, the girl might have been wearing a little white apron over a colorful dress, perhaps with red stockings. She gave her name as Paola, the daughter of Maria and Mattio Lozaro. Her testimony was transcribed in her own childish words, in Venetian dialect rather than standard Italian. She identified her father, for instance, as "mio Pare, Mattio Lozaro," rather than "mio Padre," and in the same colloquial elision of the letter *d* she referred to Franceschini as her master, "mio Paron," instead of "mio Padrone." The recording of her testimony in Venetian dialect suggests some degree of authenticity, suggests that these were the child's actual words as spoken before the tribunal, her authentic voice.

From the records of the Bestemmia in the Venetian archive, from across two centuries, the voice of the child, Paola or Paolina Lozaro, speaks directly to us and tells us what happened to her in the summer of 1785.

> TRIBUNAL. In these recent days have you had any reason for going anyplace?
> PAOLINA. Yes sir, I went to my master's [*Sior si, son stada dal mio Paron*].

TRIBUNAL. What did you do at this master's?

PAOLINA. I was knitting.

TRIBUNAL. Where did you eat?

PAOLINA. I had dinner at the table with the master, and in the evening I had supper.

TRIBUNAL. When did you go to your master's?

PAOLINA. Wednesday morning [*Mercore de mattina*].

TRIBUNAL. How did you happen to know your master?

PAOLINA. Because I saw him at my house when he passed by.

TRIBUNAL. How long did you stay at your master's?

PAOLINA. Until Thursday morning [*Zioba de mattina*].

TRIBUNAL. Tell how you used the time in the house of your master.

PAOLINA. When I came, I was given some bread and some fish, and then I went to dine with him because he wanted that, and then he went to sleep and wanted me on the bed too, but dressed, and I wanted to go out of the room and told him it was hot, but he didn't want me to. When he got up, he went out of the house, and I stayed with the housekeeper, who made me a blouse that the master ordered for me. When it was evening, the housekeeper had me say the rosary so God would help me, and then she put on me the blouse that she had made for me, and she put me in the bed of the master as he had told her, but before that she gave me some meat for supper. In the morning when the master got up, I also got up, and he had the woman do my hair with powder, and he gave me silver buckles. He went out of the house, and I went to the balcony and sat down to do some knitting. The mistress of my mother came to find me and wanted to take me away, but the housekeeper didn't want it, and then a priest came, and he said to the housekeeper that he wanted me to go with him. So the housekeeper let me go, but she had me take off the buckles, and the priest took me to a fine lady, who gave me dinner, and then my mother came with a woman, and we went to the mistress of my mother, and then I was taken to Murano, to my uncle's, and so I stayed there.[1]

This was truly a tale told by a child. It was the same story that stirred the interest and outrage of the entire neighborhood of Sant'Angelo, the story that occupied for months the judicial officials of the Venetian Republic, but, from a child's perspective, that story could be narrated merely as a succession of meals and some details of dress. There was fish for lunch and meat for supper; there was a new blouse, and there were shiny silver buckles. There was an array of interested adults, the housekeeper who made the blouse, the priest who wanted to take her away, and some of the adults were recognizable figures of authority, like "the mistress of my mother"—

Elena Artico—and, of course, the man who was simply named as "my master." Indeed, five days after having been removed from Franceschini's apartment, Paolina Lozaro spoke as if she perhaps expected to return to his service. Asked what she did while she was in Franceschini's house, Paolina Lozaro, the daughter of a working woman, replied as if to deny any insinuations of idleness: she was knitting, or making stockings (*faceva calze*). The tribunal could easily take note of the significantly missing piece in the child's narration: What happened between going to sleep in the bed of the master and waking up the next morning to receive the new silver buckles?

"What did you do with your master in the room?" was the obvious next question to Paolina Lozaro, but a note in the record remarked that "to this question she responded awkwardly [*stentatamente*] with replies and cautious questions."[2] Here the transcript may perhaps have imposed some narrative order on the child's confused responses, though the record nevertheless preserved the unmistakable confusion of a child recounting an experience that she herself did not clearly understand, that is, the experience of sexual abuse. Like any eight-year-old child—now or then—Paolina Lozaro would have been able to make only limited sense out of what happened to her, would have been confused by the experience of sexual molestation, because sex itself would have been beyond the horizon of childish consciousness. Furthermore, in the eighteenth century, even adults did not coherently understand the social or psychological dimensions of the sexual abuse of children. Maria Lozaro, for instance, was quite uncertain about how to describe, understand, or react to her daughter's experience. Yet the judges of the Bestemmia, confronted with this particular case, had to try to comprehend the circumstances as fully as possible, and they pushed Paolina Lozaro to try to articulate the difficult details of what happened in bed.

> He had me get into the bed after dinner, and he put his hand on me under my skirts, and he gave me a kiss [*el m'hà dà un basso*], but I did not sleep at all—at night when he came into the bed, he woke me, and he touched me everywhere, he pinched me everywhere, he took me in his arms, he pinched me between the legs, he wanted me to give him caresses everywhere between the legs, he stretched me out upon him, and pinched me between the legs [*el m'hà pizzegà in mezzo le gambe*].[3]

After this extraordinary exposition, which began to re-create with a child's simple precision the anatomical contact, the crude touching and pinching, that took place in that bed on that night, the transcript of the testimony was suddenly interrupted with a comment from the secretary. This interruption, very unusual in the records of the Bestemmia, marked the strange, even unprecedented, nature of the testimony. There was a pause in the proceedings, a pause that indicated the dramatic nature of the occasion, its impact upon those members of the tribunal who were present as Paolina Lozaro tried to articulate what had happened to her, when Gaetano Franceschini manipulated her body and pinched her again and again between the legs. "In the middle of these awkward responses," noted the transcript, "she said with a sigh, 'Oh, I wish I had gone to Paradise'" (*oh magari fussio andada in Paradiso*). The secretary then inserted with an editor's caret symbol, before "she said with a sigh" (*con sospiro disse*) the notation "raising her eyes" (*innalzando li occhi*).[4] The insertion was extremely unusual, for the verbatim transcription of Venetian courtroom testimony was rarely annotated with observations about the eyes and the sighs of the witness. Clearly, this was more than just testimony; it was a dramatic occasion for those who were present. The caret symbol insertion that noted the raising of the child's eyes was the secretary's sentimental gesture to posterity, for it served no conventional judicial purpose.

That she raised her eyes meant that she was addressing not the tribunal but God in heaven. She prayed to God: "I wish I had gone to Paradise." The tribunal presumably understood this as the prayer of innocence, testimony before God that the child would rather have died and gone to Paradise than experience the hellish torment of her night in bed with Franceschini. The contrast could not have been more clearly drawn between his lecherous depravity and her childish innocence. For the tribunal, her raised eyes, her pathetic sighs, and her prayer to God were dramatic proof of her authenticity as an innocent child. She might also have meant that she would rather have died and gone to Paradise than have to relive the night with Franceschini by testifying before the tribunal. Her interjection, after all, served as an interruption of the testimony, a pause, a moment's relief, before she was prodded to continue her retelling of what happened in Franceschini's bed.

> Then extending his left hand, he showed me how to make the indicated caresses, and promptly lifting toward me the index finger with his left hand, he took the finger in his right fist, and raising and lowering the fisted hand [*l'impugnata mano*], he said he wanted me to do it like that, and he took my hand so that I should do it, and if I turned away, he turned me back, and with his hand he put my hand there, and all night long he did not let me sleep after he came to bed and woke me with pinches [*pizzigoni*] and tickling [*gattorigole*].[5]

Paolina Lozaro's testimony annotated by the tribunal secretary (lines 5 and 6): "innalzando li occhi, con sospiro disse, oh magari fussio andada in Paradiso" (raising her eyes [inserted in text with caret symbol] she said with a sigh, "Oh, I wish I had gone to Paradise"). Paolina's further testimony describes how Franceschini showed her what he wanted her to do in bed (lines 12 and 13): "alzando ed abbassando l'impugnata mano" (raising and lowering the fisted hand). And how he kept her awake all night (last lines): "coi Pizzigoni e colle Gattorigole" (with pinches and tickling). Archivio di Stato di Venezia, Esecutori contro la Bestemmia, Busta 40, *Processi*, 1785, 18r.

This then was the crucial piece of testimony, the only eyewitness account of what actually happened in bed between Gaetano Franceschini and Paolina Lozaro, though hardly witnessed by eye since the drama took place in the dark. He had an account of his own, of course, dramatically opposed to hers on the most important point: he said they both slept the night through, while she claimed that they were awake all night. Her story illustrated some of the problems that still surround testimony in cases of sexual abuse, notably how to evaluate testimony concerning sex from a child who clearly has no notion of what sex actually is. Paolina Lozaro, if asked to sum up in a word what happened in bed with Gaetano Franceschini, would simply have answered, "pinching." Unquestionably she found the experience uncomfortable, and confusing, and above all unrestful since it kept her awake, but the weighty implications of sexual advances and violations must have been mysterious to her.

An adult, then as now, would have no trouble interpreting the testimony as evidence that Franceschini attempted to have the girl masturbate him, which he demonstrated by the raising and lowering of his own fisted hand. The girl, however, seemed unable to distinguish in the dark between his hand and his penis, and seemed more puzzled than anything else by the complex manipulation of digits and limbs demanded by her master. It was only her prayer—"I wish I had gone to Paradise"—that suggested the emotional weight of the occasion for the child, both when it actually happened and when she had to relive it by her testimony to the tribunal. The night that she spent in Franceschini's bed, in the apartment upstairs from the coffeehouse in Calle della Cortesia, took her far from her childhood's experience along the embankment at Santa Maria Maggiore. The day that she spent testifying before the Bestemmia about Franceschini, in the Doge's Palace, the awesome monumental center of Venetian political life, must have seemed also fearfully strange to an eight-year-old child from an impoverished Friulian family.

There was still something more, however, for Paolina Lozaro to undergo, an examination in silence, but no less intrusive upon her innocence. In a note in the record, after the girl's testimony about the night with Franceschini, the secretary remarked that "having pursued the inquiries with reserve, about whether any consequences occurred, it seemed to me to emerge that nothing had ensued, and so, not being able to draw out anything further, I had her moved to another place, where the public surgeon was summoned, Pietro Recaldini."[6] The consequences that interested the tribunal,

Report of the surgeon, Pietro Recaldini: "Visitai oggi una figlia di età tenera cioè di circa nove anni come mi appariva e fattogli diligentissime esame alle parti muliebri" (I visited today a girl of tender age, that is, of about nine years as she appeared to me, and having made a most diligent examination in her female parts). Recaldini concludes, concerning the clitoris [*clitoride*]: "non dubito di asserire costantemente che quella parte fu molestata non potendo poi assolutamente stabilire con qual sorte di stromento" (I would not hesitate to assert reliably that that part was molested, but I cannot then establish absolutely with what sort of instrument). Archivio di Stato di Venezia, Esecutori contro la Bestemmia, Busta 40, *Processi*, 1785, 19r.

the "further" information that remained to be discovered, concerned the question of whether Franceschini actually had intercourse with the girl. For then he would have been clearly guilty of a criminal charge, the defloration of a virgin, presuming that she was a virgin at the age of eight. The girl's testimony, however, seemed to suggest that "nothing" had occurred beyond the pinching and tickling, that is, no sexual intercourse. The surgeon would be able to provide physical evidence and medical testimony addressed to this very specific question. Recaldini's report, which still sits in the case file in the records of the Bestemmia, was dated September 5 and must have immediately followed upon the girl's testimony before the tribunal.

"I visited today a girl of tender age, that is, of about nine years as she appeared to me, and having made a most diligent examination in her female parts, I did not find any alteration or dilation of her vagina. However, there was some extraordinary redness around the circumference and some swelling of her clitoris. From which I would not hesitate to assert reliably that that part was molested, but I cannot then establish absolutely with what sort of instrument."[7] Molestation was a medical term in this context, not a criminal charge, nor even a category of sexual deviance. With such a report on file there could be no question of intercourse, of rape, of defloration, and thus the vaginal examination of the child's body seemed to confirm her verbal interrogation before the tribunal.

Ten days later on September 15, Recaldini, described as Professor of Medicine and Surgery, was summoned as an expert witness to elaborate on the results of his examination. Asked about the instrument that might have caused the redness, he replied that it could not have been anything like a wooden object, which would have caused an abrasion "in those parts delicate by nature, and all the more so at such a tender age." Rather, he thought it possible that the cause might have been "friction either of the hand or of the penis, or even attempted rape." He even speculated about why intercourse had not occurred: "not consummated either by volition" or "by a lack of elasticity and force in the active body," that is, because Franceschini could not sustain an erection. Recaldini reminded the tribunal that though there was some "molestation" of the clitoris, the cause was a matter of speculation, and the vagina was in any event unaffected so that the girl remained "perfectly virginal."[8]

Questioned further about whether he could specify the timing of the molestation, he pleaded the impossibility of determining it precisely. He thought it could not have happened long before the exam, "since that redness and swelling would naturally keep on diminishing in such a fashion that by now it would have been completely restored to its natural state." Neither did he think it could have happened only a few hours before the exam, since "the redness was declining from the most inflamed condition that would have appeared in the moment closest to the molestation, so that I would believe that this could have happened to her five or six days earlier, more or less."[9] Since the examination dated from September 5, and Paolina Lozaro spent the night of August 31 with Gaetano Franceschini, the estimate of five or six days since the molestation was almost too perfectly timed, considering the doctor's general reluctance to draw any definitive conclusions. Furthermore, in his testimony of September 15 he was reflecting on a medical exam that was itself already ten days old and remembering a redness that must have been already fading in his memory as it was on the girl's body. From the minimal empirical observations of physical evidence in the original report, Recaldini was permitting himself some speculative conclusions when he now suggested that a human hand or a penis might have been the molesting instrument and that the molestation might be interpreted as an "attempted rape."

Franceschini's defense did not fail to reflect on the dramatic difference between the "inconclusiveness" of the original medical report and Recaldini's later testimony before the tribunal: "what a horrible and arbitrary variation exists between the one and the other." Although the surgical report spoke only of redness of the clitoris and could not specify the cause, the professor's testimony did not refrain from speculation about the possible role of a penis in the course of an attempted rape. Furthermore, the defense insisted that an insinuation of attempted rape was inconsistent with the physical evidence, since there were no "signs of force and violence." The manipulation of the medical evidence was interpreted by the defense as further proof that the accusations against Franceschini were nothing but "arbitrariness and confusion," that the case itself actually created the scandal that it claimed to investigate. All was "malice" rather than "an innocent and legitimate scandal."[10] The contradictions and speculations that emerged from the medical testimony, however, reflected what was most modern and least clearly articulable in the case against Franceschini. For implicit in the indictment, and in the entire scandal, was the notion that an eight-year-old girl possessed a particular innocence that could be compromised by a night of pinching and fondling, by redness and swelling around her genitals, even if she was left entirely virginal according to the more traditional standards of sexual violation. The tribunal indicted him for taking something intangible from the children he pinched and tickled: "taking from them that innocence that was supposed to form the most sturdy rampart of their virtue."[11]

The compromising of childhood's innocence would be understood today as a spiritual and psychological matter, no less than a physical and medical matter. Paolina Lozaro's testimony about Franceschini's nocturnal fumbling was, in that modern sense, the best evidence of what she had suffered, literally at his hands. At the same time, her minimal comprehension of what had occurred dramatized the quality of childlike innocence that her eighteenth-century contemporaries had begun to appreciate as an issue of culture, though not necessarily as a point of law. Rousseau helped formulate this newly emerging cultural perspective when he wrote about Emile: "He has lived the life of a child; he has not purchased his perfection at the expense of his happiness." The perfection of childhood was simply the liberty to preserve the uncontaminated perspective of a child, without the untimely intrusions of adult affairs, whether concerning education or sexuality. Rousseau believed that if Emile were tragically to die in childhood, a not uncommon occurrence in the eighteenth century, it would still be possible to say with some consolation: "At least he enjoyed his childhood; we have caused him to lose nothing of what nature gave him."[12] Paolina Lozaro, virginally intact, was still enough of a child to tell the story of her abusive encounter with an emphasis on the silver buckles, but a modern public—and the eighteenth-century Venetian public stood on the verge of modernity—would recognize that she had been robbed of her childhood.

EIGHTEEN

Paolina Lozaro
in the History of Childhood

The case of Paolina Lozaro occurred at a turning point in the history of childhood, when ideas about children and childhood, evolving over several centuries, received a distinctly modern articulation in the age of Enlightenment, and especially in the writings of Rousseau. The language of the indictment concerning children in 1785—"taking from them that innocence"—was clearly related to the formulation of Rousseau, concerning Emile, that if he could just enjoy his childhood, at least he would "lose nothing of what nature gave him." Yet these sentiments depended upon a cultural conception of childhood as a distinctive stage in life to be enjoyed on its own terms, with a distinctive character that could also be compromised and lost. The eight-year-old child Paolina Lozaro could be robbed of her childhood, because childhood itself had acquired a particular significance, a modern meaning, over the course of a long period that began in the Renaissance and culminated in the Enlightenment.

History has relatively little to tell us about the individual lives of eight-year-old children during these early modern centuries; very few children have left personal traces in the official or published accounts that constitute the historical record. For that reason, it is all the more illuminating to consider Paolina Lozaro, an eight-year-old child who lived in Venice in the age of Enlightenment, in counterpoint to another eight-year-old child, Valerio Marcello, who died in Venice during the Renaissance. His Renaissance childhood within the Venetian patriciate, like Paolina's later childhood within the immigrant working class, actually made a mark on the historical record. In the period framed by the lives of these two children, from the fifteenth century to the eighteenth century, the historian can discern the gradual emergence of the modern idea of childhood.

In Venice in 1461, Valerio Marcello died at the age of eight, after a feverish illness, in a patrician palace not far from the Campo Sant'Angelo. His father, Jacopo Marcello, a Venetian statesman, military commander, and humanist patron, was posted the next year to Friuli as governor in Udine, and there he coordinated the creation of a monumental literary work of mourning and tribute to his dead son. This album or manuscript codex recorded the virtues and promise of the child whose life had been cut short, and also the lamentations of the father in dialogue with other humanists who sought, in vain, to offer religious and philosophical consolation. During the eighteenth century the codex was sold in Venice and transported to England, eventually ending up at Glasgow University in Scotland.[1] There the historian Margaret King has studied the manuscript and made it the centerpiece of her own book, analyzing the culture of childhood and fatherhood in Renaissance Venice by exploring the circumstances surrounding the death of an eight-year-old child.

In 1960 historian Philippe Ariès published his pioneering, and controversial, book about childhood and family life under the ancien régime in early modern Europe. "In medieval society the idea of childhood did not exist," he declared in a purposefully polemical pronouncement that provoked outrage among medieval historians, though Ariès carefully qualified the thesis. "This is not to suggest that children were neglected, forsaken, or despised. The idea of childhood is not to be confused with affection for children: it corresponds to an awareness of the particular nature of childhood, the particular nature which distinguishes the child from the adult."[2] Ariès argued that the Renaissance witnessed a "discovery" of childhood, that is, a discovery of the fundamental difference between children and adults, a new awareness that children were not merely "miniature adults," not cherishable only as adults in the making; he further suggested that this revolution in cultural consciousness was accompanied by a waning of medieval "indifference" to children that had made it possible to accept psychologically the high levels of infant mortality in an age without benefit of modern medicine.

Writing about early modern England, historian Lawrence Stone pursued the implications of the Ariès thesis in the 1970s and hypothesized a human emotional revolution that he called "affective individualism," in which sentimental family ties acquired new intensity, between husbands and wives, between parents and children. Stone argued that beginning in the sixteenth century, and culminating in the eighteenth century, not only did adults more readily find forms of cultural expression for their parental feelings, but children were increasingly cherished as individuals, each distinct from every other.

Although the arguments of Ariès and Stone have been contested by other historians who see the parent-child relation more as a social and psychological constant across the centuries, the thesis of an early modern discovery of childhood has encouraged particularly interesting research in cultural history, exploring the images and conceptions of children in early modern culture. In art history, for instance, Pieter Breughel's painting *Children's Games* in 1560 reflected both the discovery of play as a distinctive characteristic of childhood and the ambivalence of society about the moral character of such play.[3] A hundred years later, in the 1650s, Diego Velázquez made the Spanish infanta Margarita into the iconic center of court life in Madrid, painted at the age of two with flowers and a fan, at five with her maids of honor, and at eight in spectacular ceremonial court dress.[4] Art historian Anne Higonnet has noted the emergence of a new ideal of childhood's innocence in the eighteenth-century British portraits of Joshua Reynolds, Thomas Lawrence, and Thomas Gainsborough.[5] The importance of childhood, proclaimed by Rousseau in the name of the Enlightenment, was also commercially confirmed in the eighteenth century with an emerging market for children's individual portraits, children's distinctive clothes, children's toys, and children's books aimed specifically at a child's literary mentality.[6] In England it was the age of Mother Goose.

When Valerio Marcello died in 1461, his father's grief testified to the power of parental feeling in the fifteenth century:

O death impure and savage . . . why did you wish to hurl this unleashed violence in the death of so sweet a child? O stealthy and execrable death, why did you want with your firebrand upraised, with incensed rage, to assail such a spirit, which presaged the development of so fine a man? O death entangled in viperous knot, with what wild fury, with what pestiferous poison did you consume so noble a son? How did it enter your mind to devote yourself to the undoing of such a boy, as if you would win a glorious prize for his entombment?[7]

Such railing against death, denounced as superlatively savage in proportion to the superlative sweetness of the child, demonstrated that for Jacopo Marcello, at least, the statistics on childhood mortality had not instilled any spirit of resignation, any emotionally strategic diminution of parental sentiment.

The creation of such a codex on the death of a child was itself very rare, if not unique, and the humanist interlocutors included in the album confirmed the extremity, even the eccentricity, of the father's intense emotion, measured by contemporary standards. George of Trebizond almost reproached the father for his excessive grief: "And you, a man great in the arts of war and peace, proven on the sea and on the land, famous at home and abroad, conspicuous in the Venetian Senate for prudence, eloquence, and gravity, will you allow yourself to be defeated by this perturbation of soul?"[8] The tension between the father's lamentations and the comforter's stoicism suggests some cultural ambivalence in the fifteenth century, a changing sentimental climate for parents and children.

If Jacopo Marcello was extreme in his paternal emotion by the standards of the fifteenth century, one century later the French humanist Michel de Montaigne felt himself surrounded by contemporaries who displayed overwrought emotion toward their progeny. Montaigne contrarily declared himself unable to comprehend "that passion for caressing newborn infants, that have neither mental activities nor recognizable bodily shape by which to make themselves lovable." He was unmoved by "children's frolickings, games, and infantile nonsense" and perplexed at the doting of other adults on children: "It is as if we had loved them for our own amusement, as monkeys, not as human beings."[9] Montaigne presumably would not have been so emphatic if he did not sense a heightened interest in children among his contemporaries.

In the fifteenth century Jacopo Marcello already indulged in the passion for caressing children, and he took pleasure in the spectacle of his child at play. One interlocutor urged him to remember "how Valerio hung from your neck, how he kissed you, how he melted in your arms, how he mangled words when he babbled [*balbutiebat*], yet made them lovely to hear." Another recalled that "the strength and quality of this child's spirit was so great that when Valerio saw other household children playing, by his gestures and struggling to join them, he seemed to melt with love, and a wondrous desire to play." Yet at the time of his death, Valerio was already embarked upon a serious course of humanist education, including both Latin and Greek. The codex, while not neglecting to admire his "flowing curls" and "rosy cheek," offered testimony to the child's precocious academic dedication: "And in literary studies? He labored all the time with ambition to learn, while he daily stimulated his fellow students to exertion." The tutor of Valerio recalled that the child began studying letters during his sixth year and soon achieved wonders of "eloquence" as a student. The codex actually cited some concern that the child might have ruined his health by excessive studying.[10] There was thus at least as much work as play in the child's short life, and Rousseau, publishing *Emile* three centuries later, would probably have felt that Valerio had already been robbed of his childhood before he died. The rigorous traditional curriculum of ancient languages was precisely the pedagogy that Rousseau thought most pernicious for a child, because least conducive to a childlike spirit. The cultural tensions concerning childhood in the Renaissance were thus also evident in the terms of lamentation for Valerio Marcello, remembered both for his childish babbling and his precocious eloquence.

The four hundred pages of manuscript compiled as the codex memorial to the eight-year-old Valerio Marcello, testimonials to the life of the child and the love of the father, may perhaps be compared to the three hundred pages of transcript accumulated from the testimony of the witnesses in the case of the eight-year-old Paolina Lozaro, another sort of symposium reflecting cultural ambivalence about childhood. Their stations in life were radically different, he the child of a powerful patrician statesman, from the heart of the Venetian ruling class, and she the daughter of a poor, immigrant Friulian laundress. What Valerio Marcello and Paolina Lozaro had in common was simply this: They were both eight-year-old children who, against all the odds and only on account of great misfortune, left lasting traces in the records of their respective centuries. They both became the subjects of documentary testimony such that their childhoods have not been completely consigned to historical oblivion.

Jacopo Marcello was offered religious consolation on the death of his son, a vision of the child's angelic afterlife: "An angel, Valerio triumphantly enters the heavens."[11] In the eighteenth century Casanova figuratively envisioned a child such as Lucie as "an angel incarnate who could not fail to become the victim of the first libertine who made an attempt upon her." From the fifteenth to the eighteenth century, the angelic aspect of childhood was given frequent allegorical expression in the Italian Renaissance paintings of *putti*, the winged children who hovered around the edges of pagan and religious compositions, from Botticelli to Correggio, finally achieving an apotheosis of heavenly childish play in Tiepolo's eighteenth-century Venetian ceiling frescoes. When the secretary of the Bestemmia reported Paolina Lozaro's longing to be in Paradise, and noted the raising of her eyes to God, he registered a sentimental image that matched the evolving conventions of angelic childhood.

The notion that children were especially beloved by Jesus was as old as the gospel according to Matthew: "At the same time came the disciples unto Jesus saying, 'Who is the greatest in the kingdom of heaven?' And Jesus called a little child unto him, and set him in the midst of them, And said, 'Verily I say unto you, Except ye be converted, and become as little children, ye shall not enter into the kingdom of Heaven. Whosoever therefore shall humble himself as this little child, the same is greatest in the kingdom of heaven.'"[12] In the sixteenth and seventeenth centuries, in the elaborate effusion of Catholic piety that characterized the Counter-Reformation, this special Christian priority of children was celebrated not only in the name of their humility but as a recognition of their supreme innocence. This was evident in the prayers for little girls of the Port-Royal school in France, noted in the *Règlement pour les enfants* of 1721: "Grant, O Lord, that we may always be children in our simplicity and ignorance. . . . Give us a holy childhood, which the course of the years may never take from us." In the same period, over the course of the eighteenth century, the ceremony of the First Communion was increasingly formalized in its preparations and rituals. Ariès concluded that "the First Communion ceremony was the most visible manifestation of the idea of childhood" and represented especially "the innocence of childhood" as a fundamental principle of Roman Catholic religious culture.[13] Under the aegis of the Enlightenment in the eighteenth century this religious sentiment combined with a more secular conception of childish innocence, which was essential to Rousseau's sense of childhood in *Emile*. Indeed, Rousseau preached a sort of enlightened cult of childhood, purged of its explicitly Christian forms and formulations.

Catholic reverence for the innocence of childhood was theologically controversial in early modern Europe, and Protestant wisdom was more likely to question this axiom of innocence and emphasize instead the doctrine of original sin. Calvinist, and especially Puritan, preachers in England and New England held to a concept of childhood based not on the innocence but on the essential sinfulness of the child. The Reformation historian Steven Ozment has written about the ways in which German family relations reflected evolving ideas about the nature of childhood, and the colonial American historian Philip Greven has discussed the implications of the "Protestant temperament" for raising children in the American colonies. Seventeenth-century Puritanism promulgated an authoritarian family doctrine of "breaking the will" of the wicked child, while eighteenth-century Methodism preached that a child born in sin must ultimately be "born again" as a Christian.[14]

Sex was inevitably an important issue for considering the nature of childhood, and whether children were essentially innocent or originally sinful. For the child could be understood as a sinful creature inasmuch as sexual impulses seemed to come from within, or as a model of innocence menaced by sexual corruption from the external world of already corrupted adults. Masturbation became one focus of this concern, and Lawrence Stone has noted a "rise of anxiety about adolescent masturbation in the early and mid-eighteenth century," in England and in France, which he tentatively attributed to "the growing concern for the welfare of children and their education." Historian Thomas Laqueur, writing a "cultural history of masturbation," has noted the subject's growing importance, especially after the London publication around 1712 of the anonymously authored *Onania; or The Heinous Sin of Self-Pollution, and All Its Frightful Consequences in Both Sexes Considered*, followed by numerous successive editions. Georges Vigarello, writing the history of rape, has argued that the rape of children received new attention in France in the late eighteenth century, both on account of new cultural attitudes toward childhood and new medical confidence in determining the status of a girl's virginity.[15] The innocence and experience of children became in the age of Enlightenment as much a secular, medical subject of study as a religious and moral issue. The testimony of Pietro Recaldini after the examination of Paolina Lozaro suggested the importance of the medical perspective for monitoring and evaluating juvenile sexual activity in the eighteenth century. He was expected not only to offer a judgment about virginity but also to identify the signs of any sexual contact, activity, or stimulation through the study of the little girl's genitals.

Between the death of the eight-year-old Valerio Marcello in Venice in 1461 and the testimony of the eight-year-old Paolina Lozaro in Venice in 1785 lie three centuries of cultural evolution that shaped and elaborated the modern idea of childhood. Without the idea of childhood as something absolutely distinct from adulthood, without the notion of the child as an individual with a particular and childlike character, there could be no modern conception of child abuse. At the same time, without the cultural conviction of the fundamental innocence of childhood, the adult violation of that innocence could not be construed as a crime. The great eighteenth-century ideologist of childhood was Jean-Jacques Rousseau, definitively addressing the subject in *Emile* in the 1760s, and his reverence for the natural innocence of childhood must have owed something to his own earlier experience with a little girl in Venice in the 1740s.

The case of Gaetano Franceschini in the 1780s was judicially and culturally problematic for contemporary Venetians. The enlightened culture of childhood suggested that the violation of innocence was monstrously wrong. Traditional judicial procedure, however, had not yet come to terms with the legal implications of a night of pinching in bed with an eight-year-old child. Paolina Lozaro testified before the tribunal in her own words and expressed herself in a naive manner that strongly suggested her own incomprehension of the implications of her experience, an incomprehension that seemed to confirm her innocence. The innocence of childhood, however, was a sentimental discovery, dependent upon the adult response to a certain image of the child. The tribunal of the Bestemmia, taking the testimony of Paolina Lozaro, would have reacted both legally and sentimentally, and, in the absence of an unequivocal legal provision, sentimental considerations would nevertheless have represented her as Franceschini's victim. By 1785, within the culture of the late Enlightenment, Paolina Lozaro would have appeared as an individual child whose innocence had been violated, who had suffered a spiritual, psychological, and physical violation.

It is "the imagination," Rousseau admitted, that is "the source of the charm one finds in contemplating a beautiful childhood." His own imagination worked vividly upon the image of the child:

> When I imagine a child of ten to twelve years, healthy, vigorous, well-formed for his age, it inspires in me only agreeable ideas, whether for the present or for the future. I see him fiery, alive, animated, without any gnawing care, without long and painful foreboding, entirely complete in his present existence, and enjoying the fullness of life. . . . I contemplate the child, and he pleases me. I imagine the man, and he pleases me more. His ardent blood seems to reheat my own. I believe that I am living from his life, and

his vivacity rejuvenates me. The hour strikes, and what a change! In an instant his eye is tarnished; his gaiety is effaced. Farewell the joy; farewell the playful games.[16]

One cannot fail to recognize the power of the imagination in Rousseau's visual response to the image of the child, a response that went almost beyond sentiment into the realm of erotic engagement. In fact, one would have to take note that Rousseau's metaphorical appreciation of childhood's innocence—reheating his own adult blood from the warm blood of the child, rejuvenating his flagging adult vivacity—was disturbingly similar to Franceschini's pseudo-medical motive for needing a little girl in his bed: "so that the warmth might reinvigorate him." This was no mere coincidence, for the same sentimental perspective that enshrined the innocence of childhood, and made it seem so appealing, could also provoke an aggressively erotic vision of the violation of innocence. In this sense, Rousseau's *Emile* prepared the way for Sade's *Juliette*.

When Rousseau signaled the hour of transformation, the farewell to childhood's joy, he meant only the summoning to study, the commencement of the traditional education that he regarded as totally destructive of true childhood. It need not have been only books, however, that provoked Rousseau's sense of the sudden dimming of childhood's delight. The violation of innocence, as in the case of Paolina Lozaro, would certainly have inspired in him the same sentimental sense of childhood defiled and destroyed. In 1785 some of the judges, some of the neighbors, some of the Venetian public—but not all—would have seen the child Paolina Lozaro with something like Rousseau's modern imagination.

NINETEEN

The Chimera of Innocence

Paolina Lozaro spoke once for the record, before the tribunal, and then vanished forever from the traces of history. She left behind her something very rare, the voice of a sexually abused child in the eighteenth century, describing her experience in her own words. Though she herself may have only barely understood the case that was being made on her account, her name and her story figured throughout the testimony and were constantly invoked and disputed by the witnesses, in the indictment, and for the defense. She told her story once before the Bestemmia, but she had also spoken with many of the witnesses who had lovingly, or anxiously, or pruriently, asked her to describe what happened to her in Franceschini's apartment—so her formal testimony was not the first telling, and perhaps was already somewhat rehearsed. The variations in what she said, and especially the range of interpretations that different witnesses put upon her words, suggested the ambiguity of the actual circumstances and also the ambivalence of contemporary culture concerning the innocence and experience of children.

One might expect that the girl's mother would have intimately interrogated her, but in fact Maria Lozaro, when she testified to the tribunal, had surprisingly little to say about what happened to the child. "I could not find anything out from my daughter, because I was afraid to inquire, since I didn't want to cause her harm [*ponerla in malizia*]," she explained. After the girl was rescued, her blouse was changed at Elena Artico's house, and there Maria Lozaro saw a bruise on her daughter's body. The distraught mother also heard about the night of tickling and pinching, though not from the girl herself but from the other rescuers. "I don't know anything else about what happened to her," testified Maria Lozaro, "and I hope that nothing more than this occurred, thanks to her being removed from the turpitude of that wicked man."[1] One might conclude that the mother was so troubled by what she had permitted to happen, and felt herself so implicated in responsibility, that she preferred not to learn the details of a disaster so much of her own making and only hoped that her daughter had been rescued in time. She seemed to be saying that as long as there was "nothing more" than pinching and tickling, as long as her daughter remained a virgin, then at least the worst had been averted, and there was no need to explore the incident in brutal detail.

While the narrow focus on virginity was absolutely traditional, Maria Lozaro was somewhat more attuned to the evolving early modern culture of childhood when she testified that she was afraid of harming her daughter by asking direct questions about sex. However legally unsatisfying this testimony must have been to the tribunal, it indicated the pervasive presence in eighteenth-century culture of the notion of childhood's innocence. Paradoxically, the mother seemed less concerned that her daughter's innocence would be compromised by a night of pinching and tickling than by subsequent inquiries concerning sexual matters. The imperative of innocence made it preferable that the child should misunderstand her own experience rather than recognize its implications and become corrupted by the knowledge of good and evil. Indeed, the testimony of Paolina Lozaro suggested that her mother had done the job well and left the girl with only a minimal understanding of what all that pinching and fumbling meant.

No less invested than Mario Lozaro in the hope that "nothing" had happened was Maria Bardini, Franceschini's housekeeper. For it was she who had put Paolina Lozaro to sleep in the master's bed, and surely if it were determined that some sort of crime had been committed, then the housekeeper would have to be regarded as some sort of accomplice. It was she who had the first opportunity in the morning to observe and interrogate the girl: "When they were up the next morning, I made all the most minute observations to see if anything had happened to either of them. In truth I could reassure myself that nothing had happened." Pressed further on the question of whether "anything sinister" had happened to the girl, Maria Bardini thought not: "Nothing decisive, inasmuch as I could learn from the girl without causing her harm [*ponerla in malizia*]. I was able to understand that some liberties could have occurred, but nothing more."[2] The phrase "some liberties" could hardly have come from the mouth of the girl, who seemed more inclined to speak of pinching and tickling. Instead, the housekeeper offered the tribunal her own distinction between "some liberties" and "nothing decisive," between molestation and intercourse.

The housekeeper was completely in agreement with the mother that specific inquiries would be harmful to the child, and even used exactly the same phrase: *ponerla in malizia*. Yet the nature of that harm remained unspecified, leaving the tribunal to puzzle over the questions of how exactly a child could be harmed, either by liberties or by inquiries, what damage could be done besides the ultimately "decisive" damage, and what the difference was between "something" happening and "nothing" happening.

After Paolina Lozaro was removed from the apartment, Father Fiorese brought her first to the home of Elena Comarolo, a woman who lived nearby in the neighborhood of Sant'Angelo; later the girl was moved to the home of her mother's patroness, Elena Artico, in the neighborhood of Santa Maria Zobenigo. It was therefore Elena Comarolo who had the first opportunity to question Paolina after her removal from Franceschini's apartment: "Seeing that she was sleepy, I asked her if she was tired, and she said yes. I asked if she had slept during the night, and she said she slept little, because she slept with the master, who annoyed her so she couldn't sleep. I asked her what he did to her, and she answered that he was pinching her." Yet Elena Comarolo did not push for additional details. "Further than that I did not extend my inquiries," she explained to the tribunal, "for the sake of reserve [*per riserva*]."[3] She, too, was concerned about protecting the innocence of the child and feared that more intimate questions would cause harm.

This sense of discretion in the eighteenth century reflected a generalization of Roman Catholic ecclesiastical concern in the previous centuries; the Counter-Reformation focused new attention on the sacrament of confession, which required new caution in exploring the secrets of conscience. The confessional was supposed to produce penitence without actually stimulating sexuality by discussing sexual issues that went beyond the experience of the penitent person. Michel Foucault, in *The History of Sexuality*, quotes the seventeenth-century Jesuit Paolo Segneri and the eighteenth-century saint Alfonso de' Liguori, both recommending discretion, reserve, and vagueness about sexual subjects to contemporary confessors. The younger the person confessing, the more careful the priest had to be. Though Father Fiorese said nothing about questioning Paolina Lozaro when he removed her from Franceschini's house, another Venetian priest, Vicenzo Comin, testified about his encounter with thirteen-year-old Meneghina Dalla Giana, the earlier object of Franceschini's lecherous advances. The girl confided in Father Comin that Franceschini had troubled her with "some insolences," and that was enough for the priest to know. "I did not make any further inquiries, dealing with a girl of good custom, as I can assert in all truth, fearing to insinuate to her some harm [*qualche malizia*]."[4] This was the language of the Catholic confessional manuals, interpolated into a matter of extra-sacramental social relations, framing the innocence of childhood in the age of Enlightenment.

When Paolina Lozaro was moved from Elena Comarolo's house to Elena Artico's house, it was the latter's chambermaid, Orsola Baresi, who was assigned to redo the powdered hair and change the girl's clothes. At that time Paolina Lozaro spoke about the pinching, and it was on the chambermaid's mind while she attended to the little girl's costume and appearance: "Her hair was done with powder, and she was wearing a fine blouse that Franceschini had gotten made for her, and her mother wanted to redo her hair in the usual manner and put her back in her ordinary blouse that she wore to Franceschini's house, so while changing her clothes, I observed her body to see whether there could be seen some signs of the pinching she said she received, and since I did not see any signs, I questioned her about where he had pinched her, but she turned her shoulders to me, as if embarrassed, and said nothing in reply, and I did not go further in my inquiries."[5] Thus, four days before the surgeon examined the girl's genitals, a curious chambermaid conducted an examination of the body for marks of abuse.

"Where precisely did you observe her?" the tribunal asked. "From the waist to the thighs, behind," she promptly replied, "supposing that those alone could have been the parts where she might have been molested with pinches."[6] Orsola Baresi seemed to have a very clear idea of where gentlemen generally pinched chambermaids. Though Maria Lozaro claimed to have seen a bruise on her daughter's body, Orsola Baresi, who seemed perfectly objective, extremely interested, and quite comprehensive, saw nothing that excited her suspicions.

When the girl seemed embarrassed by questions, Orsola Baresi did not press her further. Elena Artico, however, felt more strongly about issues of innocence, and not only for the sake of Paolina Lozaro. According to the chambermaid, "The mistress felt reserve about the girl being able to speak to her own children and to the other servants, lest something inconvenient should come out, or lest the girl herself should be further harmed by other interrogations."[7] Thus, while Elena Artico did worry about harming the girl through explicit questions, she worried more about protecting the innocence of her own children from Paolina Lozaro, inasmuch as the latter was presumed to be no longer impeccably innocent of sex. At least one of the Artico children must have been very close to the same age as Paolina Lozaro, nursed at the very same time from the very same breasts, when Maria Lozaro served as a wet nurse to the Artico family eight years earlier. The children were in some sense siblings, those two, but from radically separate social classes, the native Venetian citizenry and the immigrant Friulian underclass, now further separated by the boundary of childhood's innocence. Paolina Lozaro, while her hair was redone and her clothing changed, was being kept in a kind of quarantine in the Artico house, for fear of contaminating the innocence of others.

Elena Artico was clearly committed to modern middle-class motherhood, and her social privilege offered special protection for the innocence of her own children. Her interventions on behalf of Maria Lozaro to rescue the laundress's daughter must have been motivated in part by her own sense of sentimental maternity. When the rescue party arrived at Franceschini's apartment, Paolina Lozaro burst into tears, which were interpreted by Elena Artico for the tribunal: "It seemed that she was embarrassed to be seen by me in that apartment, with her hair dressed like that, and all powdered." The changing of the girl's hair and clothes eventually took place in Elena Artico's own home, though she herself was not present in the room. "My servant who found herself present told me that she had observed toward the lower back a mark indicating some pinching, of which the girl also complained, and she made some expression connoting some familiarity that occurred, but since the reserve due to her tender age did not permit certain inquiries, nothing positive was learned."[8] This sign of pinching was precisely what Orsola Baresi told the tribunal she did not see on the girl's body. Elena Artico, in her mind's eye, could more clearly discern the mark that ought to have been visible, the evidence of molested innocence. Yet her sense of the reserve and embarrassment surrounding childhood's innocence was such that she could not even enunciate the inquiries that could not be made, resorting to exceptional obscurity—"some expression connoting some familiarity that occurred"—to indicate the delicacy of the dilemma.

To violate reserve and ask explicit questions would constitute further harm to the child, and that harm was the cost of determining what actually happened in Franceschini's apartment. The work of the tribunal required the direct and unreserved interrogation of the girl, followed by a far from casual examination of her genitals, though everyone who testified seemed to agree that such procedure compromised the very same innocence that constituted the reason for prosecuting Franceschini in the first place. Opening up the issue of sexual abuse, in a modern sentimental climate, the case of Paolina Lozaro confronted the same moral and procedural dilemmas that continue to complicate the prosecution of sexual abuse in our own times.

Maria Lozaro's friends and neighbors in the parish of Santa Maria Maggiore also talked to the child about what happened, though these conversations would have occurred a week later, after she returned home from Murano. Maddalena Schiavon, who came from the same town in Friuli and lived with Maria Lozaro in Venice, was the witness to Franceschini's first approach to Paolina Lozaro on the embankment and naturally wanted to know what happened. "I asked the girl if he had done anything to her, and she answered that he gave her a pinch on one side, and I asked nothing else so as not to cause her harm, but she told me that she did not sleep all night from that pinch."[9] Though Maddalena Schiavon did not want to ask or hear anything further, Paolina Lozaro nevertheless continued to speak of the force of the pinching. She seemed to suggest that Franceschini's handling of her that night was not gentle.

Cattarina Burubù, who had originally given Franceschini a character reference for Paolina Lozaro, was another neighbor now eager to know what had happened. She testified to the tribunal a few days after the girl had returned from Murano: "I asked her mother, who replied that nothing had occurred. When the girl came to my house, afterward, I said to her that it must have gone well, and she replied that she did not sleep at all. I did not pursue the inquiry on account of the necessary reserve, and she did not say anything else."[10] Even the working women of Santa Maria Maggiore, though curious, still believed that questions would be harmful to the child.

For Franceschini the legal challenge was to affirm and demonstrate his own innocence in this particular case, while the innocence of the child, as a general cultural principle, was invoked by the prosecution. The defense not only noticed but directly denounced the sentimental manipulation of the child's "innocence" in the case for the prosecution. According to the defense, the tribunal "claimed to extract from her, pure and innocent, the truth," while making procedural use of an unprecedented "new method" to "avoid causing harm." The child, "before the altar of justice," could only be questioned allusively and suggestively for fear of compromising her spiritual innocence. According to the defense, such a method inevitably compromised the integrity of the investigation itself, since the vague questions produced vague answers susceptible to prejudicial interpretations. With something like sarcasm the defense asked how the tribunal could presume "that everything enunciated has emerged from the most innocent truth, that innocent was the interpretation given to the ways that innocence spoke [*che innocente fu l'interpretazione data ai modi che parlava l'innocenza*]."[11] Franceschini, or, more likely, his lawyer, had studied the evidence against him with great attention and had not failed to notice that the interrogation of the girl was constantly being stymied and evaded out of deference to her innocence, for fear of causing harm. For that reason her utterances were subject to considerable interpretation, and as long as they were interpreted in the spirit of perfect innocence, they naturally confirmed Franceschini's guilt.

Franceschini's defense observed that the case against him became easy to confuse, but impossible to confute, when the voice of supposed innocence could not be questioned or challenged. This procedural paradox heralded an age in which it would indeed become unthinkable to cast aspersions on the sacred innocence of childhood, enshrined and cherished in a mist of pious sentiment. The defense, while attempting to vindicate Franceschini, discerned the ideological fault line of a historical epoch, recognizing the historical process by which the roles and representations of children in society were being culturally transformed. In the nineteenth century it would become more difficult to perceive, let alone remark, that the "innocence" of childhood was the artful construction of culture rather than the natural discovery of "the most innocent truth." Indeed, already in 1785, the housekeeper Maria Bardini spoke with rhetorical grandiloquence in her testimony about her own "repugnance at cooperating in the sacrifice of an innocent."[12]

The defense observed that, in this legal case, "innocence spoke" but was then sentimentally interpreted rather than critically interrogated. Innocence supposedly spoke through the voice of the child, but as the defense observed, her testimony, and the testimony of others concerning her words, was not absolutely consistent. So Franceschini reflected on the testimony of the child who accused him: "Three times her voice speaks in this case. In all three it is absolutely different and disparate. For the first time, in my house, where either nothing was mentioned, or the voices are such that in order to give them some sort of interpretation, it is necessary that the witness assume the right to interpret the girl's silence as shame, that shame that is a chimera of her innocence."[13] This reference to the "interpretation" of silence as "shame," and shame as "innocence," must have referred to Elena Artico's attempt to explain why the girl was crying: "It seemed that she was embarrassed to be seen by me in that apartment." The embarrassment of innocence, with its sexual implication, could be, after all, a matter of interpretation; the child remained silent, or wept, and the witness was permitted, even encouraged, to speculate about the meaning of that silence and those tears. Thus, innocence was made to speak, and the defense argued that the prosecution was ventriloquizing the voice of innocence by interpreting the girl's silences. The peculiarly insightful observation of the defense was that innocence could be a "chimera"—something imaginary—that is, a culturally constructed representation of childhood that manipulated the imagery of the imagination.

According to the defense, innocence spoke three times and in three different contexts. The first time was from within Franceschini's apartment. The second was from outside the apartment, when the girl had been removed to Elena Comarolo's house and then to Elena Artico's house. The third and final time was before the tribunal of the Bestemmia. The argument of the defense was that once the girl had been removed from Franceschini's apartment, she no longer spoke in the voice of authentic innocence, because she was surrounded and influenced by so many other voices and concerns. Franceschini therefore presented his own perspective on Paolina's innocence: "Innocent absolutely her voice, indeed I request positively that it be considered to be thus; but innocent when, interrogated for the first time, she had no other guide but nature alone; not when she was terrified by the extraordinary fashion in which she was removed from my household and surrounded by voices unknown to her until that moment."[14] It was thus affirmed that only in Franceschini's apartment could the girl's testimony, the voice of innocence, be considered purely natural. For in the apartment she remained silent, and in saying nothing to Elena Artico, according to the defense, the girl definitively demonstrated that nothing had happened to her. It was thus convenient for the defense to argue that only the girl's silence in the apartment could be considered the authentic testimony of innocence, that all her later remarks were already corrupted by the concerns of others.

Though the case of Paolina Lozaro before the Bestemmia was unprecedented in its detailed attention to the issues of sexual relations between adults and children, other cases that came before the tribunal in the 1780s and 1790s made reference to children in ways that also suggested a cultural emphasis on the conservation of innocence. In 1789, four years after the case against Franceschini, Antonio Bernardini, the polenta vendor with the ominous nickname *Morte*, was charged with blasphemy and quoted in shocking outbursts against God, Jesus, and the Virgin Mary. One witness, who rented a room in Bernardini's house, also mentioned the presence there of a young niece: "I will also say that since he had no children from his own marriage, he kept in the house a girl of the tender age of ten years, the daughter of his wife's brother, and he boasted all the time that he had carnally enjoyed the girl's mother and said it in the presence of the girl without any regard, usually adding that having screwed the mother, he hoped one day to do the same with the girl, and he would make her become a fine whore in her time." The tribunal then questioned Bernardini's wife about the presence of the child in the house. "Not having children of my own," the wife testified, "I took to live with me a girl of nine, the daughter of one of my brothers, and she was living with us, but I was sending her to school." It was, however, sometimes necessary to protect the child from contact with Bernardini himself. "When I was aware that he was drunk," said his wife, "I hurried to put the girl in bed in order to avoid provocations."[15] This was only a sideline of testimony in a case that was largely focused on outbursts of blasphemy, other instances of sexual misconduct, scandal in the neighborhood, and Bernardini's general violence of temperament, but the Bestemmia seemed to take note of the possibility that the child might be at some risk from contact with him. The executors were no longer the same who had judged Franceschini, since new judges were regularly elected in rotation, but police personnel remained constant, and Bernardini was arrested in 1789 by the same Captain Pietro Bonaretti who had taken Franceschini into custody in 1785.

In 1794 two women were denounced for blasphemy and sexual scandal on the island of Burano, cited for "the most unrestrained familiarities with both sexes of all ages." One was said to "seduce and corrupt the innocent," while the other was accused of guiding her own daughter into a life of sexual immorality.[16] In 1795 Lodovica detta Schiavona, "Lodovica the Slav," probably a prostitute, probably Dalmatian, was denounced for scandal to the

Bestemmia. According to the accusation, "Lodovica of the Slavic nation, and her companions, persons of bad living , serve as a bad example and cause the spiritual ruin of the innocence of Christian children."[17] It was the neighbors who protested, on behalf of their own children, and the accusation before the tribunal was framed in the rhetoric of childhood's innocence.

In 1796 the Bestemmia received a denunciation concerning a certain Giuseppe Furlani, probably Friulian, who ran a tavern where prostitutes gathered and blasphemies were often heard. The neighbors were concerned about "the ruin of their children by the scandals," and the Bestemmia ordered the tavern to be closed.[18] In 1796 a case was brought against two laundresses who worked near a ferry point for crossing the Grand Canal; they habitually exchanged obscene and blasphemous remarks with the boatmen of the *traghetto*. The principal complaint came from a barber who was worried that his daughters would overhear these exchanges, "and the blasphemies uttered might awaken some source of harm in the tender spirit of those girls."[19] These concerns about children's innocence in the 1790s echoed the rhetorical formulas of the case against Franceschini.

Such sentiments suggest that during the last decade of the tribunal's existence, before the collapse of the Republic in 1797, the agenda of the Bestemmia included the protection of children from corruption and sexual harm. Originally, as founded in the sixteenth century, the Bestemmia was supposed to prosecute blasphemy in order to avert divine wrath and thus safeguard the Venetian state. Over the course of the following centuries the judicial focus became more diffuse, and the tribunal came to invigilate generally over morality and sexuality, suppressing scandal in the name of public order and propriety. In the eighteenth century increasing cultural attention to the innocence of childhood made children a prominent focus for concern about the harmful effects of scandal and the corruptive influence of sex.[20]

The case against Gaetano Franceschini, for his offenses against the innocence of Paolina Lozaro, provided an occasion for the unprecedented exploration of these contemporary sentiments. The child herself testified— the voice of innocence—but other witnesses also reported on her remarks, described her bruises, and interpreted her silences. Many of the witnesses further emphasized the innocence of the child by noting their own reluctance to ask intrusive questions about her experience with Franceschini. Yet the tribunal itself, in a legally ambiguous and procedurally uncertain case, did attempt to establish what actually happened in Franceschini's bed, evaluating the factual circumstances that emerged from testimony inevitably influenced by contemporary cultural values. Above all, it was the "voice of innocence" that emerged as the ideological force—or cultural chimera—giving modern meaning to testimonies and circumstances that could not be clearly comprehended according to eighteenth-century social and legal conventions.

The Secret History of Sexual Abuse

Bernardo Manella was the baker, a native Venetian with his bakery across the street from the coffeehouse on Calle della Cortesia. Manella claimed that he was too busy to pay attention to what was going on across the street, at the entrance to the coffeehouse and the apartments above it: "I do not observe who comes and goes through that door."[1] Above the bakery, however, was the room in which he sifted and prepared the flour for baking, a room that just happened to look across the street toward Franceschini's apartment. The baker was not too busy to take a peek on the day that Elena Artico and Cattarina Bartoli came around to make inquiries about Paolina Lozaro.

A few days ago there came to my place two women, who asked me if I knew whether Franceschini was at home; I told them I did not know, and they entreated me to find this out for them, without his being able to find out about their inquiry. I thought I would oblige them by going into my flour room, which corresponds to the level of his apartment, to see if any of his servants might appear at the window, so I could ask them. However, I found that on his arbor balcony [*pergola*] there was sitting, and knitting, a little girl [*ragazzetta*] who seemed to be about nine years old, whom I had not observed before. After I made my inquiry to her by gesturing, the girl gave me to understand that he was not at home. I reported the requested information to the ladies, who at this response went hurriedly through the door that also leads to the apartment of Franceschini.[2]

A little later in the day, still with his eyes on that door, the baker saw Father Fiorese emerge, holding the hand of the little girl. Manella recognized her as the knitting girl from the arbor balcony.

Knitting was an essential part of women's work in the eighteenth century, performed either by wives and mothers of modest means or by the female servants of more leisured ladies; it could also provide income as piecework production in a preindustrial economy. Richard Rutt, in his *History of Hand Knitting*, notes that in eighteenth-century England "poor children were taught knitting as though it were a Christian virtue"; Rutt further cites a work on sheepbreeding of 1792 that mentioned the knitting of stockings by "children who are put to this work as early as at four years old." Adam Smith himself took note of knitting: "Stockings in many parts of Scotland are knit much cheaper than they can anywhere be wrought upon the loom. They are the work of servants and labourers, who derive the principal part of their subsistence from some other employment."[3] Mothers taught their daughters to knit, and Maria Lozaro, a laundress, may even have employed her eight-year-old daughter in some simple darning and mending of items in the laundry. When asked by the tribunal what she did in Franceschini's apartment, Paolina Lozaro promptly replied that she was knitting, or making stockings [*lavorando di calze*]. The child would probably have been gratified to know that her domestic industry was confirmed by the baker in his testimony.

The balcony was described as a *pergola* (an arbor), so it would have been shaded with trellises of greenery, a sort of pastoral refuge, a hanging garden just above the city street. If the knitting child in the arbor had been depicted as an artistic composition of seventeenth-century Dutch genre painting, the image of the industrious little girl would have conveyed a moral message of education for domestic virtue. In an eighteenth-century French painting, however, the domestic scene of the child with her knitting needles might have carried a more mixed and complex message. The child could have represented precarious innocence, with the dangerously compromising forces of erotic interest lurking hidden somewhere behind the pastorally decorative trellises of the *pergola*. When Bernardo Manella first saw her there, and registered the image, he would have had only a vague idea of the menace that attended that picture of innocence. By the time he testified before the tribunal, however, there would have been plenty of time for the gossip of the coffeehouse to reach the bakery and fill him in on the details that were missing from the picture. Though the little girl in the arbor, with her knitting, might have seemed to represent the artistic quintessence of childhood's innocence, the fact is that, by the time Elena Artico and Cattarina Bartoli came calling, that innocence had already been violated by the previous night's pawing and pinching in Franceschini's bed. The image that the baker provided for the tribunal's consideration was therefore complex in its sentimental components, an image of innocence, tinged with brutal eroticism, in proportion to how much was known about Paolina Lozaro.

The case before the Bestemmia in 1785, though prosecuted secretly according to the conventions of Venetian justice, nevertheless brought the issue of sex between adults and children to the attention of the Venetian state, even as that same issue circulated through gossip around the neighborhood of Sant'Angelo. The ideological articulation of the innocence of childhood in the late Enlightenment contributed something to the sentimental framing of the case. At the same time, some of the literary, philosophical, and artistic representations of children in eighteenth-century culture also offered intimations of what it might mean to violate that innocence. The Victorian cult of children's innocence in the nineteenth century might permit the inference of sexually predatory adults, but it was not until the late Victorian age that such predation was sensationally reported in the public sphere, and not until the twentieth century that sexual abuse was generally acknowledged as a sociological phenomenon under that name. Only then would it be possible for historians to look back in search of the documentary clues to a concealed history of sexual abuse in earlier centuries.

In 1765, twenty years before the prosecution of Franceschini, the philosophe Denis Diderot brought out the concluding ten volumes of the *Encyclopédie*, summing up the wisdom of the Enlightenment. In that year Diderot also reviewed the paintings on display in the Salon of the Louvre and wrote with exceptional enthusiasm about a painting by Jean-Baptiste Greuze, *A Young Girl Crying over Her Dead Bird*. Diderot exclaimed over her dimples, her fingers, her hand. "One would approach this hand to kiss it, if one didn't respect this child and her suffering. Everything about her enchants." Such was the enchantment of childhood for Diderot, who claimed to have stood before the painting, crying out, "Delicious! Delicious!" This emotional response was not so far from Rousseau's excited rejuvenation at the vision of Emile: "when I imagine a child of ten to twelve years."

Yet Diderot's sense of deliciousness was perhaps more frankly erotic in its implications, and all the more so when he began to hold an imaginary conversation with the girl to try to fathom her grief over the dead bird. "Come, little one, open up your heart to me, tell me truly, is it really the death of this bird that's caused you to withdraw so sadly, so completely into yourself?" asked the solicitous philosophe. "You lower your eyes, you don't answer. Your tears are about to flow. I'm not your father, I'm neither indiscreet nor severe. Well, well, I've figured it out, he loved you, and for such a long time, he swore to it!"[4] Diderot's "conversation" with the grieving girl was curiously related to the interpretive gambit described in Franceschini's defense: the girl's silence and her imminent tears were interpreted as shame concerning sex. In the case of the painting, of course, the girl had no alternative but to remain silent, for paintings do not actually speak, so Diderot enjoyed the privilege of the most freely imaginative communion with the grieving child. He imagined her innocence, and he relished the delicious contemplation of her innocence despoiled. The submerged eroticism of the image hinted at a secret history of sexual abuse.

The girl needed to be consoled "for having lost her bird, for having lost what you will," and Diderot, who played the part of her comforter, could also envision another and more active role in the drama: "I don't like to trouble anyone; despite that, I wouldn't be too displeased to have been the cause of her pain." In other words, he imagined himself having sex with the painted child, imagined himself as the cause of her silence and tears. Diderot thought that the subject of the painting was "so cunning that many people haven't understood it," so ambiguous that many viewers "think this young girl is crying only for her canary." Yet Greuze surely knew what he was doing with his brush when he evoked the erotic allure of injured innocence. Greuze played the same game in *Broken Eggs*—depicting a girl who was probably not crying only for her broken eggs. Diderot's point about the dead bird of 1765 was that the girl, though young, was nevertheless too old to be so heartbroken merely about a pet canary: "Such pain! At her age! And for a bird!" He then speculated about her age and decided that she had to be fifteen or sixteen, old enough to be grieving about other things, old enough for him to feel comfortable imagining himself as the cause of her pain.[5] Greuze visualized a girl to stir the blood, in the spirit of Rousseau, and Diderot found himself stirred. He took it upon himself to interpret the innocence of the child in accordance with his own stirrings, and her silence was no obstacle to the chimerical play of his fantasies.

Diderot's passionate interest in a young girl's wounded innocence in the 1760s emerged from the same sentimental climate that conditioned the case of Paolina Lozaro in the 1780s. The affirmation of childhood's innocence in the culture of the Enlightenment inevitably also provoked the perverse intimations of erotic interest in violating that same innocence. What Diderot found fascinating in Greuze's grieving girl was the paradoxically simultaneous representation of both principles, innocence and its violation, intermingled on the same sentimental canvas. The Venetian tribunal of 1785 may have experienced some of the same sentimental complexity in contemplating the image of Paolina Lozaro, knitting on the balcony, as described by the baker in his testimony.

At the very beginning of the last act of the *Marriage of Figaro*, Mozart and Da Ponte wrote a little song, denominated as a *cavatina*, for Barbarina, the gardener's young daughter. She was searching with a lantern in the garden for a lost pin: "L'ho perduta; l'ho perduta" (I have lost it; I have lost it), she sings.[6] The poignancy of her little song suggested that what she had irretrievably lost was not just a pin but her sexual innocence. Diderot, who died in 1784, would have wanted to console her "for having lost her pin, for having lost what you will." By the end of the opera the virtue of Susanna was safeguarded from the Count, and the happy ending ensured, but the exquisite *cavatina* of Barbarina might still linger in the ears of the audience, as a reminder that there was also something irresistible in the plight of innocence lost.

In September 1786, a year after the trial of Franceschini, Goethe arrived in Venice, one of the first stops on the itinerary of his personally transformative and artistically inspirational Italian journey. In Venice he delighted in the architecture of Palladio, in the dramas of Goldoni, in the urban "labyrinth" of intricately curving canals and intersecting alleys. "I rode through the northern part of the Grand Canal, around the island of Santa Clara in the lagoons, into the canal of the Giudecca, up toward St. Mark's Square, and was now suddenly a co-sovereign of the Adriatic Sea, like every Venetian when he reclines in his gondola," Goethe recorded, taking possession of the city and the sea. His appreciation of the beauty of Italy extended to the Italians themselves, whom Goethe tended to admire in a spirit of some condescension for a natural and simple, even childish, relation to life and landscape. In Franceschini's native Vicenza, a week before coming to Venice, Goethe had already concluded, "The Italians seem to me a very good nation; I need only look at the children and common folk." In Vicenza he especially admired the women. "I find quite pretty creatures, especially a brunette type, which particularly interests me. There is also a blonde type, which is not as much to my taste."[7]

Continuing his Italian voyage, on the way to Naples, Goethe admired orange trees and olive trees and reflected that "Mignon was certainly right to long for this."[8] Mignon was a figment of Goethe's imagination, a figure from his then unfinished novel *Wilhelm Meister's Apprenticeship*. She was the mysterious child who captivated Wilhelm Meister, and she longed in lyric verse for the Mediterranean landscape of her native Italy: "Kennst du das Land wo die Zitronen blühn?" (Do you know the land where the lemon trees bloom?). Goethe explored through Mignon his own fascination with Italy and, at the same time, the mystique of the child in the culture of the late eighteenth century. She was on his mind as he traveled through Italy, observing the children, admiring the landscape, and he decided by authorial prerogative that she should come from Vicenza. Mignon was a dark child, not a blonde but a brunette, the type that was more to Goethe's taste.

Wilhelm Meister encountered her among a troop of acrobats and dancers and was immediately fascinated by her androgynous figure and mysterious reticence: "Wilhelm could not take his eyes off her; her whole appearance and the mystery that surrounded her completely absorbed his mind and feelings. He thought she was probably twelve or thirteen years old." When he discovered her being beaten with a whip by the Italian manager of the troop, for refusing to perform her "egg dance," Wilhelm intervened and purchased her freedom: "The negotiations with the manager began, and the child was transferred to Wilhelm's keeping for the sum of thirty thalers. The black-bearded, intemperate Italian gave up all his rights to her." Wilhelm's friend Laertes explained the terms of the bargain to Mignon:

> "Now you are ours," said Laertes. "We have bought you."
> "How much did you pay?" she asked curtly.
> "A hundred ducats," said Laertes. "And when you pay us back, you may go free."
> "That's a lot, isn't it?" the child asked.
> "Yes indeed, so just see that you behave well."
> "I'll be your servant," she replied.[9]

The purchase of Mignon from the abusive Italian was intended as a redemptive, humanitarian act, rescuing her from her own traumatic history, but there could be no doubt that the child was passing from one mastery to another in a condition of dependent bondage. The negotiations were not so far in form from Casanova's purchase of the thirteen-year-old Zaire in St. Petersburg in the 1760s or Rousseau's acquisition of rights over Anzoletta, eleven or twelve years old, in Venice in the 1740s.

To be sure, Wilhelm did not intend for Mignon's service to be a condition of sexual slavery, but neither was his interest in her completely innocent. He was transfixed by the private performance that she offered of her egg dance, blindfolding herself and then dancing among the eggs without ever breaking the shells; this was a scenario of erotic innocence that even Greuze, the painter of broken eggs, might have hesitated to portray. Wilhelm was so moved by the dance that "he wanted to take this abandoned creature to his bosom as his own child, caress her and by a father's love awaken to her the joys of life." Eventually, when she suffered a convulsive paroxysm, he did find the occasion to embrace her: "In the confusion of the moment Wilhelm feared that she might melt away in his arms, so that nothing of her would remain. He grasped her more and more firmly to himself. 'My child!' he cried, 'My child! You are mine. Let that console you. You are mine!'" The chapter concluded with her being held "ever closer in his arms," giving him "a feeling of the most perfect, indescribable bliss."[10] At the beginning of the next chapter it was already the next morning, and she was singing, "Kennst du das Land?"

Goethe could hardly have been unaware of the ambiguous nature of Wilhelm's sentiments for the child, the powerful erotic appeal of her apparent innocence. By the end of the volume Mignon was dead, lying embalmed in her sarcophagus, looking like an angel. The historian Carolyn Steedman has traced the significance of the figure of Mignon from the eighteenth to the nineteenth century, studying the complicated and compromising appeal of childhood's vulnerable innocence. The literary critic James Kincaid has argued, further, for the central importance of eroticism as a facet of modern fascination with childhood.[11]

"Oh, I wish I had gone to Paradise," were the words that Paolina Lozaro uttered, her eyes uplifted, as she testified to the tribunal. She meant she would rather have died than submit to Franceschini's molestation, but she probably also possessed some literal sense of Paradise. The child would have envisioned Paradise in Christian terms as the eternal kingdom of Jesus, or perhaps with Friulian folk inflections as a realm of abundance, in contrast to the earthly poverty of the folk tales of *Jesus and St. Peter in Friuli*. In 1789 in England, William Blake tried to conjure a seven-year-old child's mythological paradise in the poem "The Little Girl Lost."

> Sleeping Lyca lay
> While the beasts of prey,
> Come from caverns deep,
> View'd the maid asleep.
> The kingly lion stood
> And the virgin view'd,
> Then he gamboll'd round
> O'er the hallow'd ground.

This was a paradise of marvels, of nightmares made miraculously benign, of predatory beasts become tame and perhaps protective. Blake composed the poem as one of his *Songs of Innocence* in 1789, but then thought better of the classification, and republished the same poem with the more anxiously disturbing *Songs of Experience* in 1794.[12]

The ideology of childhood's innocence, as it developed in the eighteenth century, both stimulated and camouflaged an erotic aspect that was nevertheless discernible in the painting of Greuze, the criticism of Diderot, the fiction of Goethe, and the poetry of Blake. The nineteenth-century intensification of that ideology in the Victorian cult of childhood's innocence encouraged a more comprehensive containment and concealment, if not repression, of any implicit eroticism. Victorian culture celebrated an angelic ideal of childhood, seeking to evade any ambivalence of sensibility in the eyes of the beholder.[13] The ideal Victorian child required unequivocal reverence. Indeed, the model children of Victorian literature were too good to live in the real world and died saintly deaths in a swirl of sentimental intensity. Dickens lovingly drew out the lingering literary deaths of Paul Dombey in *Dombey and Son*, and especially Little Nell in *The Old Curiosity Shop*, a novel whose installments were famously awaited at the docks by American readers desperate to know the child's fate. American literature had its own supply of children too good to live, such as Little Eva in *Uncle Tom's Cabin* by Harriet Beecher Stowe.

No trace of sexuality seemed to cross the lives of these young saints, perfect in their purity and innocence, but real children in the nineteenth century had to have their innocence protected by a regime of fanatically imposed chastity. In the 1830s and 1840s, when Dickens was delineating ideally innocent children in English novels, German doctors were already prescribing elaborate belts, with straps, and spikes, and shields, and locks, designed for the mechanical prevention of masturbation, to guarantee the sexual innocence of a child against erotic impulses from within. In 1838 a French doctor, Marc Colombat, published in Paris his concerns about preserving "the seductive innocence which is the most charming ornament of a young girl." It was necessary to keep her from reading romances and from going to the theater, since all such imaginative distractions pointed in the same direction: "onanism, that execrable and fatal evil."[14] Cultivated as a cultural ideal, the innocence of childhood exercised an overwhelming ideological force over the lives of real children.

At the same time, Victorian culture was most unwilling to confront the sociological role of respectable adults in the sexual corruption of young children, to take cognizance of a figure like that of Gaetano Franceschini. In 1838, the same year that Colombat published his concerns about young girls in Paris, Charles Dickens created perhaps his most famous fictional child, Oliver Twist, and described his terrible battle to preserve his innocence in the criminal underworld of London. Oliver, nine years old at the beginning of the novel, fell under the custody of the maleficent Fagin, who managed a network of young boys, introducing them to lives of crime. Everyone who loves Victorian novels knows that Fagin trained Oliver Twist to become a pickpocket. Yet this novel has rarely been read with a modern eye to what sort of a business in boys might actually be managed by an unscrupulous old criminal in the middle of a sinful city. As the Artful Dodger explained to Oliver, "Fagin will make something of you, though, or you'll be the first he ever had that turned out unprofitable." Oliver, in all his innocence, desperately resisted being made into a thief, but the fervor of his resistance suggested that something more might have been at stake.[15]

Paolina Lozaro, even after being abused by Franceschini, presented the picture of innocence when she was knitting on the balcony the next morning. When Oliver Twist was rescued by respectable people, they studied his sleeping form, admired his innocent appearance, and wondered whether he could really have been corrupted by criminals.

> "Vice," sighed the surgeon, replacing the curtain, "takes up her abode in many temples; and who can say that a fair outside shall not enshrine her?"
> "But at so early an age!" urged Rose.

"My dear young lady," rejoined the surgeon, mournfully shaking his head; "crime, like death, is not confined to the old and withered alone. The youngest and fairest are too often its chosen victims."[16]

It would be difficult to say for certain whether Charles Dickens really thought his characters were concerned only about the vice of picking pockets. Today, any decent doctor would have other concerns about a young child rescued from the captivity of an urban criminal syndicate.

Curiously, if the case of Oliver Twist had been displaced to Venice, fifty years before, in the 1780s, the surgeon Pietro Recaldini would also have had some idea of what might have been at stake for such a child. It is of course absolutely unthinkable that in a Victorian novel the good doctor would have drawn the curtain and carefully examined the anus of Oliver Twist for redness, for swelling, for evidence of penetration, for signs of sexual abuse. Dickens and the Victorian reading public were ready to imagine Fagin capable of monstrous evil, and perhaps ready to see Oliver as susceptible to great degradation, but it would have been much harder to accept the sociological presence of respectable English gentlemen who were willing to pay for the sexual services of little boys like Oliver Twist.

In 1885, exactly a century after Franceschini's trial, the subject of sex with young girls became, for the first time, a sensation in the popular press of modern Europe, brought before the London public by the Victorian social investigator W. T. Stead, who wrote "The Maiden Tribute of Modern Babylon" in the pages of the *Pall Mall Gazette*. The full public exploration of this secret subject—beginning with "The Maiden Tribute" in the late nineteenth century and continuing right up to the revelations about pedophilia within the Roman Catholic Church in the early twenty-first century—contributed to an emerging modern perspective on sexual abuse and incorporated many of the cultural elements already present in the Franceschini case.

Stead revealed a Victorian underworld of juvenile prostitution in which young girls were sold as virgins to feed the monstrous sexual appetite of the Minotaur, that is, the respectable male clientele of modern London's commercial sex traffic. The Minotaur could be anyone, the Hyde lurking inside any respectable Jekyll, coming out only at night to stalk his prey. (Robert Louis Stevenson's novella was published in London in 1886.) Stead himself put on the mask of the Minotaur for the purposes of research and purchased the virginity of a thirteen-year-old girl, whose mother was also implicated in the sale. Stead could then write an article from firsthand experience, "A Child of Thirteen Bought for Five Pounds."[17] There was nothing here that would have surprised either Casanova or Rousseau in Venice in the 1740s, let alone Franceschini in the 1780s, but the popular press of the 1880s brought the issue before a broader public than ever before in a form that was fully intended to outrage and shock. The spirit was one of righteous indignation, but it was also, of course, the purpose of the press to capitalize on the sensational nature of sexual exploitation in order to sell more newspapers. As a direct consequence of the scandal, the age of sexual consent in England was raised from thirteen to sixteen.

The mythological figure of the Cretan Minotaur, who devoured an annual tribute of Athenian maidens and youths, put a name to precisely the monstrosity that was never fully articulated in the eighteenth-century case of Franceschini, who frankly claimed the libertine prerogatives of a "free man." At the end of the nineteenth century modern psychiatry also took up the subject of the Minotaur, and in 1886 Richard von Krafft-Ebing found a place in his *Psychopathia Sexualis* for the "psycho-sexual perversion, which may at present be named erotic paedophilia (love of children)." He recognized such conduct as both a criminal and psychiatric matter and discussed it, with reference to German and Austrian law, as the "violation of individuals under the age of fourteen"; he noted that "the term violation, in the legal sense of the word, comprehends the most horrible perversions and acts, which are possible only to a man who is a slave to lust and morally weak, and, as is usually the case, lacking in sexual power." Krafft-Ebing also specified some categories of "non-psychopathological cases of immoral acts with children," thus countenancing the notion that such conduct could fall within the range of sane, though still monstrous, sexuality.[18]

Krafft-Ebing's principal non-psychopathological category was a sort of old-fashioned libertinism: "Debauchees who have tasted all the pleasures of normal and abnormal sexual pleasures with women. The only motive for the infamous act can be found in a morbid psychical craving to create a novel sexual situation and to revel in the shame and confusion of the child victim. A subordinate motive may be sexual impotence with the adult seeking a new stimulus in the extraordinary coitus with an immature female." Krafft-Ebing recognized that "in large cities the markets for these filthy needs are well stocked" and reported as well "that lewd mothers often prepare their little daughters for the use of these libertines."[19]

The eighteenth-century Venetian instances of sex with young girls could be classified within this non-psychopathological category, with Casanova

representing the search for novelty and Franceschini perhaps the fear of impotence. In fact, Franceschini's type of predatory sex play was clearly not
unfamiliar to Krafft-Ebing, who remarked that "the manner in which acts
of immorality are committed on children differs widely, especially where
libertines are concerned," principally including "libidinous manipulations
of the genitals, active masturbation (using the child's hand for onanism),
flagellation, etc." In his professional opinion, such libertine offenders
should not be permitted the excuse of psychopathology to explain their
conduct in court. "The finer feelings of man revolt at the thought of count-
ing the monsters among the psychically normal members of human society," wrote Krafft-Ebing, even as he himself, by conceding the existence of
non-psychopathological cases, seemed to admit some degree of normality in
these sexual monsters. He insisted, in such cases, upon "the moral responsibility of the perpetrator," condemning sex with children as "sheer moral
depravity."[20] By the end of the nineteenth century the cult of childhood's innocence was ideologically balanced by the public horror at adult pedophilia.
   Sigmund Freud, in Vienna in the 1890s, wrestled with that balance when
he formulated and then ultimately abandoned the "seduction theory," in
the course of creating psychoanalysis. In 1896 he presented in Vienna "The
Aetiology of Hysteria," a paper in which he hypothesized that adult hysteria, which was then perceived as a common malady in women, was caused
by traumatic sexual abuse in childhood. He could not, of course, perform
any of the medical examinations that indicated abuse, for he was diagnos-
ing sexual contact decades after it occurred. His evidence came from the
stories of his patients, related in therapy and interpreted by him with the
daring intellectual liberty for which psychoanalysis would become both famous and notorious. He thus envisioned a society whose great secret was
the widespread sexual abuse of little girls at the hands of predatory male
adults. These little girls were neither working-class chambermaids nor juvenile prostitutes but the daughters of bourgeois families, so the discovery
seemed all the more astonishing. Krafft-Ebing, who heard Freud present the
paper, represented the psychiatric establishment in dismissing the conclusion as "a scientific fairy tale."[21] Though Krafft-Ebing accepted that pedophilia could occur in non-psychopathological cases, he was by no means
ready to ratify Freud's conviction of its frequency as a traumatic cause of
hysteria in middle-class psychiatric patients.
   Over the course of the following year, Freud himself changed his mind.
He had originally supposed that the abusive adult had to be a stranger,

an attendant, or a near relation, but gradually became convinced that the Minotaur was inevitably the near relation and, most probably, the father. He now hesitated in 1897 over "the surprise that in all cases, the father, not excluding my own, had to be accused of being perverse . . . whereas surely such widespread perversions against children are not very probable."[22] From this retraction of the seduction theory Freud eventually moved on to the new insight that his patients were not really seduced by their fathers but only fantasized about such seductions. Thus, he arrived at the Oedipus complex and the entire intellectual framework of psychoanalysis.

The late Victorians had some limited awareness of child abuse, both battering abuse and sexual abuse, but could not quite acknowledge either the common incidence or the family dimension of the problem. The great breakthrough in the modern medical and sociological recognition of child abuse came about only in the 1960s, when an American medical team formulated what was called "The Battered Child Syndrome"—and this discovery of the prevalence of battering abuse was closely allied to a parallel acknowledgment of sexual abuse. After the 1960s child abuse was increasingly acknowledged as a widespread phenomenon in modern society, such that it could no longer be treated in medicine or law as something sensationally exceptional. Yet sexual abuse, in particular, remained sensational in the context of the modern media, which highlighted its extreme monstrousness, even while recognizing that it was statistically common and relentlessly recurrent. The difficulties of recognizing, denouncing, defining, and prosecuting sexual abuse, either within a neighborhood or within a legal system, were already apparent in the Franceschini case of 1785 and remained similarly problematic in modern efforts to deal with the same issue: from the day-care scandals of the 1980s, to the issue of sex offender registration in the 1990s, to the voluminous revelations about pedophilia and the priesthood in the early twenty-first century.

C. Henry Kempe, one of the pediatricians who authored the study "The Battered Child Syndrome" in 1962, also further investigated the problem of sexual abuse. Kempe recognized pedophilia as both a family problem and a neighborhood problem, the latter paradigm fitting also the case of Gaetano Franceschini in the parish of Sant'Angelo in the 1780s. In Kempe's discussion the case of a certain anonymous Mr. T. was cited as the illustrative example of pedophilia in the neighborhood: "A brilliant lawyer, father of two, on several occasions engaged in genital fondling of six- to eight-year-old girls, friends of his daughter, while they were in his house for social visits to his children. The neighbors contacted us with a view to stopping this behavior." In fact, the neighbors wanted Mr. T. to get out of town, and he was, accordingly, "moved to a distant city where he entered psychotherapy and has had a long-term cure of his addictive pedophilia."[23] This therapeutic response was, of course, very different from anything contemplated in the Franceschini case of 1785.

Kempe sought to raise the consciousness of doctors regarding the prevalence of abuse so that they would be alert to the possibility of sexual abuse among their patients, even without intercourse. "Hymenal rupture or vaginal entry need not occur to have the rape statute apply," noted Kempe. "Orogenital molestation may leave no evidence, except the child's story. This is to be believed! Children do not fabricate stories of detailed sexual activities unless they have witnessed them."[24] Kempe advocated the comprehensive modern medical investigation of abuse that was already adumbrated by Pietro Recaldini two centuries before. In the modern world of forms and regimens such examinations could not be arbitrary, and Kempe recommended a sample "Sexual Assault Data Sheet" with a checklist of concerns: "Description of clothing: torn, blood stained; semen stained; normal. Description of perineum: normal, laceration, ecchymosis, bleeding, hematoma, rectum. Pelvic examination: vagina, uterus."[25] Modern medicine thus prescribed a technology of knowledge for examining and describing the body of the sexually abused child. It was recognized, however, that the visible and detectable signs of abuse would not always be evident to the medical gaze.

The injunction to believe the child was important for the medical and sociological recognition that sexual abuse, like battering abuse, was far more common than generally supposed. The uncertainty of procedure, however, in the interrogation of children about abuse produced other kinds of controversies in the 1980s. Sensational charges of abuse in day-care centers, most famously in the McMartin Preschool in California and the Fells Acres Day Care Center in Massachusetts, were tried in court with children testifying to extreme and sometimes bizarre instances of pedophile abuse by the responsible adults. Some legal observers, however, considered the children's testimony to have been arbitrarily elicited by provocative questioning; this resulted in mistrials, appeals, and even the overturning of convictions many years later. The issue raised by Franceschini in his defense, concerning the manipulation of innocence in the interpretation of testimony, was still legally problematic two hundred years later.

Also in the 1980s therapists began to encourage adult patients to "recover memories," supposedly long suppressed, concerning childhood sexual abuse; this resulted in a ballooning of incest accusations, not always altogether plausible, sometimes dating back decades, sometimes involving Satanic cults.[26] Though the incidence of sexual abuse was increasingly recognized as a general sociological fact—from Franceschini in the 1780s, to the London Minotaur of the 1880s, to the American day-care scandals of the 1980s—the demonstration of abuse in any individual case turned out to be still judicially problematic, all the more so in the context of the modern sensationalist media.

In Europe in the 1990s, the sociological landscape for the sexual abuse of children was dramatically transformed by the end of communism in Eastern Europe and the dissolution of the Soviet Union. Largely illegal migrations of impoverished young people, moving from east to west in the absence of the Iron Curtain, sometimes transported exploitatively by criminal networks, brought a new influx of prostitutes to the streets of Germany, France, and Italy. In Italy especially there was an Adriatic dimension to this phenomenon inasmuch as impoverished Albanians, either of their own volition, or kidnapped and coerced into sexual slavery, became the prostitutes of Milan, Bologna, Rome, and even Venice. The scandal when they were apprehended was all the greater for the fact that they were often found to be illegally young. The same economic imbalance that brought poor Friulians along the Adriatic to seek their fortunes in Venice in the eighteenth century has more recently brought poor Albanians across the sea, sometimes smuggled ashore, with the hope of economic betterment and the risk—especially for young women—of sexual exploitation.

In 1994 a seven-year-old girl in New Jersey, Megan Kanka, was raped and strangled by a man who lived across the street from her. No one in the neighborhood knew that he had previously been convicted of sexual offenses against children, so parents had no reason to feel that children needed to be protected from him. The murder of the child moved her parents to launch a national movement for a registry of sex offenders that would make past criminal convictions a part of the public record. The campaign for public knowledge, taken together with the tremendous publicity surrounding the trial of the murderer, makes a striking contrast to the secrecy that surrounded the trial of Franceschini two hundred years earlier. Yet even then the more limited neighborhood awareness, deriving from the gossip that circulated in the coffeehouse, momentarily mobilized a small community concerning a menace in its midst.

The outbreak of new scandals at the beginning of the twenty-first century, concerning the sexual abuse of children by American and European priests, in cases concealed and ignored by the Roman Catholic hierarchy, has revealed that the power of institutional silence and secrecy still obstructs public efforts to confront the problem of pedophilia. The fraught complications of addressing this issue today, in its current legal and cultural aspects, suggest some of the challenges faced by historians trying to fathom the secret history of sexual abuse in past centuries. In fact, it was a Roman Catholic priest, Father Fiorese, who raised the issue of sex between adults and children in Venice in 1785, and the case that then ensued offers now a rare glimpse into the history of sexual abuse, unprecedented in detail for the age of the ancien régime. The baker Bernardo Manella, looking across the street, saw a little girl knitting on the arbor balcony, a picture of childhood's innocence, but the Bestemmia, by the time it had completed its work, could see much more than that in the picture. The Bestemmia pursued its prosecution without any reference to the word or concept of child abuse, without any reference to the word or concept of pedophilia. Those concepts had not yet been culturally articulated, though some inklings of their modern meanings were implicit in the discussion of the case of 1785. In modern society sexual abuse is considered both a legal crime and a moral evil, an axiom that was formulated confusedly, controversially, but with pioneering conviction in the eighteenth century, when an adult was put on trial for violating the innocence of a child.

Conclusion

On December 16, 1785, the four executors of the Bestemmia gathered to decide on a verdict in the case of Gaetano Franceschini. Almost four months
had passed since August 31, when he had spent his single night in bed with
Paolina Lozaro. For Franceschini, deprived of the liberty that he claimed
as the right of a free man, these had been four very unpleasant months
of imprisonment. The case had been thorny and tangled, with numerous
witnesses, ambiguous charges, and long legal arguments from the defense,
but the tribunal seemed to be set on finally concluding before Christmas,
which would mark the beginning of the carnival season with its new round
of festivities. The changing season would also bring the return of migrant
Friulians to Venice, like the Furlana who sold ladles and spoons, and the
man who provided adoptive daughters. The month of December did not,
however, herald the end of 1785 and the coming of 1786; for Venice, alone in
Europe, kept to an eccentric calendar by which the old year ended in February and the new year began in March, *more veneto* (by Venetian custom).

The first proposal the Bestemmia considered for penalizing Franceschini
was a sentence of an additional three months' imprisonment "closed to the
light" (*serrata alla luce*). The patrician executors proceeded to a ballot on this

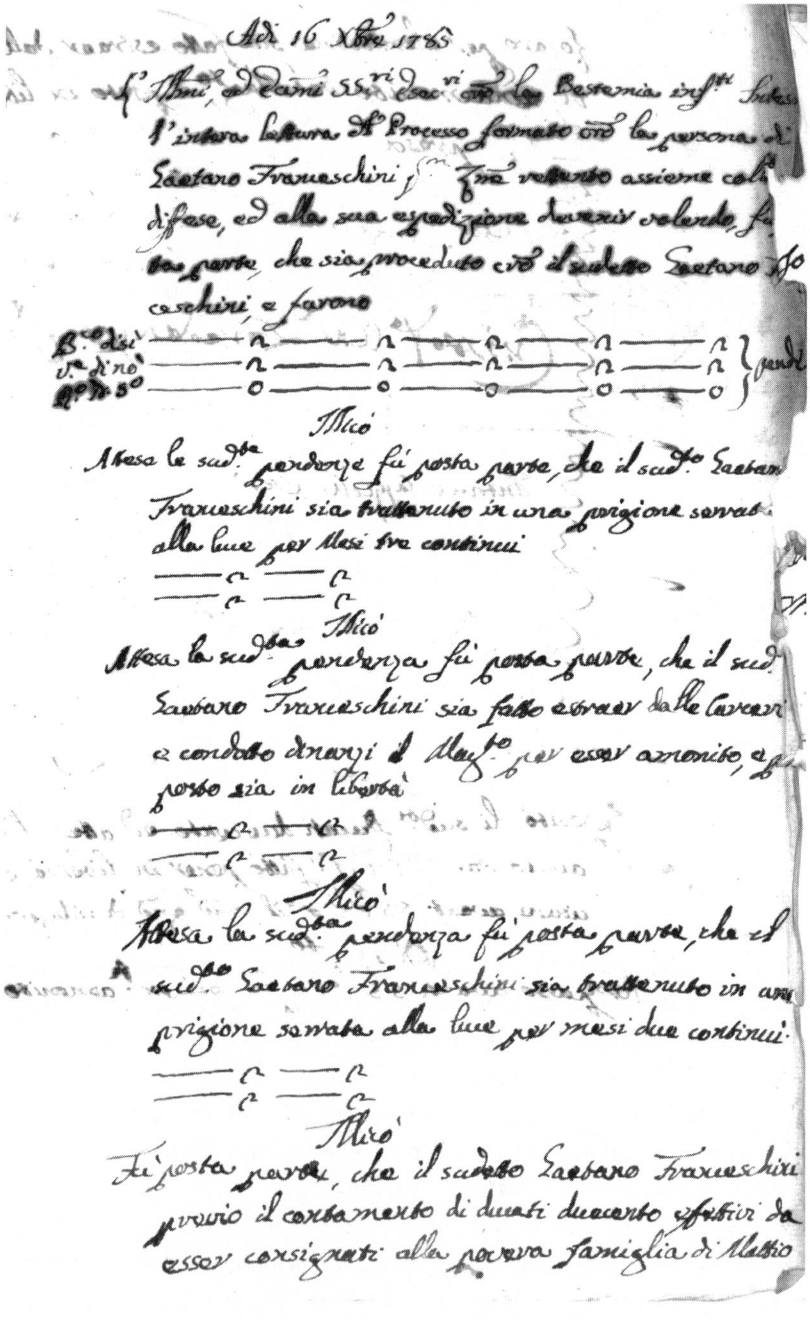
Adì 16 Xbre 1785

Gl'Ill.mi, ed Ecc.mi SS.ri Esec.ri con.o la Bestemmia inf.ti [illegible] l'intera lettura del Processo formato con.o la persona di Gaetano Franceschini, [illegible] assieme colle difese, ed alla sua espedizione devenir volendo, fu posta parte, che sia proceduto con.o il sudetto Gaetano Franceschini, e furono

B.co di sì

V.e di no

N.o S.o

pende

Ill.co

Attesa la sud.ta pendenza fu posta parte, che il sud.to Gaetano Franceschini sia trattenuto in una prigione serrata alla luce per Mesi tre continui

Ill.co

Attesa la sud.ta pendenza fu posta parte, che il sud.to Gaetano Franceschini sia fatto estraer dalle Carceri e condotto dinanzi il Mag.to per esser amonito, e posto sia in libertà

Ill.co

Attesa la sud.ta pendenza fu posta parte, che il sud.to Gaetano Franceschini sia trattenuto in una prigione serrata alla luce per mesi due continui.

Ill.co

Fu posta parte, che il sudetto Gaetano Franceschini previo il contamento di ducati duecento effettivi da esser consignati alla povera famiglia di Mattio

Balloting of the four members of the Bestemmia on penalties for Franceschini, 16 December 1785. Archivio di Stato, Esecutori contro la Bestemmia, Busta 40, *Processi*, 1785.

proposal, and the vote revealed that they were evenly divided two against two. Three months in a dark prison, taken together with the time he had already served since his arrest on September 8, would have amounted to a total incarceration of half a year.[1] The division in the voting suggests the tension and ambivalence that must have prevailed through the hearing of the entire case. Half the judges believed that half a year in prison was too harsh a punishment for the crime that Franceschini had committed, if crime it was. They may have believed him absolutely innocent, or they may have simply favored a lesser penalty. In any event, the even division of the court must be understood not only as an indication of the legal ambiguity surrounding such a case of sexual abuse, conceived as an issue of scandal, but also the cultural uncertainty surrounding the figure of the libertine and concerning the innocence of childhood. The tie vote meant that the penalty was not adopted.

The indulgent wing of the tribunal next proposed a ballot formulation that reflected their own perspective: "that Gaetano Franceschini be taken out of the prisons, conducted before the magistrature in order to receive a warning, and then set at liberty." In the balloting, the tribunal was divided again, two against two, with the two negative votes this time probably holding out for a stronger punishment. The rigorists then came back with a proposal for two additional months of imprisonment, instead of three, but still they could not win over to their side either of the indulgent judges. Finally, presumably after some discussion, the executors came up with a compromise alternative that Franceschini be ordered to pay the sum of two hundred ducats "to be consigned to the poor family of Mattio Lozaro as charity" and then, reverting to the earlier proposal, that the prisoner be summoned, warned, and set free. This proposal was adopted by a vote of three to one—though we cannot be sure whether the one dissident executor would have preferred a harsher or a gentler penalty, real time in prison or no fine at all.[2] That same day, Franceschini had the two hundred ducats deposited with the court and was liberated from his imprisonment. He returned to appear before the tribunal on December 19 to receive his formal warning, the last word that he would ever hear about Paolina Lozaro.[3]

The Bestemmia's case file on Gaetano Franceschini was closed on December 19, leaving no intimations of what would happen to him after that. Probably he left the apartment in Calle della Cortesia, where his neighbors knew all too much about his recent past. They would know nothing about his future, whether he moved to a different Venetian neighborhood, whether he returned to his native city of Vicenza, or whether he decided to strike out anew, with his family wealth, in some other city altogether, eager to explore the brothels of Paris or London. Twenty years later Lorenzo Da Ponte, having been driven from Venice by the Bestemmia, having departed from Vienna after the death of Mozart, having tried his luck in the theatrical world of London, decided at the age of fifty-six to immigrate to America, and he settled in New York. Franceschini at sixty could also have decided to seek a better fortune in the New World.

In any event, whether Franceschini moved across the Grand Canal or across the Atlantic Ocean, after December 19, 1785, his further crimes and adventures remain unknown to history. Probably he continued in his established pattern of sexual relations, perhaps molesting more young girls, but presumably he had learned some lessons of caution and discretion. Casanova, his contemporary, died in 1798 in Bohemia at the age of seventy-three, and Franceschini, based on average estimates of longevity, probably also did not survive the eighteenth century.

On December 28, 1785, when Franceschini had already been free for two weeks, a new face appeared in the office of the tribunal. It was none other than Mattio Lozaro, the father of Paolina, the man who had remained completely invisible throughout the proceedings. He might have been working in the fields of Friuli through the autumn harvest. He might have been wayward and derelict in his paternal duties. He might have been lying low for reasons of his own. Whatever the motive for his autumn absence during the investigation, by the advent of winter he was on hand in Venice to pick up the compensation that had been deposited for his poor family with the tribunal. In the Venetian Archive of State there is preserved the father's receipt for two hundred ducats—"assigned as charity by the most excellent magistrature for the assistance of my poor family"—but he did not sign the document. For the text of the receipt concluded thus: "And not knowing how to write this Mattio Lozaro made the following sign of the Cross." The document is marked with an X.[4]

The sum of two hundred ducats would have been small for Franceschini, with his family fortune in the silk business, indeed a bargain price to buy his liberty from prison. For the poor, illiterate Lozaro family it would have been a handsome sum. Maria Lozaro considered it a stroke of Providence when Franceschini promised one single ducat monthly for the services of Paolina. The fine imposed by the court amounted to the sum that the girl might have earned by serving for seventeen years as a chambermaid in training. Interestingly, the court did not specify that the sum should provide for her dowry, probably because she was not actually deflowered and therefore not compromised as a marriageable woman. The tribunal seemed rather to have concluded that the abuse of the child had harmed the honor of the family as a whole; therefore, compensation was paid to the head of the family. Whether Mattio Lozaro was a concerned father who put aside a portion of the total for his daughter, whether a loving husband who urged his wife to take on less laundry labor, or whether a selfish scoundrel who put the money toward drink—history does not tell. His single momentary appearance in the case, to take the money and run, would not seem to indicate a keen sense of family commitment. In the end, two hundred ducats was the valuation of the loss to the family's honor, or, as some sentimental spirits might have said, the loss of the child's innocence.

Franceschini believed that the innocence of Paolina Lozaro was manipulated and thus made to speak against him by the prosecution, and certainly that innocence exercised a sentimental power that shaped the legal balance

Receipt for two hundred ducats paid to Mattio Lozaro, father of Paolina, signed with an X. The money was given "per elemosina" (as charity): "E non sapendo esso Mattio Lozaro scrivere fece il seguente segno della Croce" (And not knowing how to write this Mattio Lozaro made the following sign of the Cross). 28 December 1785. Archivio di Stato di Venezia, Esecutori contro la Bestemmia, Busta 40, *Processi*, 1785.

of the case. Images of the child may have lodged in the minds of the judges and haunted their reflections—as when, "raising her eyes," she exclaimed, "Oh, I wish I had gone to Paradise." Paolina Lozaro's testimony, remembering the twenty-four hours she spent in Franceschini's apartment, was simple but vivid: the meal of bread and fish, her knitting and her recitation of the rosary, her powdered hair and the silver buckles. The anatomical details that she provided of pinching and tickling, of fists and fingers, of bodies in contact under cover of darkness, demanded from the judges some reconstructive visualization to produce the apposite pornographic picture. The transcription of her voice still registers with remarkable clarity, speaking to us from the world of the ancien régime, the vividly innocent narrative of a child who was the victim of sexual abuse as we understand it today.

The descriptions of the child provided by other witnesses must have made similarly powerful impressions as images of innocence. Maddalena Schiavon described the first meeting between Franceschini and the child, by the embankment of the canal: "A little way off was the daughter of Maria Lozaro, about eight years old, named Paolina, who, seeing him give the coins to my children, ran over to demand one for herself. When he saw her, he said, 'Oh, this one, this one,' and touched her on both cheeks, and asked her if she wanted to go and serve him. She replied that she did." Bernardo Manella looked out from his upstairs flour room and saw the child sitting on Franceschini's balcony: "I found that on his arbor balcony there was sitting, and knitting, a little girl who seemed to be about nine years old, whom I had not observed before. After I made my inquiry to her by gesturing, the girl gave me to understand that he was not at home." These two images—the girl by the embankment and the girl on the balcony—represented innocence, before and after, and they had to be interpreted in court according to the disturbing reverberations of what happened in between. The sexual grappling in bed, as in a case of pentimento, remained implicitly present beneath the images of innocence.

Rousseau must have felt something similar when he contemplated little Anzoletta at play in Venice and permitted himself to imagine the eventual harvesting of her innocence in sexual slavery. The incongruity became insupportable: "Imperceptibly my heart became attached to little Anzoletta, but it was a paternal attachment, in which the senses played so little part that accordingly as it grew, there would have been less and less possibility for the senses to enter into it. . . . I am certain that however beautiful that poor child might have become, we, far from ever being the corruptors of her innocence, would have been its protectors." The interplay of innocence and eroticism was both potent and equivocal, for though there was a porno-graphic element in the combination, the new cult of childhood would also make a new kind of monster out of men like Franceschini.

Paolina Lozaro survived the night in Franceschini's bed and was knitting on the balcony the next morning, a picture of childlike innocence. Two weeks later she was home at Santa Maria Maggiore, and her mother was telling the neighbors that "nothing" had happened. Paolina Lozaro then dis-appears from history and returns to the anonymity of her own life, leaving no trace of how her experience with Franceschini might have affected her for the rest of her life. Eight years old in 1785, she would have been born in Venice in 1777. She could have lived for a long time, probably outliving the Venetian Republic, which passed into history in 1797.

After the case of 1785 Maria Lozaro might have decided to return with her child to Friuli, as many immigrants did; so Paolina, born in Venice, could have grown up as an urban Venetian or as a provincial Friulian. At twenty she might have been married, become a mother herself, or she might have eventually entered into the career of domestic service, which went so spectacularly awry with Franceschini. She would have lived through the Na-poleonic maelstrom in Europe, perhaps heard something about the rights of man, though probably nothing about the rights of women or children. As an adult, she would have found herself a subject of the Habsburg monarchy, which ruled both Venice and Friuli after the Congress of Vienna in 1815. If she migrated again from Friuli in search of urban employment, she could easily have ended up in Vienna, the Habsburg capital. She would have been almost seventy in 1848, and, if she was in Venice, she might have witnessed the momentary exaltation in which the Republic of San Marco was resur-rected in revolutionary spirit, the same republic in which she had been born. If she was in Vienna, she might have witnessed the revolutionary rising of the students and the workers, the fall of Metternich, the accession of the young emperor Franz Joseph, who would reign into the twentieth century.

In 1848 Karl Marx and Friedrich Engels wrote *The Communist Manifesto* in German, and, if she was in Vienna, Paolina Lozaro might even have heard something of its message, its fierce denunciation of the bourgeoisie. Among many other class crimes, according to the manifesto, bourgeois men engaged in sexual exploitation, "having the wives and daughters of their proletarians at their disposal, not to speak of common prostitutes."[5] Would Paolina Lozaro, at the age of seventy, have understood the bourgeois exploitation of proletarian daughters as something that might have had some relevance to her own childhood? Would she even have remembered that single summer night she spent in Franceschini's bed when she was eight years old?

"Who would believe that this punishment of a child, received at eight years by the hand of a maid of thirty, determined my tastes, my desires, my passions, my self, for the rest of my life?" Rousseau reflected, when he recalled in his *Confessions* the spanking that he received from Mademoiselle Lambercier.[6] He was fully persuaded that a child of eight could not only remember but could be formatively influenced by such an episode at such an early age. Goethe, in *Wilhelm Meister's Apprenticeship*, included a fictional female memoir called "Confessions of a Beautiful Soul," which began at the age of eight: "Up to my eighth year I was a healthy child; but I have as little memory of those years as I have of my birth. Then, when I had just turned eight, I had a hemorrhage, and from that moment on I was all feeling and memory. Every little detail of what happened then is as present to me now as if it had occurred only yesterday."[7] Like Rousseau, Goethe believed that an eight-year-old could remember experiences and that eight was a developmental milestone for the formation of character.

Casanova, in his memoirs, similarly emphasized the significance of the eighth year: "Let us now come to the beginning of my existence as a thinking being. At the beginning of August in the year 1733 the organ of my memory developed. I was eight years and four months old. I remember nothing that may have happened to me before that epoch." The occasion was also a hemorrhage, an unstanchable bloody nose, for which Casanova's grandmother decided to seek an extraordinary remedy. She took the eight-year-old boy in a gondola to the island of Murano, the same little trip that the eight-year-old Paolina Lozaro would make fifty years later to visit her uncle, after her ordeal. On Murano Casanova was subjected to the medical magical spells of an old woman with a black cat. Her language was Friulian or Furlan, and that was the language in which she addressed Casanova's grandmother. "At the end of their conversation in the Friulian language, the witch, after having received from my grandmother a silver ducat, opened a chest, took me in her arms, put me in the chest, and locked me in there, telling me not to be afraid," recalled Casanova, exercising his organ of memory back to the moment of its original development.

> I was dazed. I remained tranquil, holding my handkerchief to my nose because I was bleeding, quite indifferent to the din that I heard being made outside. I heard laughing and crying by turns, shouting, singing, and beating

upon the chest. It was all the same to me. Finally they took me out, and my bleeding was stanched. This extraordinary woman, after having given me a hundred caresses, undresses me, puts me on the bed, burns some herbs, gathers the smoke in a sheet, wraps me in it, recites some incantations, unwraps me afterward, and gives me five candies to eat, very agreeable to the taste. She immediately rubs my temples and the nape of my neck with an ointment that gives off a sweet odor, and she dresses me again. She tells me that my hemorrhage will continue to subside, provided that I inform nobody of what she had done to cure me, and she warns me that otherwise I will suffer loss of blood and even death, if I should dare to reveal to anyone her mysteries.[8]

These were, apparently, Friulian folk mysteries, which Casanova eventually revealed in the opening pages of his memoirs.

Such was Casanova's very first memory, the commencement of his life as a thinking being; he obviously also believed that an eight-year-old was capable of remembering a traumatic experience in full detail throughout a long life. Indeed, his own episode in some ways resembled the experience of Paolina Lozaro, being placed in a strange bed, having his clothes removed, having his body stroked and handled by an elderly stranger, and being given to understand that what had happened was to be treated as a guilty secret. His reward was candies instead of silver buckles.

The most important memoirists of the eighteenth century, and the most important writers about childhood, thus agreed that the age of eight was a crucial threshold for memory, character, and formative experience. Paolina Lozaro may have remembered in excruciating detail what happened to her in Franceschini's bed, or, if she happened to fall just short of the threshold, she may have forgotten the experience completely. Perhaps she only remembered the silver buckles, given to her as a sparkling gift in the strange apartment, a gift that she was forced to return when she was taken away.

The everyday details of eighteenth-century Venetian apartments, with all their rococo embellishments and fashionable artifacts, from powdered hair to buckled shoes, are preserved for historical memory in the paintings of Pietro Longhi. In the museum of Ca' Rezzonico or in the Accademia, Longhi's canvases represent the domestic scenes of the morning cup of chocolate, the morning toilette, the dressing of a lady's hair, the dancing lesson; there are rococo chairs, china cups, silver trays, bowls of fruit, large cushions, and little dogs. In the scenes from Venetian life that he painted between his maturity in the 1740s and his death in 1785, Longhi represented the privileged elite making music, sipping chocolate, or playing cards, but

The Letter (also known as *The Milliner*), by Pietro Longhi (1740s). The older gentleman in black, on the right, holding the bag of coins in his left hand, is visiting the young milliner seated at the table, reading a letter, but his attention seems to have been distracted by the little girl playing with her doll. Image © The Metropolitan Museum of Art / Art Resource, New York.

he also showed the working-class roles that someone like Maria Lozaro would have filled, like the washerwoman of Ca' Rezzonico or the wet nurse in the Accademia. The wet nurse, judging from her costume, could have come from Friuli. In Ca' Rezzonico there is also a painting by Longhi that shows a young woman seductively dancing the Furlana, the dance that became so exceptionally popular in the eighteenth century.

In the 1740s Longhi executed a series of paintings related to the theme of temptation, that is, a woman appearing as the temptation to a man, and one of these pictures, innocuously known as *The Letter*, or alternatively as *The Milliner*, hangs in the Metropolitan Museum in New York.[9] A charming milliner, with a flower in her hair and a letter in her hand, is receiving a visit from an older gentleman, mediated by the presence of an old woman who might be playing the role of procuress. There is laundry hanging on a line overhead, suggesting the humble status of the milliner, and there are mannequin heads for displaying hats, the equipment of a working woman. The gentleman, on the far right, is clearly of higher status, perhaps of the prosperous bourgeoisie, and he holds a little bag in his hand, probably a bag of coins.

There is also a child in the picture, a beautiful little girl, perhaps the daughter of the milliner, maybe eight years old, playing with a doll just as Rousseau might have imagined Sophie: "Watch a little girl pass the day with her doll, continually changing its costume, dressing it and undressing it hundreds of times."[10] Longhi's little girl is so busy with her doll that she seems oblivious to the drama taking place around her, with all its erotic angles, the charming milliner, the lecherous gentleman, the avaricious old woman, the little bag of coins. Dating from the 1740s, the painting depicts a little girl in Venice at just the time that Rousseau purchased such a child, intended for his eventual sexual entertainment. Her childlike innocence and absorbed attention to her doll would surely have dissuaded Rousseau from any sexually exploitative intentions. Yet there is no doubt about it: When you peer closely at the painting, you can see that the older gentleman is not actually looking at the pretty milliner, the ostensible object of his visit. He has discovered another temptation, the temptation of innocence. He is looking intently at the little girl.

Notes

Introduction

1. Denunciation by Bartolo Fiorese, 2 September 1785, Archivio di Stato di Venezia, Esecutori contro la Bestemmia, Busta 40: *Processi*, the case of Gaetano Franceschini, 1785. All subsequent citations from the documents of the case refer to this archival citation. All translations, unless otherwise noted, are by the author, Larry Wolff. For translations from Venetian dialect the essential reference was Giuseppe Boerio, *Dizionario del dialetto veneziano* (Venice: Tipografia di Giovanni Cecchini, 1856); preliminary article studies by the author are Larry Wolff, "Depraved Inclinations: Libertines and Children in Casanova's Venice," *Eighteenth-Century Studies* 38, no. 3 (Spring 2005), pp. 417–40; and Wolff, "Sexual Relations between Adults and Children in Eighteenth-Century Venice: The Rhetoric of Deviance," *Acta Historiae* 15, no. 2, *Retorike Deviantnosti / Retoriche della devianza*, ed. Claudio Povolo and Urška Železnik (Koper, Slovenia: 2007), pp. 375–84; and Wolff, "Private Life, Personal Liberty, and Sexual Crime in Eighteenth-Century Venice: The Case of Gaetano Franceschini," in *Studies on Voltaire and the Eighteenth Century: Representing Private Lives of the Enlightenment*, ed. Andrew Kahn (Oxford: Voltaire Foundation, 2010), pp. 107–21, also published in Russian: "Chastnaya zhisn, svoboda lichnosti i seksualnoe prestuplenie v Venetzii XVIII veka: delo Gaetano Francheskini," *Novoe Literaturnoe Obozrenie* 92 (Moscow 2008), pp. 158–70.

2. Guido Ruggiero, *The Boundaries of Eros: Sex Crime and Sexuality in Renaissance Venice* (New York: Oxford University Press, 1985); Edward Muir and Guido Ruggiero, eds., *History from Crime*, trans. Corrada Biazzo Curry, Margaret Gallucci, and Mary Gallucci (Baltimore: Johns Hopkins University Press, 1994); Gaetano Cozzi, "Note su tribunali e procedure penali a Venezia nel '700," *Rivista storica italiana* 77, no. 4 (1965), pp. 931–52; Gaetano Cozzi, "Religione, moralità, e giustizia a Venezia: Vicende della magistratura degli Esecutori contro la Bestemmia (secoli XVI–XVII)," *Ateneo veneto* 178/179, no. 29 (1991), pp. 7–95; Claudio Povolo, *L'intrigo dell'onore: Poteri e istituzioni nella Repubblica di Venezia tra cinque e seicento* (Verona: Cierre, 1997); Renzo Derosas, "Moralità e giustizia a Venezia nel '500–'600: Gli Esecutori contro la Bestemmia," in *Stato, società, e giustizia: Nella Repubblica veneta (sec. XV–XVIII)*, ed. Gaetano Cozzi (Rome: Jouvence, 1980), pp. 431–528; Alain Cabantous, *Blasphemy: Impious Speech in the West from the Seventeenth to the Nineteenth Century*,

trans. Eric Rauth (New York: Columbia University Press, 2002); Joanne Ferraro, *Nefarious Crimes, Contested Justice: Illicit Sex and Infanticide in the Republic of Venice, 1557–1789* (Baltimore: Johns Hopkins University Press, 2008); Elizabeth Horodowich, *Language and Statecraft in Early Modern Venice* (Cambridge: Cambridge University Press, 2008).

3. Carlo Goldoni, *La bottega del caffè*, in *Commedie*, vol. 1, ed. Guido Davico Bonino (Milan: Garzanti, 1981), act 1, scene 3, p. 190.

4. Jürgen Habermas, *The Structural Transformation of the Public Sphere: An Inquiry into a Category of Bourgeois Society*, trans. Thomas Burger (Cambridge, Mass.: MIT Press, 1993); Danilo Reato, *La bottega del caffè: I caffè veneziani tra '700 e '900* (Venice: Arsenale Editrice, 1991); Brian Cowan, *The Social Life of Coffee: The Emergence of the British Coffeehouse* (New Haven, Conn.: Yale University Press, 2005); James Johnson, *Venice Incognito: Masks in the Serene Republic* (Berkeley: University of California Press, 2011); Sarah Maza, *Private Lives and Public Affairs: The Causes Célèbres of Prerevolutionary France* (Berkeley: University of California Press, 1993).

5. *Eros philosophe: Discours libertins des lumières*, ed. François Moureau and Alain-Marc Rieu (Geneva: Editions Slatkine, 1984); *Libertine Enlightenment: Sex, Liberty, and License in the Eighteenth Century*, ed. Peter Cryle and Lisa O'Connell (New York: Palgrave Macmillan, 2004); Pierre Saint-Amand, *The Libertine's Progress: Seduction in the Eighteenth-Century French Novel*, trans. Jennifer Curtiss Gage (Providence, R.I.: Brown University Press, 1994); Stephanie Genand, *Le libertinage et l'histoire: Politique de la séduction à la fin de l'ancien régime* (Oxford: Voltaire Foundation, 2005); Didier Foucault, *Histoire du libertinage: Des goliards au marquis de Sade* (Paris: Perrin, 2007); Georges Vigarello, *A History of Rape: Sexual Violence in France from the 16th to the 20th Century* (Oxford: Polity Press, 2001).

6. Philippe Ariès, *Centuries of Childhood: A Social History of Family Life*, trans. Robert Baldick (New York: Vintage, 1965); Paula Fass, ed., *Encyclopedia of Children and Childhood in History and Society* (New York: Macmillan, 2004); Margaret King, *The Death of the Child Valerio Marcello* (Chicago: University of Chicago Press, 1994); David Kertzer, *The Kidnapping of Edgardo Mortara* (New York: Knopf, 1997).

Chapter 1

1. Denunciation by Bortolo Fiorese, 2 September 1785, Archivio di Stato di Venezia, Esecutori contro la Bestemmia, Busta 40: *Processi*, case of Gaetano Franceschini, 1785.

2. Testimony of Bortolo Fiorese, 2 September 1785, 2r–2v, case of Gaetano Franceschini, 1785.

3. Ibid., 2v–3r.

4. 1 Kings 1:1–4 (King James Version).

5. Alvise Zorzi, *Venezia scomparsa*, vol. 2, *Repertorio degli edifici veneziani distrutti, alterati o manomessi* (Milan: Electa Editrice, 1972), pp. 309–11; Giuseppe Tassini, *Curiosità veneziane*, ed. Lino Moretti (Venice: Filippi Editore, 1964), pp. 23–24.

6. Testimony of Bortolo Fiorese, 3r–3v.

7. Monica Chojnacka, *Working Women of Early Modern Venice* (Baltimore: Johns Hopkins University Press, 2001), chap. 3, "Around the Neighborhood," pp. 50–80; see also *La Chiesa di Venezia nel settecento*, ed. Bruno Bertoli (Venice: Edizioni Studium Cattolico Veneziano, 1993).

8. Testimony of Bortolo Fiorese, 3v.

9. Ibid., 4r.

10. Ibid., 4r–4v.

11. Bruno Bertoli, "Clero e popolo tra santità e peccato," in *La Chiesa di Venezia nel settecento*, pp. 56–62.

12. Testimony of Bortolo Fiorese, 4v.

13. Archivio di Stato di Venezia, Esecutori contro la Bestemmia, Busta 36: *Processi*, case of Giuseppe Terrizzo, 1779.

14. Testimony of Bortolo Fiorese, 5r–5v.

Chapter 2

1. Charles Secondat, baron de Montesquieu, *The Spirit of the Laws*, trans. Thomas Nugent (New York: Hafner, 1949), vol. 1, book 11, chap. 6, pp. 152–53.

2. Armand Baschet, *Les archives de la Sérénissime République de Venise* (Paris: Amyot, 1857), pp. 87–88.

3. Cozzi, "Religione, moralità, e giustizia," pp. 26–27; see also Cabantous, *Blasphemy*, pp. 49–69; Horodowich, *Language and Statecraft in Early Modern Venice*, pp. 56–90.

4. Cozzi, "Religione, moralità, e giustizia," pp. 70–71.

5. Ibid., p. 18; Ruggiero, *The Boundaries of Eros*, p. 113; Derosas, "Moralità e giustizia," pp. 433–34, 441–43.

6. Cozzi, "Religione, moralità, e giustizia," pp. 23–24, 80–81, 83–85; Derosas, "Moralità e giustizia," pp. 446–47, 455–56.

7. James Davis, *The Decline of the Venetian Nobility as a Ruling Class* (Baltimore: Johns Hopkins University Press, 1962), pp. 58, 73.

8. Cesare Beccaria, *Dei delitti e delle pene*, chap. 15, "Accuse segrete" (Milan: Mursia, 1973), pp. 51–53; Beccaria, *On Crimes and Punishments and Other Writings*, ed. Richard Bellamy, trans. Richard Davies (Cambridge: Cambridge Texts in the History of Political Thought, Cambridge University Press, 1995), pp. 37–38, 126; Gianfranco Torcellan, "Cesare Beccaria a Venezia," *Rivista storica italiana* 76, no. 3 (1964), pp. 720–48; Franco Venturi, *Italy and the Enlightenment: Studies in a Cosmopolitan Century*, ed. Stuart Woolf, trans. Susan Corsi (New York: New York University Press, 1972), pp. 154–64.

9. Beccaria, *On Crimes and Punishments*, Cambridge ed., p. 33.

10. Zeffirino Giambatista Grecchi, *Le formalità del processo criminale nel dominio veneto*, 2 vols. (Padua: Tommaso Bettinelli, 1790–91), 2:188–90.

11. Ibid.; Franco Venturi, *Settecento riformatore*, book 5, *L'Italia dei lumi*, vol. 2, *La Repubblica di Venezia (1761–1797)* (Turin: Giulio Einaudi, 1990), p. 217.

12. Michel Foucault, *Madness and Civilization: A History of Insanity in the Age of Reason*, trans. Richard Howard (Abingdon, U.K.: Routledge, 2001), p. 246.

13. Archivio di Stato di Venezia, Esecutori contro la Bestemmia, Busta 36: *Processi*, case of Giuseppe Terrizzo, 1779.

14. Ibid., case of Bortolo Sigla, 1779.

15. Ibid., case of Giuseppe Constantini, 1779.

16. Sheila Hodges, *Lorenzo Da Ponte: The Life and Times of Mozart's Librettist* (London: Grafton Books, 1985), pp. 30–31; Rodney Bolt, *The Librettist of Venice: The Remarkable Life of Lorenzo Da Ponte* (London: Bloomsbury, 2006), pp. 60–63; Fausto Nicolini, "La vera ragione della fuga di Lorenzo Da Ponte da Venezia," *Archivio storico italiano*, ser. 7, vol. 14 (1930), pp. 129–38.

17. Archivio di Stato di Venezia, Esecutori contro la Bestemmia, Busta 36: *Processi*, case of Lorenzo Da Ponte, 1779.

18. Lorenzo Da Ponte, *Memorie*, in *Memorie–Libretti mozartiani* (Milan: Garzanti, 1981), p. 58.

19. Allegazione per Gaetano Franceschini, article 62, Archivio di Stato di Venezia, Esecutori contro la Bestemmia, Busta 40: *Processi*, case of Gaetano Franceschini, 1785.

20. Cozzi, "Religione, moralità, e giustizia," pp. 55, 89–91.

Chapter 3

1. Giuseppe Tassini, *Curiosità veneziane*, ed. Lino Moretti (Venice: Filippi Editore, 1964), pp. 401–2.

2. Testimony of Maria Lozaro, 5 September 1785, 13r–13v, Archivio di Stato di Venezia, Esecutori contro la Bestemmia, Busta 40: *Processi*, case of Gaetano Franceschini, 1785; see also Chojnacka, *Working Women of Early Modern Venice*, chap. 4, "Immigrant Women," pp. 81–102.

3. Testimony of Maria Lozaro, 13v–14r.

4. Ibid., 14r.

5. Ibid.

6. Ibid., 14v.

7. Nicolò Papadopoli Aldobrandini, *Le monete di Venezia*, part 3, *Da Leonardo Donà a Lodovico Manin, 1606–1797* (Venice: Tipografia Libreria Emiliana, 1919), pp. 770, 787, 820, 1092.

8. Testimony of Maria Lozaro, 14v.

9. Ibid., 15r–15v.

10. Ibid., 15r.

11. Testimony of Elena Artico, 3 September 1785, 6r–7r, case of Gaetano Franceschini, 1785.

12. Ibid., 7v–8r.

13. Testimony of Cattarina Bartoli, 3 September 1785, 9r–9v, case of Gaetano Franceschini, 1785.

14. Ibid.

15. Testimony of Elena Artico, 8r.

16. Testimony of Maria Lozaro, 15v.

17. Ibid., 15v–16r.

18. Mozart and Da Ponte, *Don Giovanni*, act 1, scene 20.

19. Testimony of Maria Lozaro, 16r.

20. Ibid.

21. Testimony of Elena Artico, 8v.

22. Cozzi, "Religione, moralità, e giustizia," pp. 55, 89–91.

Chapter 4

1. Jacques Casanova de Seingalt, *Histoire de ma vie*, 12 vols. (Wiesbaden: F. A. Brockhaus, 1960–62), 2:270–71; Casanova, *Histoire de ma vie*, ed. Francis Lacassin, 3 vols. (Paris: Robert Laffont, 1993), 1:436–47; see also Chantal Thomas, "Préferer le libertinage à la philosophie (Note sur les *Mémoires* de Casanova)," in *Eros philosophe: Discours libertins des lumières* (Geneva: Editions Slatkine, 1984), pp. 109–16.

2. Casanova, *Histoire de ma vie*, Brockhaus ed., 2:184–88; Laffont ed., 1:371–74.

3. Ibid., Brockhaus ed., 2:271–72; Laffont ed., 1:437.

4. Ibid., Brockhaus ed., 2:272–73; Laffont ed., 1:438.

5. Ibid., Brockhaus ed., 2:273–74; Laffont ed., 1:439.

6. Ruggiero, *The Boundaries of Eros*, p. 9.

7. Ibid., p. 102.

8. Merry Wiesner, *Women and Gender in Early Modern Europe*, 2nd ed. (Cambridge: Cambridge University Press, 2000), p. 71.

9. Ruggiero, *The Boundaries of Eros*, pp. 31, 44, 107.

10. Ibid., pp. 41, 105, 150–51.

11. Ibid., pp. 17, 91–92.

12. Ibid., pp. 78–81, 85–86, 109–13.

13. Benedetto Pasqualigo, *Della giurisprudenza criminale, teorica e pratica*, vol. 1 (Venice: Stefano Orlandini, 1731); Lorenzo Priori, *Pratica criminale secondo le leggi della Serenissima Repubblica di Venezia* (Venice: Gasparo Girardi, 1738); see also *L'amministrazione della giustizia penale nella Repubblica di Venezia (secoli XVI–XVIII)*, ed. Giovanni Chiodi and Claudio Povolo, vol. 1, *Lorenzo Priori e la sua Prattica criminale* (Verona: Cierre Edizioni, 2004).

14. Pasqualigo, *Della giurisprudenza criminale*, pp. 76–90.

15. Ibid., pp. 76–90; Priori, *Pratica criminale*, pp. 162–63.

16. Pasqualigo, *Della giurisprudenza criminale*, p. 97.

17. Archivio di Stato di Venezia, Esecutori contro la Bestemmia, Busta 36: *Processi*, case of Giuseppe Terrizzo, 1779.

18. Ibid., Busta 33: *Processi*, case of Paolo Zane et al., 1775.

19. Ibid., Busta 33: *Processi*, case of Sebastian Marchetti, 1772; Busta 33: *Processi*, case of Iseppo Franceschini, 1771; Busta 34: *Processi*, case of Anastasio Valensa, 1775.

20. Ibid., Busta 34: *Processi*, case of Francesco Toselli, 1776; Busta 33: *Processi*, case of Zuane Fratovich, 1774.

21. Zeffirino Giambatista Grecchi, *Le formalità del processo criminale nel dominio veneto*, 2 vols. (Padua: Tommaso Bettinelli, 1790–91), 2:188–90.

22. Archivio di Stato di Venezia, Esecutori contro la Bestemmia, Busta 39: *Processi*, case of Alvise Loredan, 1784; Busta 39: *Processi*, case of Antonio Gavardina, 1783.

23. Ibid., Busta 39: *Processi*, case of Salvador Silva and Maddalena Piazza, 1783–84; Busta 40: *Processi*, case of Anzolo Strozzi and Domenico Siega, 1785; Busta 41: *Processi*, case of Marco Menocchi, 1784; Busta 51: *Processi*, case of Catterina and Lucrezia (Lavanderi), 1784.

24. Ibid., Busta 40: *Processi*, case of Domenico Pievi, 1785; Busta 52: *Processi*, case of Antonio Valentini, 1785; Busta 52: *Processi*, case of Giovanni Battista Locatello and Teresa Bedena, 1785; Busta 42: *Processi*, case of Bortolo Mergotti; Busta 52: *Processi*, case of Antonio Bernardini, detto Morte, 1789.

Chapter 5

1. Testimony of Maria Bardini, 7 September 1785, 25r–25v, Archivio di Stato di Venezia, Esecutori contro la Bestemmia, Busta 40: *Processi*, case of Gaetano Franceschini, 1785.

2. Ibid.

3. Ibid., 26r–26v.

4. Ibid., 26v–27r.

5. Ibid., 27r–27v.

6. Testimony of Giuseppe Masironi, 7 September 1785, 23r–24v, case of Gaetano Franceschini, 1785.

7. Testimony of Maria Bardini, 28r.

8. Dennis Romano, *Housecraft and Statecraft: Domestic Service in Renaissance Venice, 1400–1600* (Baltimore: Johns Hopkins University Press, 1996), pp. 207–8; see also Sarah Maza, *Servants and Masters in Eighteenth-Century France: The Uses of Loyalty* (Princeton: Princeton University Press, 1983).

9. Carlo Goldoni, *The Venetian Twins*, in *Four Comedies*, trans. Frederick Davies (New York: Penguin, 1968), act 1, scene 1, p. 23.

10. Mozart and Da Ponte, *Le nozze di Figaro*, act 1, scene 2.

11. Ibid., act 3, scene 4.

12. Mozart and Da Ponte, *Don Giovanni*, act 1, scene 1.

13. Ibid., act 2, scene 1; act 2, scene 9; act 2, scene 18.

14. Daniel Roche, *The Culture of Clothing: Dress and Fashion in the Ancien Régime*, trans. Jean Birrell (Cambridge: Cambridge University Press, 1997), pp. 110–11.

15. Testimony of Maria Bardini, 28r.

16. Testimony of Bortolo Fiorese, 2 September 1785, 5v, case of Gaetano Franceschini, 1785.

17. Pasqualigo, *Della giurisprudenza criminale*, 1:37.

18. Testimony of Maria Bardini, 28v.

19. Order of arrest, Esecutori contro la Bestemmia, 8 September 1785, 30r, case of Gaetano Franceschini, 1785.

Chapter 6

1. Habermas, *Structural Transformation of the Public Sphere*, pp. 32–34.

2. Testimony of Domenico Ravasin, 7 September 1785, 21v–22r, Archivio di Stato di Venezia, Esecutori contro la Bestemmia, Busta 40: *Processi*, case of Gaetano Franceschini, 1785.

3. Franco Fido, *Nuova guida a Goldoni: Teatro e società nel settecento* (Turin: Giulio Einaudi, 2000), pp. 199–200.

4. Goldoni, *La bottega del caffè*, Garzanti ed., act 1, scene 1, p. 185.

5. Fernand Braudel, *The Structures of Everyday Life: Civilization and Capitalism* (New York: Harper & Row, 1982), 1:256–57; see also Reato, *La bottega del caffè*, pp. 13–15; Giuseppe Tassini, *Curiosità veneziane*, ed. Lino Moretti (Venice: Filippi Editore, 1964), pp. 109–10.

6. Braudel, *The Structures of Everyday Life*, pp. 256–57; Cowan, *The Social Life of Coffee*, p. 30.

7. Antonio Pilot, *La bottega da caffè* (Venice: Zanetti Editore, [1926?]), pp. 16–17, 77–78, 104.

8. Cesare Musatti, "Il conticino d'un caffettiere veneziano del settecento," *Ateneo veneto* 32, no. 1 (January/February, 1909), pp. 125–29.

9. Pilot, *La bottega da caffè*, p. 99; see also Cowan, *The Social Life of Coffee*, chap. 7, "Policing the Coffeehouse," pp. 193–224.

10. Reato, *La bottega del caffè*, pp. 24–27.

11. Pilot, *La bottega da caffè*, p. 101; Reato, *La bottega del caffè*, pp. 20, 32.

12. Pilot, *La bottega da caffè*, p. 42.

13. Ibid., pp. 100–102.

14. Ibid., pp. 19–26.

15. Ibid., p. 96.

16. Reato, *La bottega del caffè*, pp. 44–46.

17. Pilot, *La bottega da caffè*, p. 21.

18. Carlo Goldoni, *La sposa persiana*, in *Tutte le opere di Carlo Goldoni*, ed. Giuseppe Ortolani, vol. 9 (Milan: Arnoldo Mondadori, 1960), act 4, scene 4, pp. 574–75.

19. Reato, *La bottega del caffè*, p. 44.

20. Gasparo Gozzi, "Elogio delle botteghe di caffè," in *Opere scelte*, ed. Enrico Falqui (Milan: Rizzoli, 1939), p. 296.

21. Reato, *La bottega del caffè*, pp. 99–100.

22. Da Ponte, *Memorie*, pp. 13–14; Johnson, *Venice Incognito*, p. 51.

23. Gozzi, "Elogio," pp. 298–99.

24. Gozzi, *La Gazzetta Veneta*, ed. Antonio Zardo (Florence: Sansoni, 1967), August 13, 1760, p. 245.

25. Archivio di Stato di Venezia, *Inquisitorato alle Arti*, Busta 16: "Catastico di tutte le botteghe e posti dell'Arte Acquavita di questa città, 1761"; "Risposte ai quesiti dell'Ecc'mo Signore Inquisitor sopra le Arti," 16 June 1781.

26. Goldoni, *La bottega del caffè*, Garzanti ed., act 2, scene 1, p. 216.

27. Ibid., scene 2, p. 219.

Chapter 7

1. Testimony of Domenico Ravasin, 7 September 1785, 22v, Archivio di Stato di Venezia, Esecutori contro la Bestemmia, Busta 40: *Processi*, case of Gaetano Franceschini, 1785.

2. Testimony of Francesca Ravasin, 17 September 1785, 56v–57r , case of Gaetano Franceschini, 1785.

3. Goldoni, *La bottega del caffè*, Garzanti ed., p. 183.

4. Ibid., act 1, scene 9, p. 199.

5. Lady Mary Wortley Montagu, *Selected Letters*, ed. Robert Halsband (New York : Penguin Books, 1986), p. 91.

6. Carlo Goldoni, *I pettegolezzi delle donne*, act 3, scene 26, in *Commedie*, Garzanti ed., 1:333; see also Horodowich, *Language and Statecraft*, chap. 4, "Conversation and Exchange: Networks of Gossip," pp. 126–64; Cowan, *Social Life of Coffee*, pp. 241–43.

7. Ferraro, *Nefarious Crimes, Contested Justice*, pp. 25–26.

8. Testimony of Francesca Ravasin, 57r–58r.

9. Ibid., 58v.

10. Testimony of Cattarina Callegari, 19 September 1785, 63r–63v, case of Gaetano Franceschini, 1785.

11. Testimony of Zuane Lorenzini, 14 September 1785, 44v–45r, case of Gaetano Franceschini, 1785.

12. Archivio di Stato di Venezia, Esecutori contro la Bestemmia, Busta 52: *Processi*, case of Giovanni Battista Locatello and Teresa Bedena, 1785.

13. Testimony of Zuane Lorenzini, 45r–45v.

14. Ibid.

15. Ibid., 44v–45v.

16. Johnson, *Venice Incognito*, p. 214.

17. Lina Padoan Urban, "Il carnevale veneziano," in *Storia della cultura veneta*, ed. Girolamo Arnaldi and Manlio Pastore Stocchi, vol. 5, pt. 1, *Il settecento* (Vicenza: Neri Pozza Editore, 1985), pp. 631–46; Maurice Andrieux, *Daily Life in Venice in the Time of Casanova*, trans. Mary Fitton (London: Allan & Unwin, 1972), pp. 119–25.

18. Testimony of Anzolo Marason, 17 September 1785, 54r–54v, case of Gaetano Franceschini, 1785.

19. Ibid., 54v.

20. Testimony of Bastian Todesco, 14 September 1785, 46v–47r, case of Gaetano Franceschini, 1785.

21. Testimony of Bernardo Manella, 11 September 1785, 40v–41r, case of Gaetano Franceschini, 1785.

22. Testimony of Giacomo Bassagia, 17 September 1785, 55r–56r, case of Gaetano Franceschini, 1785.

23. Ibid., 55v.

24. Reato, *La bottega del caffè*, p. 20.

25. Ibid., p, 18.

26. Gozzi, "Elogio," pp. 296–99.

27. Habermas, *The Structural Transformation of the Public Sphere*, pp. 32–33, 42–43; Reato, *La bottega del caffè*, pp. 34–36; Cowan, *The Social Life of Coffee*, pp. 172–75.

28. Dena Goodman, *The Republic of Letters: A Cultural History of the French Enlightenment* (Ithaca, N.Y.: Cornell University Press, 1994), p. 123; John Brewer, *The Pleasures of the Imagination: English Culture in the Eighteenth Century* (Chicago: University of Chicago Press, 2000), p. 35.

29. James Boswell, *Boswell's London Journal, 1762–1763*, ed. Frederick Pottle (New Haven, Conn.: Yale University Press, 1992), pp. 74–75.

30. Reato, *La bottega del caffè*, p. 34; Franco Venturi, *Italy and the Enlightenment: Studies in a Cosmopolitan Century*, ed. Stuart Woolf, trans. Susan Corsi (New York: New York University Press, 1972), pp. 19–20, 154–55.

31. Goldoni, *La bottega del caffè*, Garzanti ed., act 2, scene 16, p. 235.

32. Johnson, *Venice Incognito*, pp. 124–27.

33. Pilot, *La bottega da caffè*, pp. 39, 41–42; see also Cowan, *The Social Life of Coffee*, pp. 222–24.

34. Testimony of Francesca Ravasin, 58v–59r.

35. Ibid., 58r.

36. Goldoni, *La bottega del caffè*, Garzanti ed., act 3, scene 26, p. 265.

Chapter 8

1. Testimony of Maddalena Schiavon, 12 September 1785, 41r, Archivio di Stato di Venezia, Esecutori contro la Bestemmia, Busta 40: *Processi*, case of Gaetano Franceschini, 1785.

2. Ibid., 41r–41v.

3. Gian Carlo Menis, *History of Friuli: The Formation of a People*, trans. Marisa Caruso, 6th ed. (Pordenone: Grafiche editoriali artistiche pordenonesi, 1988), p. xviii.

4. Edward Muir, *Mad Blood Stirring: Vendetta in Renaissance Italy* (1993; repr., Baltimore: Johns Hopkins University Press, 1998), pp. 23–24.

5. Carlo Ginzburg, *The Cheese and the Worms: The Cosmos of a Sixteenth-Century Miller*, trans. John Tedeschi and Anne Tedeschi (New York: Penguin, 1982), p. 16.

6. Carlo Ginzburg, *The Night Battles: Witchcraft and Agrarian Cults in the Sixteenth and Seventeenth Centuries*, trans. John Tedeschi and Anne Tedeschi (New York: Penguin Books, 1985), p. 30.

7. Ibid., p. 134.

8. Testimony of Cattarina Burubù, 12 September 1785, 42v–43r, case of Gaetano Franceschini, 1785.

9. Testimony of Maria Beloisi, 14 September 1785, 51r–51v, case of Gaetano Franceschini, 1785.

10. Testimony of Zuane Meniuto, 18 September 1785, 59v–60r, case of Gaetano Franceschini, 1785.

11. Fernand Braudel, *The Mediterranean and the Mediterranean World in the Age of Philip II*, trans. Siân Reynolds (Berkeley: University of California Press, 1995), 1:335–36.

12. Lovorka Čoralić, "La Scuola Dalmata nei testamenti degli immigrati dalla

sponda orientale dell'Adriatico," *Scuola Dalmata dei SS. Giorgio e Trifone* 27 (1994), pp. 21–23.

13. Chojnacka, *Working Women of Early Modern Venice*, pp. 95–96.

14. Testimony of Francesca Ravasin, 17 September 1785, 58r–58v, case of Gaetano Franceschini, 1785.

15. Giovanni Grevembroch, *Gli abiti de veneziani di quasi ogni età con diligenza raccolti e dipinti nel secolo XVIII*, vol. 3 (Venice: Filippi Editore, 1981), plate 76.

16. Ibid.

17. Ibid.

18. Ibid., plate 74.

19. Ibid.

20. Ibid., plate 155.

21. Ibid., plate 77; see also Pompeo Molmenti, "La Furlana et les anciennes danses vénitiennes," *La revue sud-américaine* 2 (April/June 1914), pp. 13–21.

22. Pietro Chiari, *Le contadine furlane* (Venice: Antonio Graziosi, 1771), p. 13.

23. Ibid., p. 16.

24. Ibid., p. 20.

25. Ibid., p. 38.

Chapter 9

1. Testimony of Giacomina Menochi, 4 September 1785, 10r–10v, Archivio di Stato di Venezia, Esecutori contro la Bestemmia, Busta 40: *Processi*, case of Gaetano Franceschini, 1785.

2. Ibid., 11r.

3. Ibid., 12v.

4. Ibid., 11v.

5. Ibid., 11v–12r.

6. Testimony of Elisabetta Segati, 18 September 1785, 60r–61r, case of Gaetano Franceschini, 1785.

7. Testimony of Giacomina Menochi, 12r–12v.

8. Romano, *Housecraft and Statecraft*, pp. 108–9, 152–67; Ferraro, *Nefarious Crimes, Contested Justice*, pp. 22, 202.

9. Carlo Goldoni, *Pamela fanciulla*, in *Pamela fanciulla—Pamela maritata*, ed. Ilaria Crotti (Venice: Marsilio, 1995), act 1, scene 6, p. 92; act 1, scene 17, p. 111.

10. Testimony of Maria Dalla Giana, 7 September 1785, 20r, case of Gaetano Franceschini, 1785.

11. Ibid., 20r–20v.

12. Ibid., 21r.

13. Ibid.

14. Testimony of Domenica (Meneghina) Dalla Giana, 8 September 1785, 29r–29v, case of Gaetano Franceschini, 1785.

15. Ibid., 30r.

16. Testimony of Vicenzo Comin, 15 September 1785, 52r–52v, case of Gaetano Franceschini, 1785.

17. Testimony of Petronilla Zilson, 18 September 1785, 62r–62v, case of Gaetano Franceschini, 1785.

18. Ibid., 63r.

19. Testimony of Malgarita Bianchi, 18 September 1785, 61v, case of Gaetano Franceschini, 1785.

20. Ibid., 61v–62r.

21. Guido Ruggiero, *Binding Passions: Tales of Magic, Marriage, and Power at the End of the Renaissance* (New York: Oxford University Press, 1993), pp. 35–55.

22. Letter to M. de Blancey, 14 August 1739, in Charles de Brosses, *Lettres familières d'Italie* (Brussels: Editions Complexe, 1995), p. 85; see also Chojnacka, *Working Women of Early Modern Venice*, pp. 22–24.

23. Testimony of Malgarita Bianchi, 62r.

Chapter 10

1. Larry Wolff, "Venice and the Slavs of Dalmatia: The Drama of the Adriatic Empire in the Venetian Enlightenment," *Slavic Review* 56, no. 3 (Fall 1997), pp. 428–55; see also Wolff, *Venice and the Slavs: The Discovery of Dalmatia in the Age of Enlightenment* (Stanford, Calif.: Stanford University Press, 2001).

2. Archivio di Stato di Venezia, *Avogaria di Commun: Nascite, Libro d'Oro.*

3. Testimony of Antonia Bon, 14 September 1785, 47v, Archivio di Stato di Venezia, Esecutori contro la Bestemmia, Busta 40: *Processi*, case of Gaetano Franceschini, 1785.

4. Ibid., 47v–48r.

5. Mozart and Da Ponte, *Don Giovanni*, act 1, scene 5; see also Edward Dent, *Mozart's Operas: A Critical Study* (1947; repr., Oxford: Clarendon Press, 1991), pp. 158–60; Daniel Heartz, "Donna Elvira and the Great Sextet," in *Mozart's Operas* (Berkeley: University of California Press, 1990), pp. 207–15.

6. Mozart and Da Ponte, *Don Giovanni*, act 1, scene 6.

7. Ibid., act 2, scene 10.

8. Testimony of Antonia Bon, 48r–48v.

9. Ibid., 48v.

10. Testimony of Giacomina Menochi, 4 September 1785, 11v, case of Gaetano Franceschini, 1785.

11. Testimony of Antonia Bon, 48v.

12. Ibid., 48v–49r.

13. Ibid., 49r.

Chapter 11

1. Testimony of Gaetano Franceschini, 10 September 1785, 32r–32v, Archivio di Stato di Venezia, Esecutori contro la Bestemmia, Busta 40: *Processi*, case of Gaetano Franceschini, 1785.

2. Archivio di Stato di Venezia, Esecutori contro la Bestemmia, Busta 33, *Processi*, case of Maffio Amadei, 1770; Busta 39, case of Alvise Loredan, 1784; Busta 52, case of Antonio Valentini, 1785.

3. Casanova, *Histoire de ma vie*, Brockhaus ed., 4:203–6; Laffont ed., 1:863.

4. Ibid., Brockhaus ed., 4:205–8; Laffont ed., 1:864–66.

5. Ibid., Brockhaus ed., 4:205–8, 215; Laffont ed., 1:866, 871–72.

6. Maurice Andrieux, *Daily Life in Venice at the Time of Casanova*, trans. Mary Fitton (London: Allen & Unwin, 1972), p. 58.

7. Appeal of Franceschini regarding conditions of imprisonment, 19 September 1785; medical note regarding Franceschini's health, 19 September 1785; case of Gaetano Franceschini, 1785.

8. Casanova, *Histoire de ma vie*, Brockhaus ed., 3:295–97; Laffont ed., 1:699–701.

9. Sebastiano Rumor, *Il blasone vicentino* (Venice: Federico Cav. Visentini, 1899), p. 81; Patrizia di Savino, "Manifattura e commercio dei tessuti serici a Vicenza nel XVIII secolo" (graduation thesis, Università degli Studi di Venezia, Tesi di Laurea, 1985–86), p. 116.

10. Emanuele Lodi, *Cenni storici e statistici sul setificio in Vicenza nella seconda metà del secolo passato* (Vicenza: G. Burato, 1872), pp. 5–7; Alessandro Ometto, "Il setificio vicentino nel settecento: Organizzazione produttiva, scambi e mercati" (graduation thesis, Università degli Studi di Verona, Tesi di Laurea, 1985–86), p. 214.

11. Archivio di Stato di Vicenza, *Notai di Vicenza*, Busta 14961, *Testamenti*, pp. 94–96.

12. Testimony of Gaetano Franceschini, 32r–32v.

13. Ibid., 33r–33v.

14. Ibid., 34r.

15. Ibid., 34r–35r.

16. Ibid., 35v–36r.

17. Ibid., 36r–37v.

18. Casanova, *Histoire de ma vie*, Brockhaus ed., 3:196–97; Laffont ed., 1:620–21.

19. Ibid., Brockhaus ed., 3:197–201; Laffont ed., 1:621–24.

20. Testimony of Gaetano Franceschini, 37v.

Chapter 12

1. Testimony of Gaetano Franceschini, 10 September 1785, 38r–38v, Archivio di Stato di Venezia, Esecutori contro la Bestemmia, Busta 40: *Processi*, case of Gaetano Franceschini, 1785.

2. Michel Foucault, *The History of Sexuality: An Introduction*, trans. Robert Hurley (New York: Vintage, 1980), pp. 43–44; Richard von Krafft-Ebing, *Psychopathia Sexualis*, trans. Franklin S. Klaf (New York: Arcade Publishing, 1998), p. 371.

3. Casanova, *Histoire de ma vie*, Brockhaus ed., 2:199; Laffont ed., 1:383.

4. Ibid., Brockhaus ed., 2:199–200; Laffont ed., 1:383–84; see also Peter Cryle, "Codified Indulgence: The Niceties of Libertine Ethics in Casanova and His Contemporaries," in Cryle and O'Connell, *Libertine Enlightenment*, pp. 48–60; Chantal Thomas, *Casanova: Un voyage libertin* (Paris: Denoël, 1985); Pierre Saint-Amand, *The Libertine's Progress: Seduction in the Eighteenth-Century French Novel*, trans. Jennifer Curtiss Gage (Providence, R.I.: Brown University Press, 1994).

5. Mozart and Da Ponte, *Don Giovanni*, act 1, scene 21; see also Johnson, *Venice Incognito*, pp. 169–236.

6. Mozart and Da Ponte, Don Giovanni, act 1, scene 5.

7. Casanova, *Histoire de ma vie*, Brockhaus ed., 1:74–75; Laffont ed., 1:71.

8. Ibid., Brockhaus ed., 1:76; Laffont ed., 1:71–72.

9. Ibid., Brockhaus ed., 1:78; Laffont ed., 1:73.

10. Jean-Jacques Rousseau, *Emile ou de l'éducation*, ed. Michel Launay (Paris: GF-Flammarion, 1966), p. 92.

11. Casanova, *Histoire de ma vie*, Brockhaus ed., 1:78; Laffont ed., 1:73.

12. Ibid., Brockhaus ed., 1:81; Laffont ed., 1:75.

13. Ibid., Brockhaus ed., 1:82–83; Laffont ed., 1:76.

14. Ibid., Brockhaus ed., preface, 1:xi; Laffont ed., 1:4.

15. Ibid., Brockhaus ed., 2:4; Laffont ed., 1:231.

16. Ibid., Brockhaus ed., 2:7–8; Laffont ed., 1:233–34.

17. Ibid., Brockhaus ed., 2:8; Laffont ed., 1:235.

18. Ibid.

19. Ibid., Brockhaus ed., 2:11; Laffont ed., 1:237.

20. Ibid., Brockhaus ed., 2:12; Laffont ed., 1:237–38.

21. Ibid., Brockhaus ed., 2:12; Laffont ed., 1:238.

22. Ibid., Brockhaus ed., 10:114; Laffont ed., 3:397.

23. Ibid., Brockhaus ed., 10:116–19; Laffont ed., 3:399–401.

24. Ibid., Brockhaus ed., 10:131; Laffont ed., 3:412.

25. Ibid., Brockhaus ed., 10:116; Laffont ed., 3:399.

26. Samuel Eliot Morison, *John Paul Jones: A Sailor's Biography* (1959; rpt. Annapolis, Md.: Naval Institute Press, 1999), pp. 457–62.

27. Casanova, *Histoire de ma vie*, Brockhaus ed., 4:154; Laffont ed., 1:824.

28. Ibid., Brockhaus ed., 4:176–79; Laffont ed., 1:841–42.

29. Ibid., Brockhaus ed., 4:181; Laffont ed., 1:843–44; see also Judith Summers, *Casanova's Women: The Great Seducer and the Women He Loved* (New York: Bloomsbury, 2006), pp. 320–21.

30. Carlo Gozzi, *Useless Memoirs*, ed. Philip Horne, trans. John Addington Symonds (London: Oxford University Press, 1962), pp. 115–16; Gozzi, *Memorie inutili*, ed. Paolo Bosisio (Milan: Università degli Studi di Milano, 2006), 2:878–79.

31. Gozzi, *Useless Memoirs*, pp. 116–17; Gozzi, *Memorie inutili*, 2:879–80; see also Larry Wolff, *Venice and the Slavs*, pp. 29–40.

32. Carlo Gozzi, *Useless Memoirs*, p. 117; Gozzi, *Memorie inutili*, 2:880.

33. Carlo Gozzi, *Useless Memoirs*, p. 119; Gozzi, *Memorie inutili*, 2:882.

34. Mozart and Da Ponte, *Don Giovanni*, act 1, scene 5.

35. Ibid.

36. Testimony of Gaetano Franceschini, 39r.

37. Ibid.

38. Casanova, *Histoire de ma vie*, Brockhaus ed., 12:235; Laffont ed., 3:1050–51.

39. Ibid., Brockhaus ed., 12:238; Laffont ed., 3:1053.

40. Ibid.

Chapter 13

1. Testimony of Gaetano Franceschini, 10 September 1785, 36r–37v, Archivio di Stato di Venezia, Esecutori contro la Bestemmia, Busta 40: *Processi*, case of Gaetano Franceschini, 1785.

2. Cozzi, "Note su tribunali," pp. 944–46; see also Claudio Povolo, "Retoriche giudiziarie, dimensioni del penale e prassi processuale nella Repubblica di Venezia: Da Lorenzo Priori ai pratici settecenteschi," in *L'amministrazione della giustizia penale nella Repubblica di Venezia (secoli XVI–XVIII)*, ed. Giovanni Chiodi and Claudio Povolo, vol. 2, *Retoriche, stereotipi, prassi* (Verona: Cierre Edizioni, 2004), pp. 19–170.

3. Opposizionale, indictment against Franceschini, 11 November 1785, case of Gaetano Franceschini, 1785.

4. Cozzi, "Note su tribunali," p. 943n27.

5. Opposizionale, indictment against Franceschini, 11 November 1785.

6. Mozart and Da Ponte, *Don Giovanni*, act 1, scene 20.

7. Opposizionale, indictment against Franceschini, 11 November 1785.

8. Ibid.

9. Ibid.

10. Ibid.

11. Ibid.

12. Ibid.

13. Ibid.

14. Ibid.

15. Ibid.

16. Ibid.

17. Ibid.

18. Ibid.

19. Ibid.

20. Ibid.

21. Response by Franceschini to indictment, 11 November 1785, case of Gaetano Franceschini, 1785.

Chapter 14

1. Maurice Lever, *Sade: A Biography*, trans. Arthur Goldhammer (New York: Harcourt Brace, Harvest Edition, 1994), pp. 345–50.

2. Sade, *Les 120 journées de Sodome* (Paris: Cercle du Livre Précieux, 1967), in *Oeuvres complètes* (Paris: Cercle du Livre Précieux, 1966–67), 13:33.

3. Ibid., pp. 34–36.

4. Ibid., pp. 349, 369.

5. Lever, *Sade*, p. 254; French edition, Lever, *Donatien Alphonse François, marquis de Sade* (Paris: Fayard, 1991), p. 269.

6. Sigmund Freud, *Three Essays on the Theory of Sexuality*, trans. James Strachey (New York: Basic Books, 1975), p. 23; Krafft-Ebing, *Psychopathia Sexualis*, Arcade ed., pp. 55–56.

7. Lever, *Sade*, p. 294.

8. Sade, *Justine ou Les malheurs de la vertu* (Paris: Cercle du Livre Précieux, 1966), in *Oeuvres complètes*, 3:58.

9. Ibid., p. 60.

10. Ibid., pp. 67–71.

11. Ibid., pp. 159–62.

12. Antonia Fraser, *Marie Antoinette: The Journey* (New York: Doubleday, 2001), pp. 426–31; see also Lynn Hunt, "The Many Bodies of Marie Antoinette: Political Pornography and the Problem of the Feminine in the French Revolution," in *Marie Antoinette: Writings on the Body of a Queen*, ed. Dena Goodman (New York: Routledge, 2003), pp. 117–38.

13. Sade, *L'histoire de Juliette* (Paris: Cercle du Livre Précieux, 1967), in *Oeuvres complètes*, 8:16.

14. Ibid., p. 38.

15. Ibid., p. 96.

16. Ibid., p. 98.

17. Ibid., p. 100.

18. Ibid., pp. 559–64.

19. Sade, *Justine*, pp. 79–81.

20. Robert Darnton, *The Forbidden Best-Sellers of Pre-revolutionary France* (New York: W. W. Norton, 1995), p. 89.

21. Sade, *Justine*, pp. 198–99.

22. Ibid., pp. 199–201.

23. Ibid., p. 208.

24. Sade, *L'histoire de Juliette*, p. 30; see also Alan Corkhill, "Kant, Sade and the Libertine Enlightenment," in Cryle and O'Connell, *Libertine Enlightenment*, pp. 61–74; Jean Goldzink, *A la recherche du libertinage* (Paris: L'Harmattan, 2005), pp. 123–42; *Sade: Écrire la crise*, ed. Michel Camus and Philippe Roger (Paris: P. Belfond, 1983).

25. Sade, *L'histoire de Juliette*, pp. 103–4.

26. Ibid., p. 76; see also Larry Wolff, "Discovering Cultural Perspective: The Intellectual History of Anthropological Thought in the Age of Enlightenment," in *The Anthropology of the Enlightenment*, ed. Larry Wolff and Marco Cipolloni (Stanford, Calif.: Stanford University Press, 2007), pp. 27–30.

27. Sade, *L'histoire de Juliette*, pp. 183–84.

28. Lever, *Sade*, pp. 519, 545, 559–60.

29. Ibid., pp. 498–500.

30. Simone de Beauvoir, "Faut-il brûler Sade?" *Les Temps modernes* 74 (1951): 1002–33; *Les Temps modernes* 75 (1952): 1197–1230; Beauvoir, *Faut-il brûler Sade?* (Paris: Gallimard, 1955).

31. Vladimir Nabokov, *Lolita* (1955; repr., New York: Vintage, 1997), p. 9.

Chapter 15

1. Allegazione per Gaetano Franceschini, article 10, Archivio di Stato di Venezia, Esecutori contro la Bestemmia, Busta 40: *Processi*, case of Gaetano Franceschini, 1785.

2. Jean-Jacques Rousseau, *Social Contract*, trans. Maurice Cranston (London: Penguin Books, 1968), p. 49; Mozart and Da Ponte, *Don Giovanni*, act 1, scene 21; see also Svetlana Boym, *Another Freedom: The Alternative History of an Idea* (Chicago: University of Chicago Press, 2010).

3. Allegazione per Gaetano Franceschini, article 1; Cozzi, "Note su tribunali," pp. 944–46.

4. Allegazione per Gaetano Franceschini, article 1.

5. Ibid., article 2.

6. Ibid.

7. Pierre-Augustin Caron de Beaumarchais, *Le barbier de Séville* (Paris: Garnier-Flammarion, 1965), p. 63. See also Beaumarchais, *The Barber of Seville* and *The Marriage of Figaro*, trans. John Wood (London: Penguin, 2004), pp. 61–62.

8. Darnton, *Forbidden Best-Sellers*, pp. 137–66.

9. Maza, *Private Lives and Public Affairs*, pp. 188, 320.

10. Allegazione per Gaetano Franceschini, articles 61, 62.

11. Ibid., articles 61, 62.

12. Casanova, *Histoire de ma vie*, Brockhaus ed., preface, 1:xv; Laffont ed., 1:6.

13. Allegazione per Gaetano Franceschini, article 66.

14. Testimony of Anzolo Zorzi, Carlo Foncel, and Felice Sartori, 14 December 1785, case of Gaetano Franceschini, 1785.

15. Testimony of Paolo Valmarana and Francesco Panizzon, 14 December 1785, case of Gaetano Franceschini, 1785.

16. Testimony of Paolo Valmarana and Francesco Panizzon.

17. Allegazione per Gaetano Franceschini, articles 63, 69.

18. Ibid., articles 23–26.

19. Ibid., article 29.

20. Ibid., article 42.

21. Beccaria, *On Crimes and Punishments*, Cambridge ed., pp. 79–80; Beccaria, *Dei delitti e delle pene*, ed. Renato Fabietti (Milan: Mursia, 1973), p. 91.

22. Beccaria, *On Crimes and Punishments*, Cambridge ed., p. 80.

23. Foucault, *The History of Sexuality*, p. 39.

24. Ibid., pp. 43–44.

25. Ibid., pp. 155–56.

26. Casanova, *Histoire de ma vie*, Brockhaus ed., preface, 1:xv–xvi; Laffont ed., 1:7.

27. Allegazione per Gaetano Franceschini, article 22.

Chapter 16

1. Rousseau, *Emile*, Garnier-Flammarion ed., p. 92; Leo Damrosch, *Jean-Jacques Rousseau: Restless Genius* (Boston: Houghton Mifflin, 2005), pp. 331–38.

2. Rousseau, *Emile*, p. 131.

3. Rousseau, *Les confessions*, book 2 (Paris: Garnier Flammarion, 1968), pp. 56–58.

4. Ibid., pp. 58–59; Damrosch, *Jean-Jacques Rousseau*, pp. 174–75.

5. Rousseau, *Les confessions*, book 2, p. 59.

6. Ibid.; Charles de Brosses, letter to M. de Blancey, 14 August 1739, in *Lettres familières d'Italie* (Brussels: Editions Complexe, 1995), p. 85.

7. Rousseau, *Les confessions*, book 2, pp. 63–65; Damrosch, *Jean-Jacques Rousseau*, pp. 176–79.

8. Rousseau, *Les confessions*, book 2, p. 66.

9. Ibid., pp. 66–67; Damrosch, *Jean-Jacques Rousseau*, pp. 179–80.

10. Rousseau, *Les confessions*, book 1 (Paris: Garnier-Flammarion, 1968), p. 43.

11. Rousseau, *Les confessions*, Garnier-Flammarion ed., book 1, pp. 52–53; Damrosch, *Jean-Jacques Rousseau*, pp. 29–30.

12. Rousseau, *Emile*, Garnier-Flammarion ed., p. 479; see also Joan Landes, *Women and the Public Sphere in the Age of the French Revolution* (Ithaca, N.Y.: Cornell University Press, 1988), pp. 66–89.

Chapter 17

1. Testimony of Paolina Lozaro, 5 September 1785, 16v–17v, Archivio di Stato di Venezia, Esecutori contro la Bestemmia, Busta 40: *Processi*, case of Gaetano Franceschini, 1785.

2. Ibid., 17v.

3. Ibid.

4. Ibid., 18r.

5. Ibid.

6. Ibid., 18v.

7. Report of Pietro Recaldini, 5 September 1785, 19r , case of Gaetano Franceschini, 1785.

8. Testimony of Pietro Recaldini, 15 September 1785, 53r–53v, case of Gaetano Franceschini, 1785.

9. Ibid., 53v.

10. Allegazione per Gaetano Franceschini, article 61, case of Gaetano Franceschini, 1785.

11. Opposizionale, indictment against Franceschini, 11 November 1785, case of Gaetano Franceschini, 1785.

12. Rousseau, *Emile*, Garnier-Flammarion ed., p. 208.

Chapter 18

1. Margaret King, *The Death of the Child Valerio Marcello* (Chicago: University of Chicago Press, 1994), pp. 1–3.

2. Philippe Ariès, *Centuries of Childhood: A Social History of Family Life*, trans. Robert Baldick (New York: Vintage Books, 1962), p. 128; see also Hugh Cunningham, *Children and Childhood in Western Society since 1500* (London: Longman, 1995); Lloyd deMause, ed., *The History of Childhood* (New York: 1974; Harper Torchbooks, 1975).

3. Lawrence Stone, *The Family, Sex and Marriage in England 1500–1800* (New York: Harper & Row, 1977); Simon Schama, *The Embarrassment of Riches: An Interpretation of Dutch Culture in the Golden Age* (New York: Alfred A. Knopf, 1987), pp.

497–500; Mary Frances Durantini, *The Child in Seventeenth-Century Dutch Painting* (Ann Arbor, Mich.: UMI Research Press, 1979), pp. 177–296.

4. Michel Foucault, *The Order of Things: An Archaeology of the Human Sciences* (New York: Routledge, 1989), pp. 3–18.

5. Anne Higonnet, *Pictures of Innocence: The History and Crisis of Ideal Childhood* (London: Thames & Hudson, 1998), pp. 23–49.

6. J. H. Plumb, "The New World of Children in Eighteenth-Century England," *Past and Present* 67 (1975): 64–93; Stone, *The Family, Sex and Marriage*, pp. 408–12.

7. King, *Death of the Child Valerio Marcello*, p. 143.

8. Ibid., p. 138.

9. Michel de Montaigne, *Essays* (New York: Penguin Classics, 1983), pp. 139–40, 157–58; see also Anthony Krupp, *Reason's Children: Childhood in Early Modern Philosophy* (Lewisburg, Penn.: Bucknell University Press, 2009).

10. King, *Death of the Child Valerio Marcello*, pp. 8, 10–11, 171.

11. Ibid., p. 21.

12. Matthew 18:1–4 (King James Version).

13. Ariès, *Centuries of Childhood*, pp. 122, 127.

14. Steven Ozment, *When Fathers Ruled: Family Life in Reformation Europe* (Cambridge, Mass.: Harvard University Press, 1983); Philip Greven, *The Protestant Temperament: Patterns of Child-Rearing, Religious Experience, and the Self in Early America* (1977; repr., Chicago: University of Chicago Press, 1988).

15. Stone, *The Family, Sex and Marriage*, pp. 514–16; Thomas Laqueur, *Solitary Sex: A Cultural History of Masturbation* (New York: Zone Books, 2004), pp. 25–44; Georges Vigarello, *A History of Rape: Sexual Violence in France from the 16th to the 20th Century*, trans. Jean Birrell (Cambridge, U.K.: Polity Press, 2001), pp. 75–86.

16. Rousseau, *Emile*, pp. 203–4; Larry Wolff, "'When I Imagine a Child': The Idea of Childhood and the Philosophy of Memory in the Enlightenment," *Eighteenth-Century Studies* 31, no. 4 (Summer 1998), pp. 377–401.

Chapter 19

1. Testimony of Maria Lozaro, 5 September 1785, 15v–16r, Archivio di Stato di Venezia, Esecutori contro la Bestemmia, Busta 40: *Processi*, case of Gaetano Franceschini, 1785.

2. Testimony of Maria Bardini, 7 September 1785, 27v–28v, case of Gaetano Franceschini, 1785.

3. Testimony of Elena Comarolo, 13 September 1785, 43v–44v, case of Gaetano Franceschini, 1785.

4. Testimony of Vicenzo Comin, 15 September 1785, 32r–32v, case of Gaetano Franceschini, 1785; Michel Foucault, *The History of Sexuality*, Vintage ed., pp. 19–20.

5. Testimony of Orsola Baresi, 14 September 1785, 49v–51r, case of Gaetano Franceschini, 1785.

6. Ibid., 50v.

7. Ibid., 51r .

8. Testimony of Elena Artico, 3 September 1785, 8v, case of Gaetano Franceschini, 1785.

9. Testimony of Maddalena Schiavon, 12 September 1785, 42v, case of Gaetano Franceschini, 1785.

10. Testimony of Cattarina Burubù, 12 September 1785, 43v, case of Gaetano Franceschini, 1785.

11. Allegazione per Gaetano Franceschini, article 57, case of Gaetano Franceschini, 1785.

12. Testimony of Maria Bardini, 26r.

13. Allegazione per Gaetano Franceschini, article 58.

14. Ibid.

15. Archivio di Stato di Venezia, Esecutori contro la Bestemmia, Busta 52: *Processi*, case of Antonio Bernardini, 1789.

16. Ibid., Busta 53: *Processi*, case of Maria Sorda and Paola detta Zaffa, 1794.

17. Ibid., case of Francesco Lanza and Lodovica detta Schiavona, 1795.

18. Ibid., case of Giuseppe Furlani, 1796.

19. Ibid., case of Regina Minotto, 1796.

20. Higonnet, *Pictures of Innocence*, pp. 23–49; Cunningham, *Children and Childhood*, pp. 61–74; Stone, *The Family, Sex and Marriage*, pp. 405–8.

Chapter 20

1. Testimony of Bernardo Manella, 11 September 1785, 40v–41r, Archivio di Stato di Venezia, Esecutori contro la Bestemmia, Busta 40: *Processi*, case of Gaetano Franceschini, 1785.

2. Ibid., 40r.

3. Richard Rutt, *A History of Hand Knitting* (Loveland, Colo.: Interweave Press, 1987), pp. 88–90, 97–99; Adam Smith, *The Wealth of Nations* (New York: Penguin Books, 1982), p. 220.

4. Denis Diderot, *On Art*, vol. 1, trans. John Goodman (New Haven, Conn.: Yale University Press, 1995), pp. 97–98.

5. Ibid., p. 99; see also Higonnet, *Pictures of Innocence*, pp. 28–29.

6. Mozart and Da Ponte, *Le nozze di Figaro*, act 4, scene 1.

7. Goethe, *Italian Journey*, trans. Robert Heitner, in *Collected Works*, vol. 6 (Princeton, N.J.: Princeton University Press, 1989), pp. 52, 60.

8. Goethe, *Italian Journey*, p. 150.

9. Goethe, *Wilhelm Meister's Apprenticeship*, trans. Eric Blackall (New York: Suhrkamp Publishers, 1989), pp. 54–59.

10. Ibid., pp. 65, 81–83.

11. Carolyn Steedman, *Strange Dislocations: Childhood and the Idea of Human Interiority* (Cambridge, Mass.: Harvard University Press, 1998), pp. 1–42; James Kincaid, *Erotic Innocence: The Culture of Child Molesting* (Durham, N.C.: Duke University Press, 1998), pp. 51–72; see also James Kincaid, *Child-Loving: The Erotic Child and Victorian Culture* (London: Routledge, 1992).

12. William Blake, "The Little Girl Lost," in *English Romantic Writers*, ed. David Perkins (New York: Harcourt, Brace & World, 1967), p. 59.

13. Higonnet, *Pictures of Innocence*, pp. 31–49; Cunningham, *Children and Childhood*, pp. 74–78; Priscilla Robertson, "Home as a Nest: Middle Class Childhood in Nineteenth-Century Europe," in *The History of Childhood*, ed. Lloyd deMause (1974; repr., New York: Harper Torchbooks, 1975), pp. 407–31.

14. Erna Olafson Hellerstein, Leslie Parker Hume, and Karen Offen, eds., *Victorian Women: A Documentary Account of Women's Lives in Nineteenth-Century England, France, and the United States* (Stanford, Calif.: Stanford University Press, 1981), p. 93; Thomas Laqueur, *Solitary Sex: A Cultural History of Masturbation* (New York: Zone Books, 2004), pp. 63–66; Robertson, "Home as a Nest," pp. 419–20.

15. Larry Wolff, "'The Boys Are Pickpockets and the Girl Is a Prostitute': Gender and Juvenile Criminality in Early Victorian England from *Oliver Twist* to *London Labour*," *New Literary History* 27, no. 2 (Spring 1996), p. 232.

16. Wolff, "'The Boys Are Pickpockets and the Girl Is a Prostitute,'" p. 244.

17. Judith Walkowitz, *City of Dreadful Delight: Narratives of Sexual Danger in Late-Victorian London* (Chicago: University of Chicago Press, 1992), pp. 100–101; see also Lloyd deMause, "The Evolution of Childhood," in deMause, *The History of Childhood*, pp. 1–73.

18. Krafft-Ebing, *Psychopathia Sexualis*, Arcade ed., pp. 369–71.

19. Ibid.

20. Ibid., pp. 370–74.

21. Larry Wolff, *Postcards from the End of the World: Child Abuse in Freud's Vienna* (New York: Atheneum, 1988), pp. 204–5; Peter Gay, *Freud: A Life for Our Time* (1988; repr., New York: Norton, 1998), p. 93.

22. Wolff, *Postcards from the End of the World*, p. 205.

23. C. Henry Kempe, "Incest and Other Forms of Sexual Abuse," in *The Battered Child Syndrome*, 3rd ed., ed. C. Henry Kempe and Ray Helfer (Chicago: University of Chicago Press, 1980), pp. 203–4.

24. Ibid.

25. Ibid., p. 212.

26. Lawrence Wright, *Remembering Satan: A Case of Recovered Memory and the Shattering of an American Family* (New York: Alfred A. Knopf, 1994).

Conclusion

1. Record of voting on Franceschini verdict, 16 December 1785, Archivio di Stato di Venezia, Esecutori contro la Bestemmia, Busta 40: *Processi*, case of Gaetano Franceschini, 1785.

2. Ibid.

3. Note of deposit of two hundred ducats, 16 December 1785, case of Gaetano Franceschini, 1785; note of warning to Franceschini, 19 December 1785, case of Gaetano Franceschini, 1785.

4. Receipt for two hundred ducats paid to Mattio Lozaro, 28 December 1785, case of Gaetano Franceschini, 1785.

5. Karl Marx, *The Communist Manifesto* (New York: International Publishers, 1973), p. 27.

6. Rousseau, *Les confessions*, Garnier-Flammarion ed., 1:52–53.

7. Goethe, *Wilhelm Meister's Apprenticeship*, Suhrkamp ed., p. 216.

8. Casanova, *Histoire de ma vie*, Brockhaus ed., 1:4–5; Laffont ed., 1:17.

9. Rolf Bagemihl, "Pietro Longhi and Venetian Life," *Metropolitan Museum Journal* 23 (1988), pp. 233–47.

10. Rousseau, *Emile*, Garnier-Flammarion ed., p. 479.

Index

Italic page numbers indicate illustrations.